Abortion Bibliography
For 1973

Abortion Bibliography

For 1973

compiled by

Mary K. Floyd

The Whitston Publishing Company
Troy, New York
1974

PREFACE

Abortion Bibliography for 1973 is the fourth annual list of books and articles surrounding the subject of abortion in the preceeding year. It appears serially each fall as a contribution toward documenting in one place as comprehensively as possible the literature of one of our central social issues. It is an attempt at a comprehensive world bibliography.

Searches in compiling this material have covered the following sources: *Art Index; Applied Science and Technology Index; Bibliographic Index; Biological Abstracts; Books in Print; British Books in Print; British Humanities Index; Business Periodicals Index; Canadian Periodical Index; Catholic Periodicals and Literature Index; Cumulative Book Index; Current Index to Journals in Education; Current Literature of Venereal Disease; Education Index; Guide to Social Science and Religion in Periodical Literature; Hospital Literature Index; Index to Catholic Periodicals and Literature; Index to Legal Periodicals; Index Medicus; Index to Nursing Literature; Index to Periodical Articles Related to Law; Index to Religious Periodical Literature; International Nursing Index; Law Review Digest; Library of Congress Catalog: Books: Subjects; Philosophers Index; Public Affairs Information Service; Readers Guide to Periodical Literature; Social Sciences and Humanities Index; Whitaker's Cumulative Book Index.*

The bibliography is divided into two sections: a title section in alphabetical order; and a subject section. Thus, if the researcher does not wish to observe the subject heads of the compiler, he can use the title section exclusively. The 159 subject heads have been allowed to issue from the nature of the material indexed rather than being imposed from Library of Congress subject heads or other standard lists.

Countries are listed alphabetically under subjects: "Abortion: Africa," etc.; with states listed alphabetically under "Abortion: United States:"

Arkansas, California, etc.; and drugs are listed under the specific drug involved.

Mary K. Floyd
Troy, New York
August, 1974

LIST OF PERIODICAL ABBREVIATIONS

ABBREVIATIONS	TITLE
AER	American Ecclesiatical Review (Washington)
AORN J	AORN Journal (Engelwood, Colorado)
Acta Endocrinal	Acta Endocrinologica (Copenhagen)
Acta Eur Fertil	Acta Europaea Fertilitatis (Roma)
Acta Obstet Gynecol Scand	Acta Obstetricia et Gynecologica Scandinavica (Lund)
Acta Physiol Scand	Acta Physiologica Scandinavica (Stockholm)
Acta Psychiatr Scand	Acta Psychiatrica Scandinavica (Copenhagen)
Akush Ginekol	Akusherstvo i Ginekologiya (Moscow)
Akush Ginekol	Akusherstvo i Ginekologia (Sofiia)
Albany L Rev	Albany Law Review (Albany, New York)
Am Biol Teach	American Biology Teacher (Washington)
Am Druggist Merch	American Druggist Merchandising (New York)
Am J Crim L	American Journal of Criminal Law (Austin, Texas)
Am J Hum Genet	American Journal of Human Genetics (Chicago)
Am J Nurs	American Journal of Nursing (New York)
Am J Obstet Gynecol	American Journal of Obstetrics and Gynecology (St. Louis)
Am J Orthopsychiatry	American Journal of Orthopsychiatry (New York)
Am J Pathol	American Journal of Pathology (New York)
Am J Psychiatry	American Journal of Psychiatry (Washington)
Am J Vet Res	American Journal of Veterinary Research (Chicago)
Am Phil Quart	American Philosophical Quarterly (Oxford)
Amer Med News	American Medical Association News (Chicago)
America	America (San Francisco)

American Philosophical Quarterly	American Philosophical Quarterly (Oxford)
An R Acad Nacl Med	Anales de la Real Academia Nacional de Medicine (Madrid)
Ann Endocrinol	Annales d'Endocrinologie (Paris)
Ann Hum Genet	Annals of Human Genetics (London)
Ann Med Interne	Annales de Medecine Interne (Paris)
Ann R Coll Surg Engl	Annals of the Royal College of Surgeons of England (London)
Arch Gen Psychiatry	Archives of General Psychiatry (Chicago)
Arch Gynaekol	Archiv fur Gynaekologie (Munich)
Arch Intern Med	Archives of Internal Medicine (Chicago)
Arch Ostet Ginecol	Archivio di Ostetricia e Ginecologia (Naples)
Armed Forces Med J India	Armed Forces Medical Journal (New Delhi)
Atlan Adv	Atlantic Advocate (New Brunswick)
Aust NZ J Obstet Gynaecol	Australian and New Zealand Journal of Obstetrics and Gynaecology (Melbourne)
Aust Vet J	Australian Veterinary Journal (Sydney)
BU L Rev	Boston University Law Review (Boston)
Banner	Banner (Grand Rapids)
Beitr Gerichtl Med	Beitraege zur Gerichtlichen Medizin (Vienna)
Berl Munch Tieraerztl Wochenschr	Berliner und Muenchener Tieraerztliche Wochenschrift/Berlin and Munich Veterinarian's Weekly (Berlin)
Br J Anaesth	British Journal of Anaesthesia (Cheshire)
Br J Cancer	British Journal of Cancer (London)
Br J Prev Soc Med	British Journal of Preventive and Social Medicine (London)
Br J Psychiatry	British Journal of Psychiatry (London)
Br Med J	British Medical Journal (London)
Br Vet J	British Veterinary Journal (London)
Broadcasting	Broadcasting (Washington)
Bull Acad Natl Med	Bulletin de l'Academie Nationale de Medecine (Paris)
Bull Fed Soc Gynecol	Bulletin de la Federation des Societes

Obstet Lang Fr	de Gynecologie et d'Obstetrique de Langue Francaise (Paris)
Bull Menninger Clin	Bulletin of the Menninger Clinic (Topeka)
Bull NY Acad Med	The New York Academy of Medicine Bulletin. (New York)
Bull Soc Ophtalmol Fr	Bulletin des Societes d'Ophtalmologie de France (Paris)
C Char	Catholic Charities Review (Washington)
C Dgst	Catholic Digest (St. Paul)
C Econ	Christian Economics (Los Angeles, California)
C Lawyer	Catholic Lawyer (Brooklyn, New York)
C Mind	Catholic Mind (New York)
C R Hebd Seances Acad Sci Ser D Sci Nat	Comptes Rendus Hebdomadaires des Seances de l'Academie des Sciences; D: Sciences Naturelles (Paris)
Cah Med	Cahiers de Medecine (Paris)
Calif Med	California Medicine (San Francisco)
Can B J	Canadian Bar Journal (Ottawa)
Can Hosp	Canadian Hospital (Toronto)
Can J Public Health	Canadian Journal of Public Health (Toronto)
Can Vet J	Canadian Veterinary Journal /Revue Veterinaire Canadienne (Ontario)
Cath Hosp	Catholic Hospital (Ottawa)
Cent Afr J Med	Central African Journal of Medicine (Salisbury, Rhodesia)
Cesk Gynekol	Ceskoslovenska Gynekologie (Prague)
Cesk Pediatr	Ceskoslovenska Pediatrie (Praha)
Cesk Zdrav	Ceskoslovenska Zdravotnictvi (Prague)
Ch Her	Church Herald (Grand Rapids, Michigan)
Chatelaine	Chatelaine (Toronto)
Child Welfare	Child Welfare (New York)
Chin Med J	Chinese Medical Journal (Peking)
Chr Cent	Christian Century (Chicago)
Chr Today	Christianity Today (Washington)

Christ Nurse	Christian Nurse (Nagpur, India)
Clin Genet	Clinical Genetics (Copenhagen)
Clin Obstet Gynecol	Clinical Obstetrics and Gynecology (New York)
Clin Sci	Clinical Science (London)
Colo Nurse	Colorado Nurse (Denver)
Columbia	Columbia (New Haven, Connecticut)
Commonweal or Comm	Commonweal (New York)
Compr Psychiatry	Comprehensive Psychiatry (New York)
Conn Med	Connecticut Medicine (New Haven)
Contraception	Contraception (Los Altos, California)
Cornell Vet	Cornell Veterinarian (Ithaca, New York)
Critic	Critic (Chicago)
Curr Ther Res	Current Therapeutic Research (New York)
Current	Current (Cambridge, Massachusetts)
Daily Telegraph	Daily Telegraph Magazine (London)
Del Med J	Delaware Medical Journal (Wilmington)
Dimension	Dimension (Johannesburg, South Africa)
Doc Cath	Documentation Catholique (Paris)
Drug Ther Bull	Drug and Therapeutics Bulletin (London)
Dtsch Gesundheitsw	Deutsche Gesundheitswesen (Berlin)
Dtsch Med Wochenschr	Deutsch Medizinische Wochenschrift (Stuttgart)
Dtsch Tieraerztl Wochenschr	Deutsche Tieraerztliche Wochenschrift (Hannover, New York)
Duodecim	Duodecim (Helsinki)
Economist	Economist (London)
Etudes	Etudes (Paris)
European Demographic Inf Bul	European Demographic Information Bulletin (The Hague, Netherlands)
F A H Rev	Federation of American Hospitals Review (Little Rock, Arkansas)
Family Plann Perspect	Family Planning Perspectives (New York)
Feldsher Akush	Fel'dsker I Akusherka (Moscow)
Fertil Steril	Fertility and Sterility (New York)
Fla B J	Florida Bar Journal (Tallahassee)
Fordham L Rev	Fordham Law Review (New York)
Forensic Sci	Forensic Science Society. Journal (London)
Furrow	Furrow (Moline, Illinois)

GNB	Good News Broadcaster (Lincoln, Nebraska)
Ga SB J	Georgia State Bar Journal (Macon)
Gac Med Mex	Gaceta Medica de Mexico (Mexico)
Geburtshilfe Frauenheilkd	Geburtshilfe Frauenheilkunde (Stuttgart)
Genet Psychol Monogr	Genetic Psychology Monographs (Provincetown)
Geo L J	Georgetown Law Journal (Washington)
Ginecol Obstet Mex	Ginecologia y Obstetricia de Mexico (Mexico City)
Ginekol Pol	Ginekologia Polaska (Warsaw)
God Zb Med Fak Skopje	Godisen Zbornik na Medicinslciot Fakultet vo Skopje
Good H	Good Housekeeping (New York)
Guardian	Guardian (New York)
Gynecol Prat	Gynecologie Pratique (Paris)
HPR	Homiletic and Pastoral Review (New York)
Harefuah	Harefuah (Tel Aviv)
Hawaii Med J	Hawaii Medical Journal (Honolulu)
Health Bull	Health Bulletin (Melbourne)
Health People	Health of the People (Auckland, New Zealand)
Health Serv Rep	Health Service Reports (Rockville, Maryland)
Health Soc Serv J	Health and Social Service Journal (London)
Hippokrates	Hippokrates (Stuttgart)
Hosp Admin Can	Hospital Administration in Canada (Ontario)
Hosp Med Staff	Hospital Medical Staff (Chicago)
Hosp Progress	Hospital Progress (St. Louis)
Hosp Top	Hospital Topics (Chicago)
Hosp World	Hospital World (London)
Hospitals	Hospitals (Chicago)
Houston L Rev	Houston Law Review (Houston, Texas)
Humangenetik	Humangenetik (Berlin)
Indian J Chest Dis	Indian Journal of Chest Diseases (Delhi)
Indian J Med Res	Indian Journal of Medical Research (New Delhi)
Indian J Public Health	Indian Journal of Public Health

	(Calcutta)
Infect Immun	Infection and Immunity (Washington)
Int Surg	International Surgery Bulletin (Chicago)
Internat Socialist R	International Socialist Review (New York)
JAMA	Journal of the American Medical Association (Chicago)
J Am Assoc Nurse Anesth	Journal of the American Association of Nurse Anesthetists (Chicago)
J Am Coll Health Assoc	Journal of the American College Health Association (Ithaca, New York)
J Am Osteopath Assoc	Journal of the American Osteopathic Association (Chicago)
J Am Vet Med Assoc	Journal of the American Veterinary Medical Association (Chicago)
J Amer Med Ass	Journal of the American Medical Association (Chicago)
J Arkansas Med Soc	Journal of the Arkansas Medical Society (Fort Smith)
J Biosoc Sci	Journal of Biosocial Science (London)
J Can BA	Journal of the Canadian Bar Association (Ottawa)
J Clin Pathol	Journal of Clinical Pathology (London)
J Community Psychol	Journal of Community Psychology (Brandon, Vermont)
J Endocrinol	Journal of Endocrinology (London)
J Family L	Journal of Family Law (Louisville, Kentucky)
J Genet Hum	Journal de Genetique Humaine (Geneve)
J Gynecol Obstet Biol Reprod	Journal de Gynecologie, Obstetrique et Biologie de la Reproduction (Paris)
J Hyg	Journal of Hygiene (Cambridge, England)
J Indian Med Assoc	Journal of the Indian Medical Association (Calcutta)
J Infect Dis	Journal of Infectious Diseases (Chicago)
J Iowa Med Soc	Journal of the Iowa Medical Society (Des Moines)
J La State Med Soc	Journal of the Louisiana State Medical Society (New Orleans)
J Med Assoc Ga	Journal of the Medical Association of Georgia (Atlanta)
J Med Assoc State Ala	Journal of the Medical Association of

	the State of Alabama (Montgomery)
J Med Assoc Thai	Journal of the Medical Association of Thailand (Bangkok)
J Med Soc NJ	Journal of the Medical Society of New Jersey (Trenton)
J Nucl Med	Journal of Nuclear Medicine (New York)
J Obstet Gynaecol Br Commonw	Journal of Obstetrics and Gynaecology of the British Commonwealth (London)
J Okla State Med Ass	Journal of the Oklahoma State Medical Association (Oklahoma City)
J Pharm Sci	Journal of Pharmaceutical Sciences (Washington)
J Reprod Fertil	Journal of Reproduction and Fertility (Oxford)
J Reprod Med	Journal of Reproductive Medicine (Chicago)
J S Afr Vet Med Assoc	South African Veterinary Medical Association. Journal (Pretoria)
J SC Med Assoc	Journal of the South Carolina Medical Association (Florence)
J Sch Health	Journal of School Health (Columbus)
J Social Work	Journal of Social Work Education (New York)
J Tenn Med Assoc	Journal of the Tennessee Medical Association (Nashville)
J Urban L	Journal of Urban Law (Detroit)
J Urol	Journal of Urology (Baltimore)
Jugosl Ginekol Opstet	Jugoslavenska Ginekologija i Opstetricija (Ljubljana, Yugoslavia)
Klin Monatsbl Augenheilkd	Klinische Monatsblaetter fuer Augenheilkunde und fuer Augnarztliche Fortbildung (Stuttgart)
Klin Wochenschr	Klinische Wochenschrift (Berlin)
Lakartidningen	Lakartidningen (Stockholm)
Lancet	Lancet (London)
Laval Theol Phil	Laval Theologique et Philosophique (Quebec)
Le Maclean	Le Maclean (Montreal)
Liquorian	Liquorian (Liquori, Missouri)
Linacre Q	Linacre Quarterly (Milwaukee)
Lumiere	Lumiere (Toulon, France)
Macleans	Macleans Magazine (Toronto)
Mademoiselle	Mademoiselle (New York)

Marriage	Marriage (Meinrad, Indiana)
Maternal-Child Nurs J	Maternal-Child Nursing Journal (Pittsburg, Pennsylvania)
McCalls	McCalls (New York)
Md State Med J	Maryland State Medical Journal (Baltimore)
Med Arh	Medicinski Arhiv (Sarajevo)
Med Econ	Medical Economics (Oradell, New Jersey)
Med J Aust	Medical Journal of Australia (Sydney)
Med Klin	Medizinische Klinik (Munich)
Med Leg Domm Corpor	Medecine Legale et Dommage Corporel (Paris)
Med Lett Drugs Ther	Medical Letter on Drugs and Therapeutics (New York)
Med Welt	Mediznische Welt (Stuttgart)
Med World News	Medical World News (New York)
Memphis St U L Rev	Memphis State University Law Review (Memphis)
Menn	The Mennonite (Basel)
Mich Med	Michigan Medicine (East Lansing)
Minerva Ginecol	Minerva Ginecologia (Turin)
Minn Med	Minnesota Medicine (St. Paul)
Mod Hosp	Modern Hospital (Chicago)
Mod Nursing Home	Modern Nursing Home (Chicago)
Mod Vet Pract	Modern Veterinary Practice (Wheaton, Illinois)
Monatsh Vet Med	Monatshefte fuer Veterinaermedizin (Jena)
Monist	The Monist (San Jose, California)
Month	Month (London)
N Engl J Med	New England Journal of Medicine (Boston)
NC L Rev	North Carolina Law Review (Chapel Hill, North Carolina)
NC Med J	North Carolina Medical Journal (Raleigh)
NS Med Bull	Nova Scotia Medical Bulletin (Halifax)
NZ Med J	New Zealand Medical Journal (Wellington)
Nar Zdrav	Narodno Zdravije (Belgrade)
Nat Cath Rep	National Catholic Reporter (Kansas City, Missouri)

Nat R	National Review (New York)
Nation	Nation (New York)
Nature	Nature (London)
Ned Tijdschr Geneeskd	Nederlands Tijdschrift voor Geneeskunde (Amsterdam)
New Cath World	New Catholic Word (Paramus, New Jersey)
New Humanist	New Humanist (Chicago)
New Repub	New Republic (Washington)
New Schol	The New Scholasticism (Washington)
Newsletter (Soc Hosp Attorneys)	Newsletter (Society of Hospital Attorneys) (Chicago)
Newsweek	Newsweek (New York)
Nord Med	Nordisk Medicin (Stockholm)
Nord Vet Med	Nordisk Veterinaermedicin (Hellerup, Denmark)
Notre Dame Law	Notre Dame Lawyer (Notre Dame)
Nouv Presse Med	Nouvelle Presse Medicale (Paris)
Nurs Clin North Am	Nursing Clinics of North America (Philadelphia)
Nurs J India	Nursing Journal of India (New Delhi)
Nurs Mirror	Nursing Mirror and Midwives' Journal (London)
Nurs Outlook	Nursing Outlook (New York)
Nurs Times	Nursing Times
Nursing	Nursing (Brussels)
OR	OR Nursing (Chicago)
OSV	Our Sunday Visitor (Huntington, Indiana)
Obstet Gynecol	Obstetrics and Gynecology (New York)
Orv Hetil	Orvosi Hetilap (Budapest)
Pa Med	Pennsylvania Medicine (Lemoyne)
Pacific L J	Pacific Law Journal (Sacramento, California)
Paediatr Paedol	Paediatrie und Paedologie (Vienna)
Parents Mag	Parents Magazine (London)
Pediatr Akush Ginekol	Pediatriia Akushertov i Ginekologiia (Kiev)
Phil Context	Philosophy in Context (Cleveland State University, Cleveland)
Phil Pub Affairs	Philosophy and Public Affairs (Princetown, New York)
Pol Tyg Lek	Polski Tygodnik Lekarski (Warsaw)

Population Bulletin	Population Bulletin (Washington)
Population Studies	Population Studies (London)
Practitioner	Practitioner (London)
Praxis	Praxis (Bern)
Pres J	Presbyterian Journal (Weaverville, North Carolina)
Priest	Priest (Huntington, Indiana)
Proc Cath Phil Ass	Proceedings of the American Catholic Philosophical Association (Washington)
Proc R Soc Med	Proceedings of the Royal Society of Medicine (London)
Prostaglandins	Prostaglandins (Los Altos, California)
Postgrad Med	Postgraduate Medicine (Minneapolis)
Psychiat News	Psychiatric News (Washington)
Psychiatr Neurol Neurochir	Psychiatria, Neurologia, Neurochirurgia (Amsterdam)
Psychiatry Med	Psychiatry in Medicine (Farmingdale, New York)
Psychol Rep	Psychological Reports (Missoula)
Quis Custodiet	Quis Custodiet (Middlesex, England)
R Rel	Review for Religious (St. Louis)
RANF Rev	RANF Review (Queensland)
RN	RN; National Magazine for Nurses (Oradell, New Jersey)
Radiology	Radiology (Syracuse)
Read Digest	Readers Digest (Pleasantville, New York)
Redbook	Redbook Magazine (New York)
Regan Rep Nurs Law	Regan Report on Nursing Law (New York)
Relations	Relations (Montreal)
Res Vet Sci	Research in Veterinary Science (Oxford)
Rev Fr Gynecol Obstet	Revue Francaise de Gynecologie et d'Obstetrique (Paris)
Rev Med Chil	Revista Medica de Chile (Santiago)
Rev Roum Virol	Revue Roumaine de Virologie (Bucharest)
Rev Thomiste	Revue Thomiste: Revue Doctrinale de Theologie et de Philosophie (Bruxelles)
Ripon Forum	Ripon Forum (Cambridge, Massachusetts)
S Afr Med J	South African Medical Journal (Capetown)

San Diego L Rev	San Diego Law Revue (San Diego)
Sat N	Saturday Night (Toronto)
Sat R Soc	Saturday Review of Sociology (New York)
Schweiz Med Wochenschr	Schweizerische Medizinische Wochenschrift (Basel)
Sci Am	Scientific American (New York)
Sci N	Science News (Washington)
Sem Hop Paris	Semaine des Hopitaux de Paris (Paris)
Sign	Sign (Union City, New Jersey)
Singapore Med J	Singapore Medical Journal (Singapore)
Sisters	Sisters Today (Collegeville, Minnesota)
Soc Just	Social Justice Review (St. Louis)
Soc Sci Med	Social Science and Medicine (Oxford)
Soc Work	Social Worker (Ontario)
Southern Hosp	Southern Hospitals (Charlotte, North Carolina)
Southern Med J	Southern Medical Journal (Birmingham, Alabama)
St Anth	St. Anthony Messenger (Cincinnati)
Stud Fam Plann	Studies in Family Planning (New York)
Studies	Studies (Paris)
Suffolk U L Rev	Suffolk University Law Review (Boston)
Superv Nurse	Supervisor Nurse (Chicago)
Tablet	Tablet (London)
Tex Hosp	Texas Hospitals (Austin)
Tex Med	Texas Medicine (Austin)
Theol Stds	Theological Studies (Woodstock, Maryland)
Theor Popul Biol	Theoretical Population Biology (New York)
Ther GGW	Therapie der Gegenwart (Berlin)
Therapeutique	Therapeutique (Paris)
Thomist	The Thomist (Washington)
Tidsskr Nor Laegeforen	Tidsskrift for den Norske Laegeforening (Oslo)
Time	Time (Chicago)
Triumph	Triumph (Washington)
Tul L Rev	Tulane Law Review (Worcester, Massachusetts)
U Cin L Rev	University of Cincinnati Law Review (Cincinnati)
U Richmond L Rev	University of Richmond Law Review

	(Richmond)
UC Her	United Church Herald (New York)
US Cath	U. S. Catholic and Jubilee (Chicago)
US Dept HEW Publ	United States Department of Health, Education, and Welfare Publications (Bethesda, Maryland)
US Med	U. S. Medicine (Washington)
Ugeskr Laeger	Ugeskrift for Laeger (Copenhagen)
Vand L Rev	Vanderbill Law Review (Nashville)
Vestn Akad Med Nauk SSSR	Vestnik Akademii Nauk SSSR (Moscow)
Vet Med Small Anim Clin	Veterinary Medicine/Small Animal Clinician (Bonner Springs, Kansas)
Vet Rec	Veterinary Record (London)
Veterinariia	Veterinariia (Moscow)
Virginia Med Mon	Virginia Medical Monthly (Richmond)
Virology	Virology (New York)
Vopr Okhr Materin Det	Voprosy Okhrany Materinstva i Detstva (Moscow)
Vox Sang	Vox Sanguinis (Philadelphia)
Wall St J	Wall Street Journal (New York)
Wash & Lee L Rev	Washington & Lee Law Review (Lexington, Virginia)
World Med J	World Medical Instrumentation (Oxford)
Yale L J	Yale Law Journal (New Haven, Connecticut)
Z Aerztl Fortbild	Zeitschrift fur Aerztliche Fortbildung (Jena)
Z Rechtsmed	Zeitschrift fuer Rechtsmedizin (Berlin)
Zh Eksp Klin Med	Zhurnal Eksperimental' noi i Klinicheskoi Meditsiny (Erevan)
Zentralbl Gynaekol	Zentralblatt fuer Gynaekologie (Leipzig)
Zentralbl Veterinaermed	Zentralblatt fuer Veterinaermedizinl. Journal of Veterinary Medicine (Berlin)

SUBJECT HEADINGS USED IN THIS BIBLIOGRAPHY

Abnormalties
Abortion (General)
Abortion Act
Abortion: Australia
Abortion: Belgium
Abortion: Canada
Abortion: Chile
Abortion: Denmark
Abortion: Finland
Abortion: France
Abortion: Germany
Abortion: Hungary
Abortion: India
Abortion: Italy
Abortion: Japan
Abortion: New Zealand
Abortion: Puerto Rico
Abortion: Romania
Abortion: Sweden
Abortion: Uganda
Abortion: United Kingdom
Abortion: United States
    Arkansas
    California
    Colorado
    Connecticut
    Florida
    Georgia
    Hawaii
    Illinois
    Iowa
    Louisiana
    Maryland
    Massachusetts
    Missouri
    New Jersey
    New York
    North Carolina
    Oklahoma
    Oregon
    Pennsylvania

    Tennessee
    Texas
Abortion: USSR
Abortion: Yugoslavia
Adoption
Alupent
American College of Obstetricians
   and Gynecologists
American Hospital Association
American Public Health Associa-
   tion
Anesthesia
Antibodies
Artificial Abortion
Aspirin
Behavior
Bibliography
Birth Control
Blood
Candidiasis
Cardiovascular System
Cephalothin
Cervical Incompetence and
   Insufficiency
Chlormadinone
Clinical Aspects
Clomiphene
College Women
Complications
Contraception
Criminal Abortion
Demography
Diagnosis
Diethylstibestrol
Doxicillin
Drug Therapy
Education
Endotoxin
Estradiol
Ethyl Alcohol
Family Planning

TABLE OF CONTENTS

BOOKS

Baumann, Jurgen. DAS ABTREIBUNGSVERBOT DES ART. 218 STGB: eine Vorschrift, die mehr schadet als nutzt. Neuwied: Luchterhand, 1972.

Bluford, Robert Jr. and Robert E. Petres. UNWANTED PREGNANCY. New York: Harper & Row, 1973.

Carmen, Arlene and Howard Moody. ABORTION COUNSELING AND SOCIAL CHANGE. Valley Forge, Pennsylvania: Judson Press, 1973.

Cartwright and Waite. GENERAL PRACTITIONERS AND ABORTION: evidence to the Committee on the working of the Abortion Act. London: Royal College of General Practitioner.

Depreux, Jean Claude. LE MEDECIN DEVANT LA DEMANDE D'A-VORTEMENT. Bruxelles: Centre d'education a la famille et a l'amour, 1971.

Ejerfeldt, Lennart and Herman Seiler, compilers. LAG OCH ETIK I ABORTFRAGEN. Stockholm: Katolska bokforlaget, 1972.

Feinberg, J., editor. THE PROBLEM OF ABORTION. Belmont, California: Wadsworth Publishing Company, 1973.

Floyd, Mary K., compiler. ABORTION BIBLIOGRAPHY FOR 1971. Troy, New York: Whitston Publishing Company, 1973.

--ABORTION BIBLIOGRAPHY FOR 1972. Troy, New York: Whitston Publishing Company, 1973.

Gardner, Rex. WHAT ABOUT ABORTION? Exeter, England:

Paternoster Press.

Grabbe, George. ABORTION: An Eastern Orthodox Statement. Eastern Orthodox.

Gutcheon, B. R. ABORTION: a woman's guide. New York: Abelard-Schuman, 1973.

Hardin, G. STALKING THE WILD TABOO. Los Altos, California: William Kaufmann, Inc., 1973.

Hart, Thomas M., editor. ABORTION IN THE CLINIC AND OFFICE SETTING. San Francisco: Society for Humane Abortion, 1972.

Hilgers, Thomas and Dennis J. Horan. ABORTION & SOCIAL JUSTICE. New York: Sheed & Ward, 1973.

Howells. ABORTION, WHAT PRICE? Llandyssul, Cards: Gomerian.

Huant, Ernest. NON A L'AVORTEMENT, etude biologique, sociologique et morale des divers aspects du probleme et de toutes les raisons du refus. Paris: Tequi, 1972.

Huffman, John W. and Gerald B. Holzman. IMPLEMENTATION OF LEGAL ABORTION: a national problem. New York: Medical Department, Harper & Row, 1971.

Ivaldy, Fernand. DE L'AVORTEMENT. Paris, A.D.E.: Apostolat des editions, 1971.

Jain, Sagar C. and Laurel F. Gooch. GEORGIA ABORTION ACT 1968: a study in legislative process. School of Public Health, University of North Carolina, Chapel Hill, North Carolina, 1973.

Jenness, Linda. ABORTION: Women's Fight for the Right to Choose. Path Press Inc., New York, 1973.

Kinton, J. F. and E. R. Kinton, compilers. ABORTION: social attitudes and practices. Social Science & Sociological Resources, 1973.

Kleinman, R. L. INDUCED ABORTION; a report of the meeting of the IPPF Panel of Experts on Abortion. London: International Planned Parenthood Federation, 1972.

2

Kraker, Ana. GESETZ UBER DEN SCHWANGERSCHAFTSABBRUCH UND DIE RUCKLAUFIGE ENTWICKLUNG DES GEBURTENUBER- SCHUSSES IN JUGOSLAWIEN. Hrsg. von Hans Harmsen. Hamburg, 1972.

Lader, L. ABORTION II: making the revolution. Boston: Beacon Press, 1973.

Lewit, editor. ABORTION TECHNIQUES AND SERVICES: Conference Proceedings. New York: Association Science Publishers, 1971.

Lewit, Sarah, editor. EXCERPTA MEDICA INTERNATIONAL CONGRESS SERIES, NO. 255. Abortion techniques and services. Proceedings of the Conference. New York, New York, June 3-5, 1971, Excerpta Medica: Amsterdam, The Netherlands, 1972.

Locht, Pierre de. AVORTEMENT: an moraliste s'interroge. Bruxelles: Centre d'education a la famille et a l'amour, 1971.

McEllhenney, J. G. CUTTING THE MONKEY-ROPE. Valley Forge, Pennsylvania: Judson Press, 1973.

Mullally. ABORTION: Killing the Unborn. London: Catholic Truth Society, 1973.

North, Douglass C. and Roger L. Miller. ABORTION, BASEBALL & WEED: Economic Issues of Our Times. New York: Harper & Row, 1973.

Osofsky, Howard J. and Joy Osofsky. ABORTION EXPERIENCE: Psychological & Medical Impact. New York: Harper & Row, 1973.

Pelt, J. THE SOUL, THE PILL AND THE FETUS. Dorrance, 1972.

Pennsylvania. Abortion Law Commission. REPORT OF THE PENNSYL- VANIA ABORTION LAW COMMISSION APPOINTED BY THE GOVER- NOR TO REVIEW PENNSYLVANIA'S ABORTION LAW. Harrisburg, 1972.

Planned Parenthood of New York City. ABORTION: A Woman's Guide. New York: Abelard-Schuman, 1973.

Potts, editor. GUIDE TO THE ABORTION ACT, 1967. Abortion Law

Reform Association, 1973.

Rahmas, D. Steve, editor. ABORTION CONTROVERSY. State College, Pennsylvania: San-Har Press, 1973.

Redford, Myron H. and Edgar K. Marcuse. LEGAL ABORTION IN WASHINGTON STATE: an analysis of the first year's experience. Seattle: School of Public Health and Community Medicine, University of Washington, 1973.

Reed, Evelyn and Claire Moriarty. ABORTION & THE CATHOLIC CHURCH: Two Feminists Defend Women's Rights. New York: Pathfinder Press Inc., 1973.

Revolte der Frauen. ABORTION--Germany. Stuttgart, Aktion, Verlag & politischer Buchladen, 1971.

Rudel, H. W. BIRTH CONTROL. New York: Macmillan Publishing Company, 1973.

Saltman, Jules and Stanley Zimering. ABORTION TODAY. Springfield, Illinois: C. C. Thomas, 1973.

Sarvis, Betty and Hyman Rodman. THE ABORTION CONTROVERSY. New York: Columbia University Press, 1973.

Sloane, R. B. and D. F. Horvitz. A GENERAL GUIDE TO ABORTION. Chicago: Nelson-Hall, 1973.

SUPPLEMENT ON ABORTION. Statistical Review of England and Wales, 1971.

Tettamanzi, Dionigi. L'ABORTO: puo essere legalizzato. Roma: Apes, 1972.

Walbert, D. F. and J. D. Butler, editors. ABORTION, SOCIETY, AND THE LAW. Cleveland: The Press of Case Western Reserve University, 1973.

Walner, B. B. IT ISN'T NICE. Victoria, Australia: Alpha Books, 1972.

Williams, Jean Morton. ABORTION AND CONTRACEPTION: a study of patients' attitudes. London: P.E.P., 1972.

Wilson, Paul. ABORTION, HOMOSEXUALITY, PROSTITUTION AND THE CRIMINAL THRESHOLD: Sexual Dilemma. Australia: Queensland University Press, 1971.

Winslow, Martha. ABORTIONIST. NAL, 1970.

World Health Organization. SPONTANEOUS AND INDUCED ABORTION. Technical Reports, London: H.M.S.O., 1971.

PERIODICAL LITERATURE

TITLE INDEX

"ABO blood groups and abortion." BR MED J 4:547, December 2, 1972.

"Abortifacient efficacy of intravaginal prostaglandin F2a," by A. C. Wentz, et al. AM J OBSTET GYNECOL 115:27-32, 1973.

"Abortion." NEW REPUB 168:9, February 10, 1973; Reply by M. P. O'Boyle 168:32, March 24, 1973.

"Abortion," by B. Littlewood. NZ MED J 77:126-127, February, 1973.

"Abortion," by H. Ratner. J SC MED ASSOC 69:69-70, February, 1973.

"Abortion," by P. B. Temm. NZ MED J 77:265-266, April, 1973.

"Abortion. The first five years at North Carolina Memorial Hospital," by W. E. Easterling, Jr., et al. TEX MED 69:61-67, April, 1973.

"Abortion Act in Somerset," by A. P. Jones, et al. BR MED J 3:90-92, July 14, 1973.

"The Abortion Act of 1967; Society for the Protection of Unborn Children." TABLET 227:237-239, March 10, 1973.

"Abortion after Roe (Roe v. Wade, 93 Sup Ct 705) and Doe (Doe v. Bolton, 93 Sup Ct 739): a proposed statute." VAND L REV 26:823-835, May, 1973.

"Abortion: the agent's perspective," by S. Hauerwas. AER 167:102-120, February, 1973.

"Abortion alert," by A. Altchek. OBSTET GYNECOL 42:452-454,

7

September, 1973.

"Abortion and chromosome aberrations," by G. Neuhauser. HIPPO-KRATES 44:85-87, March, 1973.

"Abortion and the Church." AMERICA 128:110-111, February 10, 1973.

"Abortion and coagulation by prostaglandin. Intra-amniotic dinoprost tromethamine effect on the coagulation and fibrinolytic systems," by W. R. Bell, et al. JAMA 225:1082-1084, August 27, 1973.

"Abortion and the Court." CHR TODAY 17:32-33, February 16, 1973.

"Abortion and family planning," by K. N. Rao. J INDIAN MED ASSOC 59:337-341, October 16, 1972.

"Abortion and infanticide," by M. Tooley. PHILOSOPHY AFFAIRS 2: 37-66, Fall, 1972.

"Abortion and liberation," by M. Simms. NEW HUMANIST 88:479-481, April, 1973.

"Abortion and the Mosaic law," by J. W. Cottrell. CHR TODAY 17:6-9, March 16, 1973.

"Abortion and population," by D. Munday. HEALTH SOC SERV J 83:13-14, pt 2, March 10, 1973.

"Abortion and the principles of legislation," by P. J. Micallef. LAVAL THEOL PHIL 28:267-303, October, 1972.

"Abortion and the sanctity of human life," by B. A. Brody. AM PHIL QUART 10:133-140, April, 1973.

"Abortion and sexual behavior in college women," by K. J. Monsour, et al. AM J ORTHOPSYCHIATRY 43:804-814, October, 1973.

"Abortion and U. S. Protestants." AMERICA 128:156-157, February 24, 1973.

"Abortion appeals rejected." NAT CATH REP 9:3, March 9, 1973.

"Abortion applicants in Arkansas," by F. O. Henker, 3d. J ARKANSAS

MED SOC 69:293-295, March, 1973.

"Abortion, an Aquarian perspective," by D. Nugent. CRITIC 31:32-36, January-February, 1973.

"Abortion around the world." TIME 101:76, February 19, 1973.

"Abortion associated with Brucella abortus (Biotype 1) in the T.B. mare," by F. J. Robertson, et al. VET REC 92:480-481, May 5, 1973.

"Abortion at MSU," by R. Kirk. NAT R 25:527, May 11, 1973.

"Abortion bill in Oregon would be costly to Catholic hospitals." HOSP PROGRESS 54:20, April, 1973.

"Abortion; blast and counter-blast." ECONOMIST 249:31, November 24, 1973.

"Abortion by vacuum method." NURS J INDIA 64:205-207, June, 1973.

"Abortion cases: a return to Lochner, or a new substantive due process?" ALBANY L REV 37:776, 1973.

"Abortion clinic design emphasizes restraint to minimize patients' tension," by H. McLaughlin. MOD HOSP 121:74-75, September, 1973.

"Abortion clinics and operating sessions," by A. E. Buckle. NURS MIRROR 136:36-38, March 9, 1973.

"Abortion clinics face competition: New York City." AMER MED NEWS 16:3, April 2, 1973.

"The abortion constellation. Early history and present relationships," by V. Abernethy. ARCH GEN PSYCHIATRY 29:346-350, September, 1973.

"Abortion: the continuing controversy." POPULATION BULLETIN 28:1-29, August, 1972.

"Abortion, contraception and child mental health," by L. J. Redman, et al. FAMILY PLANN PERSPECT 5:71-72, Spring, 1973.

"Abortion controversy: Ancient practice, current conflict," by

M. F. Brewer. CURRENT 154:26-28, September, 1973.

"Abortion counseling: an experimental study of three techniques," by M. B. Bracken, et al. AM J OBSTET GYNECOL 117:10-20, September 1, 1973.

"Abortion: Court decision removes legal uncertainty." SCI N 103: 54, January 27, 1973.

"Abortion culture," by N. Thimmesch. NEWSWEEK 82:7, July 9, 1973.

"Abortion cuts numbers of abandoned infants, immature births." J AMER MED ASS 224:1697-1698, June 25, 1973.

"Abortion deaths: England and Wales." LANCET 1:1199, May 26, 1973.

"Abortion debate is revealing our values," by G. L. Chamberlain. NEW CATH WORLD 215:206-208, September, 1972.

"The abortion decision." COMM 97:435-436, February 16, 1973.

"Abortion decision." SCI AM 228:44-45, March, 1973.

"Abortion decision," by R. F. Drinan. COMMONWEAL 97:438-440, February 16, 1973; Reply with rejoinder by J. T. McHugh 98:75 plus, March 30, 1973.

"Abortion decision and Puerto Rico," by J. L. Simon. REV C ABO PR 34:505-513, August, 1973.

"Abortion decision: a balancing of rights," by J. C. Evans. CHR CENT 90:195-197, February 14, 1973.

"The abortion decision: cond from a Washington Star Syndicate feature, 1973," by W. Buckley. C DGST 37:41-42, May, 1973.

"Abortion decision; a death blow?" CHR TODAY 17:48, February 16, 1973.

"Abortion decision: end of an inalienable right," by E. Melvin. OSV 61:1 plus, April 29, 1973.

"Abortion decision may set precedent to resolve 1st Amendment conflicts," by E. J. Schulte. HOSP PROG 54:85-87 passim, September, 1973.

"Abortion decisions: Roe v. Wade (93 Sup Ct 705), Doe v. Bolton (93 Sup Ct 739)." J FAMILY L 12:459, 1972-1973.

"The abortion decisions: the Supreme Court as moralist, scientist, historian and legislator," by W. J. Curran. N ENGL J MED 288:950-951, May 3, 1973.

"Abortion: decisions to live with: conference at Southern Methodist university," by R. C. Wahlberg. CHR CENT 90:691-693, June 27, 1973.

"Abortion: a deeper look at the legal aspects," by R. Orloski. US CATH 38:39-40, September, 1973.

"Abortion--demanding litigation: preparation and response," by S. M. Blaes. HOSP PROGRESS 54:70 plus, August, 1973.

"Abortion: denial of freedom to care," by D. DeMarco. OSV 62:1 plus, July 1, 1973.

"Abortion: deterrence, facilitation, resistance." AMERICA 128:506-507, June 2, 1973.

"Abortion: an ecumenical dilemma," by G. Baum. COMM 99:231-235, November 30, 1973.

"Abortion: the father's rights." U CIN L REV 42:441-467, 1973.

"Abortion: the fight goes on." HOSP WORLD 2:7, May, 1973.

"Abortion: the first five years at North Carolina Memorial Hospital," by W. E. Easterling, Jr., et al. TEX MED 69:61-67, April, 1973.

"Abortion for the asking," by H. Dudar. SAT R SOC 1:30-35, April, 1973.

"Abortion front: end of the phony war." NAT R 25:249-250, March 2, 1973.

"Abortion: history, opinions, and what's new in the United States," by E. D. Jubb, et al. CAN B J 4:8-12, July, 1973.

"Abortion in Canada as a public health problem and as a community health measure," by C. W. Schwenger. CAN J PUBLIC HEALTH 64: 223-230, May-June, 1973.

"Abortion in cattle associated with Bacillus cereus," by K. Wohlgemuth, et al. J AM VET MED ASSOC 161:1688-1690, December 15, 1972.

"Abortion in Finland today," by K. Wichmann. DUODECIM 89:649-651, 1973.

"Abortion in Hawaii," by M. Diamond, et al. FAMILY PLANN PERSPECT 5:54-60, Winter, 1973.

"Abortion in Hawaii: 1970-1971," by R. G. Smith, et al. HAWAII MED J 32:213-220, July-August, 1973.

"Abortion in New Zealand," by W. A. Facer, et al. J BIOSOC SCI 5:151-158, April, 1973.

"Abortion in the United States. Decisions of the Supreme Court," by R. Veylon. NOUV PRESSE MED 2:1952-1954, July 28, 1973.

"Abortion in Victoria after Menhennit," by J. Smibert. MED J AUST 1:1016-1017, May 19, 1973.

"Abortion information can be mailed." NEWSLETTER 6:5, January, 1973.

"Abortion: the inhumanity of it all," by J. McHugh. ST ANTH 80:12-22, February, 1973.

"Abortion is an expensive contraceptive," by L. O. Dandenell. LAKARTIDNINGEN 70:343, January 31, 1973.

"Abortion is killing," by J. Willke, et al. COLUMBIA 53:10-19, April, 1973.

"Abortion is morally wrong says Italian Bishops' Council." OR 9,257:5, March 1, 1973.

"Abortion issue." SAT N 88:10, September, 1973.

"Abortion law," by I. S. Edwards. MED J AUST 2:850, October 7, 1972.

"Abortion law in the USA." BR MED J 1:428-429, February 17, 1973.

"Abortion: law of nation or law of God; reprint from The Catholic Standard and Times, January 25, 1973." DIMENSION 5:35, Spring, 1973.

"Abortion law reform controversy rages in West Germany," by F. Lupsen. CHR CENT 90:487-488, April 25, 1973.

"Abortion: legal but still wrong," by E. Gilbert. LIGUORIAN 61:2-4, October, 1973.

"Abortion: locating the blind spots," by J. F. Kavanaugh. AMERICA 129:149, September 8, 1973.

"Abortion--a matter of life and death," by J. F. Gwynne. NZ MED J 76:355-357, November, 1972.

"Abortion may be a realistic alternative," by G. Koontz, et al. MENN p A-2, April 17, 1973.

"Abortion: mixed feelings." MED WORLD NEWS 14:4-6, February 9, 1973.

"Abortion: the moment of truth," by V. Dillon. US CATH 38:37-38, September, 1973.

"Abortion: next round." COMM 98:51-52, March 23, 1973.

"Abortion: no present changes." MED WORLD NEWS 14:4-5, March 23, 1973.

"Abortion of early pregnancy by the intravaginal administration of prostaglandin F2alpha," by R. J. Bolognese, et al. AM J OBSTET GYNECOL 117:246-250, September 15, 1973.

"Abortion on demand," by C. Whelan. AMERICA 128:, February 10, 1973.

"Abortion on demand." TIME 101:46-47, January 29, 1973.

"Abortion on demand in a post-Wade (Roe v. Wade 93 Sup Ct 705) context: must the state pay the bills?" FORDHAM L REV 41:921, May, 1973.

"Abortion on request: the physician's view," by A. F. Guttmacher. AM BIOL TEACH 34:514-517, December, 1972; Reply with rejoinder by P. R. Gastonguay 35:353-355, September, 1973.

"Abortion, oui!" NEWSWEEK 81:46 plus, June 11, 1973.

"Abortion: patterns, technics, and results," by E. B. Connell. FERTIL STERIL 24:78-91, January, 1973.

"Abortion picture still confused despite Supreme Court ruling." RN 36:17, April, 1973.

"Abortion positions; so who's the radical?" by C. Fager. NAT CATH REP 9:12, March 2, 1973.

"Abortion; postscript." ECONOMIST 247:28, June 2, 1973.

"Abortion programme in Duchenne muscular dystrophy in Japan," by K. Kondo, et al. LANCET 1:543, March 10, 1973.

"The abortion question and the evangelical tradition," by R. Wolfe. DIMENSION 5:84-89, Summer, 1973.

"Abortion: resources for reflection (bibliographical)," by D. Friesen. MENN p 480, August 8, 1972.

"Abortion - respect life - legality vs. morality," by P. O'Boyle. SOC JUST 65:372-373, February, 1973.

"Abortion: a review article," by P. Ramsey. THOMIST 37:174-226, January, 1973.

"Abortion revolution." NEWSWEEK 81:27-28, February 5, 1973.

"Abortion revolution: don't rush it," by C. L. Rosenberg. MED ECON 50:31 plus, March 5, 1973.

"The abortion ruling: analysis & prognosis: symposium: CHA to conduct anti-abortion campaign. NCCB pastoral message. Commentaries," by T. Shaffer, et al. HOSP PROG 54:81-96b, March, 1973.

"The abortion ruling: analysis & prognosis." HOSP PROG 54:81-83 passim, March, 1973.

14

"Abortion ruling: Catholic facts and constitutional truths," by R. Marshall. SOC JUST 66:84, June, 1973.

"Abortion services in Massachusetts." N ENGL J MED 288:686-687, March 29, 1973.

"The abortion situation in Denmark and conditions in Finland," by M. Johansson. LAKARTIDNINGEN 70:344, January 31, 1973.

"Abortion situation in Oklahoma reviewed." J OKLA STATE MED ASS 66:409-411, September, 1973.

"Abortion surveillance program of the center for disease control," by J. C. Smith, et al. HEALTH SERV REP 88:255-259, March, 1973.

"Abortion - the theological argument," by M. Alsopp. FURROW 24: 202-206, April, 1973.

"Abortion trends in European socialist countries and in the United States," by H. P. David. AM J ORTHOPSYCHIATRY 43:376-383, April, 1973.

"Abortion: two views: keep abortion under the Criminal code," by V. Macdonald. CHATELAINE 46:38, 106-107, November, 1973.

"Abortion: two views: let the individual conscience decide," by I. LeBourdais. CHATELAINE 46:38, 105-106, November, 1973.

"Abortion: The United States Supreme Court decision." LANCET 1:301-302, February 10, 1973.

"Abortion using a bicycle pump on the mistress and unusual suicide of a blind man," by F. J. Holzer. BEITR GERICHTL MED 30:187-196, 1973.

"Abortion: what happens now." NEWSWEEK 81:66 plus, February 5, 1973.

"The abortionist dictionary: gilded words for guilty deeds," by J. Allen. LIGUORIAN 61:36-37, May, 1973.

"Abortions," by C. D. Davis. TEX HOSP 28:28-29, March, 1973.

"Abortions at charity prices." SOC JUST 66:87-88, June, 1973.

"Abortions: fallacies and pitfalls," by W. L. Weyl. VIRGINIA MED MON 100:172, February, 1973.

"Abortions: a national dilemma," by J. A. Paulsen. J AM COLL HEALTH ASSOC 21:495-497, June, 1973.

"Abortions: new legal guidelines," by C. Weissburg, et al. FAH REV 6:41 plus, April, 1973.

"Abortions rise 33 per cent in nation-wide Canadian survey." HOSP ADMIN CAN 15:8, February, 1973.

"Abortus provocatus in cattle," by L. Schjerven. NORD VET MED 24: 537-543, November, 1972.

"Abruption of the placenta. A review of 189 cases occurring between 1965 and 1969," by R. G. Blair. J OBSTET GYNAECOL BR COMMONW 80:242-245, March, 1973.

"Accidents and sequelae of medical abortions," by B. Beric, et al. AM J OBSTET GYNECOL 116:813-821, July 15, 1973.

"Accumulation of complement-fixing antibodies in virus abortion of sheep," by R. K. Khamadeev, et al. VETERINARIIA 49:113-115, May, 1973.

"Achievements, changes and challenges in gynecology," by A. Peretz. HAREFUAH 85:1-3, July 1, 1973.

"Action in the wake of death Monday," by J. Doyle. SOC JUST 66:133-135, July-August, 1973.

"Action of prostaglandin F2a on the corpus luteum of the gestating rat," by H. Tuchmann-Duplessis, et al. C R HEBD SEANCES ACAD SCI SER D SCI NAT 275:2033-2035, 1972.

"Acute renal failure in obstetric septic shock. Current views on pathogenesis and management," by D. S. Emmanouel, et al. AM J OBSTET GYNECOL 117:145-159, September 1, 1973.

"Additional births averted when abortion is added to contraception," by

R. G. Potter. STUD FAM PLANN 3:53-59, April, 1972.

"Administrative commission issues pastoral message on abortion."
OR 10,258:9, March 8, 1973.

"Adolescent pregnancy: a study of aborters and non-aborters," by F. J.
Kane, Jr., et al. AM J ORTHOPSYCHIATRY 43:796-803, October, 1973.

"Adolescent sexuality," by M. G. Wolfish. PRACTITIONER 210:226-
231, February, 1973.

"L'adoption, une alternative meconnue a l'avortement; France," by F.
Dardot. ETUDES 338:701-714, May, 1973.

"Aftermath of the abortion decisions: action in the legislatures and in
the courts," by W. J. Curran. N ENGL J MED 289:955, November 1,
1973.

"Age of the woman and spontaneous and induced abortions," by Z.
Gizicki. GINEKOL POL 43:443-447, April, 1972.

"Aggressive management of septic abortion: report of 262 cases," by
W. J. Connolly, et al. SOUTH MED J 65:1480-1484, December, 1972.

"Air embolism in the interruption of pregnancy by vacuum extraction," by
G. H. Hartung. ZENTRALBL GYNAEKOL 95:825-828, June 15, 1973.

"Alpha-fetoprotein in abortion," by M. Seppala, et al. BR MED J 4:769-
771, December 30, 1972.

"Amazing historical and biological errors in abortion decision," by A. E.
Hellegers. HOSP PROG 54:16-17, May, 1973.

"America: there's a nigger in the woodpile," by W. Devlin. TRIUMPH
8:27, May, 1973.

"American bishops and abortion." TABLET 227:268-269, March 17, 1973.

"American Civil Liberties Union suit seeks abortions in St. Louis
public hospitals." HOSPITALS 47:116, September 16, 1973.

"The American College of Obstetricians and Gynecologists Statement
on abortion, February 10, 1973." J MED ASSOC STATE ALA

42:736, April, 1973.

"American tragedy: the Supreme Court on abortion," by R. M. Byrn. FORDHAM L REV 41:807, May, 1973.

"America's war on life; symposium: Where we have been, where we go from here. The abortion culture, by K. Mitzner. The movement coming together. The movement staying together. The Catholic obligation." TRIUMPH 8:17-32, March, 1973.

"Analysis of the etiology of abortions in cattle," by B. A. Timofeev, et al. VETERINARIIA 7:104-106, July, 1972.

"Analysis of induced abortions at a regional hospital," by B. Deidesheimer. ZENTRALBL GYNAEKOL 95:819-824, June 15, 1973.

"Analysis of products of conception," by W. Y. Burton, Jr. AM J OBSTET GYNECOL 115:1163, April 15, 1973.

"Analysis of prostaglandin F2a and metabolites in blood during constant intravenous infusion of prostaglandin F2a in the human female," by F. Beguin, et al. ACTA PHYSIOL SCAND 86:430-432, 1972.

"Anatomy of social abortion," by J. Jurukovski, et al. GOD ZB MED FAK SKOPJE 18:61-69, 1972.

"Anesthesia in artificial abortion," by B. P. Oleinik, et al. PEDIATR AKUSH GINEKOL 1:53-55, 1973.

"The Anker dilator in therapeutic abortion," by B. von Friesen. ACTA OBSTET GYNECOL SCAND 52:191-192, 1973.

"Anti-abortion lobby fights on," by M. Elliott. DAILY TELEGRAPH p 17, February 2, 1973.

"Appeal to all: protect human life: pastoral letter of the German Episcopate." OR 28,276:9-10, July 12, 1973.

"Appeals court rules private hospital has right to refuse abortions," by E. W. Springer. HOSP TOP 51:24-25, August, 1973.

"Arizona infections in sheep associated with gastroenteritis and abortion," by J. Greenfield, et al. VET REC 92:400-401, April 14, 1973.

"Aspirin and indomethacin: effect on instillation/abortion time of midtrimester hypertonic saline induced abortion," by R. Waltman, et al. PROSTAGLANDINS 3:47-58, 1973.

"Association of Salmonella dublin with abortion in cattle," by A. P. MacLaren. VET REC 91:687-688, December 30, 1972.

"The association of Salmonella dublin with bovine abortion in Victoria," by R. G. Russell, et al. AUST VET J 49:173-174, March, 1973.

"Attitudes of Indian women towards abortion," by K. S. Bhardwaj, et al. INDIAN J SOCIAL WORK 33:317-322, January, 1973.

"Attitudes of obstetric and gynecologic residents toward abortion," by P. R. Mascovich, et al. CALIF MED 119:29-34, August, 1973.

"Attitudes of unmarried college women toward abortion," by M. Vincent, et al. J SCH HEALTH 43:55-59, January, 1973.

"L'avortement," by P. Chauchard. REV THOMISTE 73:33-46, January-March, 1973.

"L'avortement: ethique et politique; compte rendue," by G. Bourgeault. RELATIONS 380:91-93, March, 1973.

"L'avortement; symposium: Une histoire d'amour et de mort, by M. Gillet. Sexualite, contraception et avortement, by M. Debout. Liberte de l'avortement et liberation des femmes, by H. Bonnet. Legalite et moralite face a l'avortement, by R. Boyer. La volonte de procreer: reflexion philosophique, by B. Quelquejeu. Reflexions theologiques sur la position de l'Eglise catholique, by J. M. Pohier." LUMIERE 21:6-107, August-October, 1972.

"Avorter, dit-elle," by M. Beaulieu. LE MACLEAN 13:14-15, 30 plus, February, 1973.

"A baby girl: one good argument against abortion; testimony, Pennsylvania Abortion Law Commission, February 24, 1972," by C. Martin. DIMENSION 4:144-148, Winter, 1972.

"Balanced translocation t(15q-;16p+) as cause of habitual abortions," by T. Hasegawa, et al. GEBURTSHILFE FRAUENHEILKD 33:541-544, July, 1973.

"Banding analysis of abnormal karyotypes in spontaneous abortion," by T. Kajii, et al. AM J HUM GENET 25:539-547, September, 1973.

"Because the Lord loved you," by K. O'Rourke. HOSP PROG 54:73-77, August, 1973.

"The beginning of mental activity in man and its importance to law. A new theory," by T. de Bour. PSYCHIATR NEUROL NEUROCHIR 75:385-390, September-October, 1972.

"Biochemical study of the amniotic fluid in threatened pregnancies," by R. H. Gevers, et al. NED TIJDSCHR GENEESKD 116:1969-1970, October 21, 1972.

"The bioelectrical activity of the brain in women with threatening interruption of pregnancy," by E. A. Panova. AKUSH GINEKOL 48:32-34, September, 1972.

"Births averted by induced abortion: an application of renewal theory," by R. G. Potter. THEOR POPUL BIOL 3:69-86, March, 1972.

"Bishop offers diocesan aid to prevent abortions." NAT CATH REP 9:5, February 23, 1973.

"Bishops condemn abortion decision," by R. Casey. NAT CATH REP 9:1-2, February 23, 1973.

"Bishops issue rules on abortion laws." NAT CATH REP 9:19, April 27, 1973.

"Body built and endocrine changes in women with habitual abortions," by G. P. Koreneva, et al. VOPR OKHR MATERIN DET 17:48-51, November, 1972.

"Body composition studies in the human fetus after intra-amniotic injection of hypertonic saline," by J. Wang, et al. AM J OBSTET GYNECOL 117:57-63, September 1, 1973.

"Boston prelate indicts court's abortion decision." HOSPITALS 47:170, May 16, 1973.

"Bovine abortion associated with Candida tropicalis," by K. Wohlgemuth, et al. J AM VET MED ASSOC 162:460-461, March 15, 1973.

"Bovine abortions in five Northeastern states, 1960-1970: evaluation of diagnostic laboratory data," by W. T. Hubbert, et al. CORNELL VET 63:291-316, April, 1973.

"Brook Lodge symposium on prostaglandins. Moderator's summary," by M. P. Embrey. J REPROD MED 9:464-465, December, 1972.

"Buckley and Hatfield lead fight for antiabortion measure in Senate." NAT CATH REP 9:21, June 8, 1973.

"California abortion law overturned." NEWSLETTER 6:6, January, 1973.

"Callahan on abortion: statements," by D. Callahan. COMMONWEAL 97:410, February 9, 1973.

"Cancer as a cause of abortions and stillbirths: the effect of these early deaths on the recognition of radiogenic leukaemias," by A. M. Stewart. BR J CANCER 27:465-472, June, 1973.

"Can't laugh at abortion," by A. Nowlan. ATLAN ADV 63:46-47, January, 1973.

"Cardiovascular and respiratory responses to intravenous infusion of prostaglandin F2a in the pregnant woman," by W. E. Brenner, et al. AM J OBSTET GYNECOL 114:765-772, 1972.

"A case of abortion consequent upon infection with Brucella abortus biotype 2," by P. M. Poole, et al. J CLIN PATHOL 25:882-884, October, 1972.

"Case of defibrination syndrome in internal abortion," by L. Tiraboschi, et al. MINERVA GINECOL 25:205-209, April, 1973.

"A case of postabortal bilateral uveitis--adaptometric fall of a para-central scotoma," by G. E. Jayle, et al. BULL SOC OPHTALMOL FR 72:731-736, July-August, 1972.

"Cases of mycoplasma abortion in swine," by V. Jelev, et al. ZEN-TRALBL VETERINAERMED 19:588-597, August, 1972.

"The Catholic burden." TRIUMPH 8:45, May, 1973.

"Catholic Hospital Association acts on abortion campaign; statement of philosophy; medical-moral center." HOSP PROGRESS 54:22-23, March, 1973.

"Catholic Hospital Association strengthens legal campaign against abortion." HOSP PROGRESS 54:18 plus, June, 1973.

"Catholic Hospital Association to conduct anti-abortion campaign." HOSP PROGRESS 54:82 plus, March, 1973.

"Catholic hospitals won't allow abortions." NAT CATH REP 9:4, February 2, 1973.

"The Catholic interest." TRIUMPH 8:15, November, 1973.

"Catholics attack abortion decision." NAT CATH REP 9:3-4, February 2, 1973.

"Causes for spontaneous abortion," by M. A. Petrov-Maslakov, et al. VOPR OKHR MATERIN DET 17:58-63, July, 1972.

"Cerebral air embolism following intrauterine air insufflation," by K. Joschko. ZENTRALBL GYNAEKOL 94:1587-1592, November 18, 1972.

"Cervical fistula as a complication of mid-trimester abortion," by J. S. Hirsch. OBSTET GYNECOL 41:478-479, March, 1973.

"Cervical migration of laminaria tents," by L. Wellman. AM J OBSTET GYNECOL 115:870-871, March 15, 1973.

"Cervical rupture following induced abortion," by S. L. Corson, et al. AM J OBSTET GYNECOL 116:893, July 15, 1973.

"Cervical-segmental insufficiency (CSI) as a cause of abortion. Surgical treatment. Clinico-statistical considerations," by L. Volpe, et al. MINERVA GINECOL 25:123-139, March, 1973.

"C'est pas mon probleme," by J. Pare. LE MACLEAN 13:16-17, 34-37, February, 1973.

"CHA to conduct anti-abortion campaign." HOSP PROG 54:82, March, 1973.

22

"Changes in the rat placenta following inoculation with Salmonella dublin," by G. A. Hall. AM J PATHOL 72:103-118, July, 1973.

"Changes in uterine volume following the intra-amniotic injection of hypertonic saline. Reply to comments of Dr. Goodlin," by M. O. Pulkkinen, et al. ACTA OBSTET GYNECOL SCAND 52:93-95, 1973.

"Characteristics of the functional state of the uterus in miscarriage in women with genital underdevelopment," by N. K. Moskvitina, et al. VOPR OKHR MATERIN DET 18:64-68, June, 1973.

"Characteristics of a paramyxovirus isolated from an aborted bovine fetus," by J. F. Evermann, et al. CORNELL VET 63:17-28, January, 1973.

"Les chretiens devant l'avortement; d'apres le temoignage des Peres de l'Eglise," by B. Sesboue. ETUDES 339:263-282, August-September, 1973.

"Les chretiens face a l'avortement," by B. Ribes. ETUDES 339:405-423, October, 1973.

"Christian responsibilities and abortion law." CHRIST NURSE :23-24, April, 1973.

"Chromosomal abnormalities in 32 cases of repeated abortions," by S. Warter, et al. REV FR GYNECOL OBSTET 67:321-325, May, 1972.

"Chromosomal findings in women with repeated spontaneous abortions," by J. Malkova, et al. CESK GYNEKOL 38:193-194, April, 1973.

"Chromosome investigation in married couples with repeated spontaneous abortions," by M. E. Kaosaar, et al. HUMANGENETIK 17:277-283, 1973.

"Chromosome studies in couples with repeated abortions," by H. D. Rott, et al. ARCH GYNAEKOL 213:110-118, 1972.

"Chronoperiodicity in the response to the intra-amniotic injection of prostaglandin F2 in the human," by I. D. Smith, et al. NATURE 241:279-280, January 26, 1973.

"Church abortion stand called sexist," by R. Parenteau. NAT CATH REP

10:3 plus, November 2, 1973.

"Church authorities must do much more," by G. Devine. NAT CATH REP 9:13, April 20, 1973.

"Church to make antiabortion drive." NAT CATH REP 9:1 plus, February 9, 1973.

"Clinical and hysterosalpingographical findings following interruptio," by H. J. Seewald, et al. ZENTRALBL GYNAEKOL 95:710-713, May 25, 1973.

"Clinical application of prostaglandin F2a (P.G.F2a) as a drug which can produce an interruption of pregnancy during the 1st trimester," by J. H. Luigies. NED TIJDSCHR GENEESKD 116:2368-2369, December 23, 1972.

"Clinical application of prostaglandin in obstetrics," by M. I. T'ang. CHIN MED J 9:563-569, 1973.

"Clinical evaluation of Vibravenous (doxicillin) preparation in obstetrics and gynecology," by Z. Sternadel, et al. GINEKOL POL 44:189-191, February, 1973.

"Clinical experience in prophylactic treatment of spontaneous abortion," by P. F. Tropea. ACTA EUR FERTIL 2:253-274, June, 1970.

"Clinical problems of preventive medicine. The prevention and control of infectious ovine abortion," by W. A. Watson. BR VET J 129:309-314, July-August, 1973.

"Clinical significance of organic hypomenorrhea," by W. Z. Polishuk, et al. AM J OBSTET GYNECOL 116:1058-1064, August 15, 1973.

"Clostridium infection after intra-amniotic hypertonic saline injection for induced abortion," by N. Sehgal, et al. J REPROD MED 8:67-69, February, 1972.

"Coagulation changes during termination of pregnancy by prostaglandins and by vacuum aspiration," by M. H. Badraoui, et al. BR MED J 1:19-21, January 6, 1973.

"Coagulation changes in saline-induced abortion," by R. K. Laros, Jr.,

24

et al. AM J OBSTET GYNECOL 116:271-276, May 15, 1973.

"Coagulation disorder in abruptio placentae," by N. N. Choudhury.
J INDIAN MED ASSOC 58:428-429, June 1, 1972.

"Coalition aims at abortion ban," by W. Mitchell. NAT CATH REP
9:1 plus, June 22, 1973.

"Colorado Nurses' Association statement on abortion." COLO NURSE
73:10, February, 1973.

"Colorado Supreme Court applies Wade and Bolton." NEWSLETTER
6:5-6, May, 1973.

"Combination of prostaglandine F 2 and paracervical block in the
missed abortion and intrauterine fetal death," by E. J. Hickl, et al.
KLIN WOCHENSCHR 51:140-141, February 1, 1973.

"Combined laparoscopic sterilization and pregnancy termination," by
N. G. Courey, et al. J REPROD MED 10:291-294, June, 1973.

"Community abortion services. The role of organized medicine," by
J. E. Hodgson. MINN MED 56:239-242, March, 1973.

"A comparative study of cervical mucus examination for arborisation in
pregnancy, abortion and secondary amenorrhoea," by L. Joshi. J
INDIAN MED ASSOC 58:420-421 passim, June 1, 1972.

"Comparison of operative morbidity in abortion-sterilization procedures,"
by L. L. Veltman, et al. AM J OBSTET GYNECOL 117:251-254,
September 15, 1973.

"Compassion is needed," by E. Bianchi. NAT CATH REP 9:14,
June 8, 1973.

"Complication rates associated with abortion," by G. Joslin. MED J
AUST 1:1165, June 9, 1973.

"Complications in induced abortion," by J. M. Bedoya-Gonzalez.
AN R ACAD NACL MED 90:297-306, 1973.

"Complications of abortion," by J. E. Hodgson. AM J OBSTET GYNECOL
117:293-294, September 15, 1973.

"Concern grows over abortion conscience bills," by J. Filteau. NAT CATH REP 9:3-4, April 13, 1973.

"Confusion at the highest level," by J. R. Nelson. CHR CENT 90:254-255, February 28, 1973.

"Congress and state legislatures pass 'conscience clause' legislation," by G. E. Reed. HOSP PROGRESS 54:18 plus, July, 1973.

"Congress faces abortion battle," by R. Casey. NAT CATH REP 9:1 plus, August 3, 1973.

"Connecticut asks new look at abortion." NAT CATH REP 9:2, April 13, 1973.

"Conscience bill survives attack." NAT CATH REP 9:20, June 8, 1973.

"Le Conseil permanent de l'Episcopat francais, Paris, 19-21 juin 1973, introduction," by F. Marty. DOC CATH 70:672-674, July 15, 1973.

"Considerable increase of renal HCS-clearance after the removal of fetus and placenta," by W. Geiger, et al. ACTA ENDOCRINOL 173: 51, 1973.

"Constitutional law--abortion--right of privacy--state statutes permitting abortion only for life saving procedure on behalf of mother without regard for other interests violate due process clause of the fourteenth amendment." MEMPHIS ST U L REV 3:359, Spring, 1973.

"Constitutional law--abortion--statute defining 'justifiable abortional act' not unconstitutional--constitution does not confer or require legal personality for unborn--whether law should accord legal personality is policy question to be determined by legislature." NOTRE DAME LAW 48:715, February, 1973.

"Constitutional law--abortion--state statute prohibiting abortion except to save life of mother unconstitutional." TUL L REV 47:1159-1167, June, 1973.

"Constitutional law--minor's right to refuse court-ordered abortion." SUFFOLK U L REV 7:1157-1173, Summer, 1973.

"Constitutional law--a new constitutional right to an abortion."

"Constitutional law--New Jersey abortion statute unconstitutionally vague on its face; women prior to pregnancy have no standing to attack statute, but plaintiff-physicians have standing to assert deprivation of their women patients right of privacy." J URBAN L 50: 505, February, 1973.

"Constitutional law--the right of privacy--Georgia's abortion law declared unconstitutional." GA SB J 10:153-162, August, 1973.

"Consultation for therapeutic abortion," by L. Daligand, et al. MED LEG DOMM CORPOR 5:372-378, October-December, 1972.

"Continuous extra-amniotic prostaglandin E 2 for therapeutic termination and the effectiveness of various infusion rates and dosages," by A. Midwinter, et al. J OBSTET GYNAECOL BR COMMONW 80:371-373, April, 1973.

"Continuous intrauterine infusion of prostaglandin E 2 for termination of pregnancy," by A. Midwinter, et al. J OBSTET GYNAECOL BR COMMONW 79:807-809, September, 1972.

"Continuous prostaglandin-F 2 infusion for middle-trimester abortion," by N. H. Lauersen, et al. LANCET 1:1195, May 26, 1973.

"Contraception, sterilization, and abortion legal interpretation of consent," by D. F. Kaltreider. MD STATE MED J 22:67, September, 1973.

"Contraceptive advice in connection with legal abortion," by K. Edstrom. LAKARTIDNINGEN 70:1404-1406, April 4, 1973.

"Contraceptive practice among New York abortion patients," by M. B. Bracken, et al. AM J OBSTET GYNECOL 114:967-977, December 1, 1972.

"Contraindication for carrying pregnancy to full term from the hematologic viewpoint," by R. Stieglitz, et al. Z AERZTL FORTBILD 67:274-276, March 15, 1973.

"Correlations between some economic, social and infectious factors and the pathology of pregnancy and of the neonate," by Y. Copelovici, et al. REV ROUM VIROL 10:23-32, 1973.

"Corticosteroid metabolism disorder in obstetrical sepsis," by M. G. Simakova. AKUSH GINEKOL 49:70-72, February, 1973.

"Counseling abortion patients," by E. Naugle. NURSING 3:37-38, February, 1973.

"Counseling for elective abortion," by R. S. Sanders, et al. J AM COLL HEALTH ASSOC 21:446-450, June, 1973.

"Council withholds paper on abortion, avoids feud." NAT CATH REP 9:3, March 16, 1973.

"La cour supreme des Etats-Unis et l'avortement libre," by M. Marcotte. RELATIONS 382:144-148, May, 1973.

"The courage to speak; cond from a speech to the John Carroll Society," by E. Hanify. C DGST 37:22-24, April, 1973.

"Course of pregnancy, delivery and puerperium following induced abortion of first pregnancy," by S. Lembrych. ZENTRALBL GYNAEKOL 94: 164-168, February 5, 1972.

"Court rejects new abortion hearing." NAT CATH REP 9:2, April 27, 1973.

"Court rulings on abortions." SOUTHERN HOSP 41:8, April, 1973.

"Criminal abortion in New Zealand," by W. A. P. Facer. HEALTH PEOPLE 6:18-20 plus, October, 1972.

"Criminal law--Texas abortion statute--criminality exceptions limited to live-saving procedures on mother's behalf without regard to stage of pregnancy violates due process clause of fourteenth amendment protecting right to privacy." AM J CRIM L 2:231-243, Summer, 1973.

"A critical analysis of induced abortion," by H. Schulman. BULL NY ACAD MED 49:694-707, August, 1973.

"Critical examination of the indications of the so-called therapeutic abortion," by J. Garcia Orcoyen. AN R ACAD NACL MED 90:263-272, 1973.

"Critical judgment of the medical indications of therapeutic abortion," by F. Bonilla Marti. AN R ACAD NACL MED 90:273-284, 1973.

"Culmination of the abortion reform movement--Roe v. Wade (93 Sup Ct 705) and Doe v. Bolton (93 Sup Ct 739)." U RICHMOND L REV 8:75-87, Fall, 1973.

"Curran: theologians on bishops' side," by P. Blice. NAT CATH REP 9:18, March 2, 1973.

"The current status of the use of prostaglandins in induced abortion," by I. M. Cushner. AM J PUBLIC HEALTH 63:189-190, March, 1973.

"Cytogenetic causes of abortion," by L. Pelz. ZENTRALBL GYNAEKOL 94:145-155, February 5, 1972.

"A cytogenetic study of recurrent abortion," by M. K. Bhasin, et al. HUMANGENETIK 18:139-148, April 16, 1973.

"Data for reform of French legislation on abortion," by R. Veylon. NOUV PRESSE MED 2:475-478, February 24, 1973.

"Death before birth (relates to U.S. Supreme Court decision)," by E. Palmer. BANNER p 15, March 23, 1973.

"Death before birth ?" CHR TODAY 18:43, October 12, 1973.

"Death from an attempt to procure an abortion by intra-uterine injection of ethyl alcohol," by T. Marcinkowski. FORENSIC SCI 2:245-246, May, 1973.

"Death of pluralism? right to abortion." NAT R 25:193, February 16, 1973.

"Deaths after legal abortion," by C. Tietze, et al. LANCET 1:105, January 13, 1973.

"Declaration de 10 000 medecins de France sur l'avortement." DOC CATH 70:629, July 1, 1973.

"Declaration des eveques belges sur l'avortement." DOC CATH 70:432-438, May, 1973.

"Declaration des eveques Suisses sur l'avortement." DOC CATH

70:381, April 15, 1973.

"Declaration du Conseil permanent de l'Episcopat francais sur l'avortement." DOC CATH 70:676-679, July 15, 1973.

"Declarations des eveques du Quebec." DOC CATH 70:382-384, April
15, 1973.

"Defending the right to abortion in New York (based on conference
paper)," by D. Welch. SOCIALIST R 34:10-13, January, 1973.

"Defibrinogenation after intra-amniotic injection of hypertonic saline,"
by J. L. Spivak, et al. N ENGL J MED 287:321-323, 1972.

"Defusing the abortion debate," by J. C. Evans. CHR CENT 90:117-
118, January 31, 1973.

" 'Delayed menstruation' induced by prostaglandin in pregnant patients,"
by P. Mocsary, et al. LANCET 2:683, September 22, 1973.

"The demographic effects of legal abortion on the Hungarian labor
force (conference paper)," by B. Kapotsy. EUROPEAN DEMOGRAPHIC
INFO BUL 4:136-143, November 3, 1973.

"DEPO-Medroxyprogesterone acetate as a contraceptive agent: its effect
on weight and blood pressure," by G. Leiman. AM J OBSTET GYNECOL
114:97-102, 1972.

"Department of Defense abortion 'guidelines' liberalized." U.S. MED
9:1 plus, February 1, 1973.

"Detection of anti-immunoglobulins by the Waaler-Rose reaction in the
serum of women with habitual abortion," by D. Vladimirova, et al.
AKUSH GINEKOL 11:214-218, 1972.

"Detection of fetal heart activity in first trimester," by O. Piiroinen.
LANCET 2:508-509, September 1, 1973.

"Determination of urinary C.G.H. in spontaneous threatened abortion.
Prognostic value," by R. Hechtermans, et al. J GYNECOL OBSTET
BIOL REPROD 1:869-876, December, 1972.

"Devaluation of human life (U.S. Supreme Court decision)," by H. Berry.

"Development concerning legal abortions under the present Danish abortion law," by V. Skalts. UGESKR LAEGER 134:2505-2507, November 20, 1972.

"Development in the incidence of abortions in recent years. Investigations and calculations concerning the incidence of criminal abortions prior to and after the Danish abortion law of 1970," by V. Sele, et al. UGESKR LAEGER 134:2493-2505, November 20, 1972.

"Development of the clinical abortion situation at the gynecologic hospital of Karl-Marx-University, Leipzig from 1.1.1960 to 30.6.1972," by S. Schulz, et al. ZENTRALBL GYNAEKOL 95:952-957, July 13, 1973.

"Diagnosis and therapy of habitual abortion related to disorders in adrenal cortex function," by I. S. Rozovskii. AKUSH GINEKOL 48: 18-23, September, 1972.

"Diagnosis and therapy of spetic abortion and bacterial shock," by G. Iliew, et al. Z AERZTL FORTBILD 67:232-235, March 1, 1973.

"Diagnosis and therapy of threatened abortion--our experience," by B. Stambolovic, et al. ZENTRALBL GYNAEKOL 95:808-810, June 15, 1973.

"Diagnosis of ovine vibriosis and enzootic abortion of ewes by immunofluorescence technique," by W. B. Ardrey, et al. AM J VET RES 33:2535-2538, December, 1972.

"Diagnosis of premature separation of the normally implanted placenta with ultrasonic B-scan," by K. H. Schlensker. GEBURTSHILFE FRAUENHEILKD 32:773-780, September, 1972.

"A diagnostic survey of bovine abortion and stillbirth in the Northern Plains States," by C. A. Kirkbride, et al. J AM VET MED ASSOC 162:556-560, April 1, 1973.

"Diethylcarbamazine: lack of teratogenic and abortifacient action in rats and rabbits," by P. J. Fraser. INDIAN J MED RES 60:1529-1532, October, 1972.

"Digest of recommended guidelines for facilities performing pregnancy terminations: Michigan." MICH MED 72:359-360, May, 1973.

"The direct fluorescent antibody test for detection of Brucella abortus in bovine abortion material," by M. J. Corbel. J HYG 71:123-129, March, 1973.

"Disappearance of prostaglandin F2a from human amniotic fluid after intraamniotic injection," by C. Pace-Asciak, et al. PROSTAGLANDINS 1:469-477, 1972.

"Discipline or liberalization of abortion? Proposal for the Fortuna law: its function and applicability in Italy," by S. Fossati. MINERVA GINECOL 25:364-370, June, 1973.

"Disorders in catecholamine and serotonin excretion in premature labor," by L. P. Grokhovskii. AKUSH GINEKOL 48:30-32, September, 1972.

"Disseminated intravascular coagulation resulting in severe hemorrhage, following the intraamniotic injection of hypertonic saline to induce abortion," by A. Sedaghat, et al. AM J OBSTET GYNECOL 114:841-843, November 15, 1972.

"Doctor blames fathers for abortion," by J. McCann. NAT CATH REP 9:1-2, March, 1973.

"Doctor's bona fides and the Abortion Act," by C. Lerry. LANCET 2:212, July, 1973.

"Does anybody care?" AM J NURS 73:1562-1565, September, 1973.

"Dossier sur l'avortement, l'apport de nos lecteurs," by B. Ribes. ETUDES 338:511-534, April, 1973.

"A double-blind study of intra-amniotic urea and hypertonic saline for therapeutic abortion," by R. J. Smith, et al. J OBSTET GYNAECOL BR COMMONW 80:135-137, February, 1973.

"Double heteroploidy, 46, XY, t(13q14q), +18, in a spontaneous abortus," by S. Avirachan, et al. CLIN GENET 4:101-104, 1973.

"Dr. Jerome L. Reeves on the new sexuality," by H. A. Matthews.

32

NC MED J 34:616-618, August, 1973.

"Dred Scott case of the twentieth century," by C. E. Rice. HOUSTON L REV 10:1059-1086, July, 1973.

"Drug abuse treatment and parental consent," by R. L. Epstein, et al. HOSPITALS 47:63-64 passim, September 1, 1973.

"Drugs in pregnancy." MED LETT DRUGS THER 14:94-96, December 8, 1972.

"The due process clause and the unborn child," by M. McKernan, Jr. DIMENSION 5:25-34, Spring, 1973.

"The dynamics of therapeutic abortions in the town of Bucharest during the 1967-1969 period," by V. Coroi, et al. OBSTET GINECOL 20: 267-272, 1972.

"Early discovery of birth defects; abortion as a consequence of discovering defects by amniocentesis," by P. R. Gastonguay. AMERICA 129:218, September 29, 1973.

"Early medical complications of abortion by saline: joint program for the study of abortion (JPSA)," by C. Tietze, et al. STUD FAM PLANN 4:133-138, June, 1973.

"Early termination of anencephalic pregnancy after detection by raised alpha-fetoprotein levels," by M. J. Seller, et al. LANCET 2:73, July 14, 1973.

"Editorial: our unborn children," by H. Berger. PAEDIATR PAEDOL 8:333-335, 1973.

"Effect of anaesthetic technique on blood loss in termination of pregnancy," by S. R. Dunn, et al. BR J ANAESTH 45:633-637, June, 1973.

"Effect of biovariectomy on the embryo-maternal junction in pregnant rats before the placental relay," by M. Clabaut. ANN ENDOCRINOL 33:221-230, May-June, 1972.

"The effect of induced abortion on subsequent pregnancy ending with delivery," by A. Atanasov, et al. AKUSH GINEKOL 11:398-402, 1972.

"Effect of infused prostaglandin F 2 on hormonal levels during early pregnancy," by A. C. Wentz, et al. AM J OBSTET GYNECOL 114: 908-913, December 1, 1972.

"The effect of intra-amniotic oestriol sulphate on abortion induced by hypertonic saline," by K. J. Dennis, et al. J OBSTET GYNAECOL BR COMMONW 80:41-45, January, 1973.

"Effect of intramammary corticosteroid administration during late gestation in cattle," by D. D. Hagg, et al. MOD VET PRACT 54:29 passim, May, 1973.

"The effect of legal abortion on the rate of septic abortion at a large county hospital," by P. N. Seward, et al. AM J OBSTET GYNECOL 115:335-338, February 1, 1973.

"The effect of prostaglandin F2a and prostaglandin E2 upon luteal function and ovulation in the guinea-pig," by F. R. Blatchley, et al. J ENDOCRINOL 53:493-501, 1972.

"Effect of prostaglandin F2a upon the corpus luteum of pregnant rats," by H. Tuchmann-Duplessis, et al. C R ACAD SCI 275:2033-2035, October 30, 1972.

"Effect of recent Supreme Court Decision on Delaware's abortion law." DEL MED J 45:141-145, May, 1973.

"The effect of spontaneous and induced abortion on prematurity and birthweight," by G. Papaevangelou, et al. J OBSTET GYNAECOL BR COMMONW 80:410-422, May, 1973.

"The effects of intravenous infusion of graded doses of prostaglandins F 2 and E 2 on lung resistance in patients undergoing termination of pregnancy," by A. P. Smith. CLIN SCI 44:17-25, January, 1973.

"The effects of legal abortion on legitimate and illegitimate birth rates: the California experience (figures for the period 1966-72)," by J. Sklar, et al. STUDIES IN FAMILY PLANNING 4:281-292, November, 1973.

"The efficacy and acceptability of the 'prostaglandin impact' in inducing complete abortion during the second week after the missed menstrual period," by A. I. Csapo, et al. PROSTAGLANDINS 3:125-139,

February, 1973.

"Efficacy of an intramuscular infectious bovine rhinotraceitis vaccine against abortion due to the virus," by J. R. Saunders, et al. CAN VET J 13:273-278, December, 1972.

"Emotional patterns related to delay in decision to seek legal abortion. A pilot study," by N. B. Kaltreider. CALIF MED 118:23-27, May, 1973.

"Emotional reactions in abortion services personnel," by F. J. Kane, et al. ARCH GEN PSYCHIATRY 28:409-411, March, 1973.

"Endangered pregnancy--an important part of perinatal medicine," by Z. K. Stembera. CESK PEDIATR 28:1-2, January, 1973.

"L'episcopat des Etats-Unis et la decision de la Cour Supreme sur l'avortement," by J. Krol. DOC CATH 70:271-273, March 18, 1973.

"Equine abortion (herpes) virus: properties of the hemagglutinin in virus suspensions," by B. Klingeborn, et al. VIROLOGY 56:164-171, November, 1973.

"Ethical considerations of some biologic dilemmas," by J. A. Noonan. SOUTHERN MED J 66:937-939, August, 1973.

"Evaluation of the effects of chlormadinone in the treatment of threatened abortion," by J. Cardenas. GINECOL OBSTET MEX 33:121-124, January, 1973.

"The evaluation of intra-amniotic prostaglandin F 2 in the management of early midtrimester pregnancy termination," by D. C. Leslie, et al. J REPROD MED 9:453-455, December, 1972.

"Evaluation of the prognosis of threatened abortion from the peripheral plasma levels of progesterone, estradiol, and human chorionic gonadotropin," by K. G. Nygren, et al. AM J OBSTET GYNECOL 116:916-922, August 1, 1973.

"Evaluation of rifampicin in septic abortion," by J. M. Ezeta, et al. GINECOL OBSTET MEX 32:561-566, December, 1972.

"Even if legalized, abortion is a crime," by S. Luoni. OR 23,271:4-5, June 7, 1973.

"The evolution of an abortion counseling service in an adoption agency," by R. K. Heineman. CHILD WELFARE 52:253-260, April, 1973.

"Expectant mothers--women seeking abortions, a sociopsychiatric comparison in Umea?" by H. Holmberg, et al. LAKARTIDNINGEN 69:5920-5924, December 6, 1972.

"An expediting procedure for late abortion," by J. F. Shipp, et al. OBSTET GYNECOL 41:477, March, 1973.

"Experience acquired in some foreign countries after liberalization of voluntary abortion," by G. Le Lorier. BULL ACAD NATL MED 156: 677-682, June-October, 1972.

"Experience with the administration of heparin for the prevention of the Sanarelli-Shwartzman reaction (SSP) in cases of septic abortions," by H. H. Koch, et al. GEBURTSHILFE FRAUENHEILKD 33:460-463, June, 1973.

"Experience with intra-amniotic prostaglandin F2 alpha for abortion," by A. C. Wentz, et al. AM J OBSTET GYNECOL 117:513-521, October 15, 1973.

"Experience with Shirodkar's operation and postoperative alcohol treatment," by N. H. Lauersen, et al. ACTA OBSTET GYNECOL SCAND 52:77-81, 1973.

"Experience with the suction curette in termination of pregnancy at a Sydney Teaching hospital," by R. H. Picker, et al. AUST NZ J OBSTET GYNAECOL 13:49-50, February, 1973.

"Experiences in the control of enzootic abortion of sheep using a viable vaccine from a weakened strain of Chlamydia ovis 'P'," by S. Yilmaz, et al. BERL MUNCH TIERAERZTL WOCHENSCHR 86: 361-366, October, 1973.

"Experiences with the vibro dilatator from the Soviet Union," by K. H. Beckmann, et al. DTSCH GESUNDHEITSW 28:227-228, 1973.

"Experimental clinical studies on spontaneous and habitual abortion with nephrogenic pathology," by M. Georgneva. AKUSH GINEKOL 11:109-114, 1972.

"Experimental study of abortifacient characteristics of vaccine strain Brucella bovis No. 21 in sheep," by G. E. Irskaya, et al. DONSKOGO S-KH INST 4:12-13, 1970.

"Experimentally induced immunity to chlamydial abortion of cattle," by D. G. McKercher, et al. J INFECT DIS 128:231-234, August, 1973.

"Extended indications for cervix cerclage uteri in pregnancy," by G. Widmaier, et al. ZENTRALBL GYNAEKOL 95:16-21, January 5, 1973.

"Extra-amniotic prostaglandin-oxytocin abortion: Comparison with the intra-amniotic method," by M. Seppala, et al. PROSTAGLANDINS 3:17-28, 1973.

"Facing a current problem," by Hougardy. NURSING 45:1-2, January-February, 1973.

"Factors affecting gestational age at termination of pregnancy," by F. D. Johnstone, et al. LANCET 2:717-719, September 29, 1973.

"Facts about abortions." BR MED J 2:438, May 26, 1973.

"A familial translocation t(6q+;8q-) identified by fluorescence microscopy," by E. Niebuhr. HUMANGENETIK 18:189-192, April 16, 1973.

"Family plann digest." US DEPT HEW PUBL 1:1-16, September, 1972.

"Father may not restrain unwed mother from obtaining an abortion: Florida." NEWSLETTER 6:3, June, 1973.

"Fecundity, abortion and standard of living among Mapuche women," by T. Monreal. REV MED CHIL 100:1273-1286, October, 1972.

"Federal appeals court rules hospital may refuse abortions." HOSPITALS 47:96, July 1, 1973.

"Federal judge rules juveniles may not be denied abortions." NAT CATH REP 9:5, February 23, 1973.

"Federally funded hospitals not required to perform abortion." NEWS-LETTER 6:3-4, July, 1973.

"Fertility control and the quality of human life," by C. Muller.

AM J PUBLIC HEALTH 63:519-523, June, 1973.

"Fertility of women over the age of 40," by S. Sehovic. JUGOSL GINEKOL OPSTET 11:191-196, 1971.

"Fetal implants in uterus." BR MED J 2:133-134, April 21, 1973.

"Fetal rights and abortion laws," by S. F. O'Beirn. BR MED J 1:740, March 24, 1973.

"The fetus: whose property?" by A. Etzioni. COMM 98:493, September 21, 1973.

"Figures and fetuses," by R. J. Neuhaus; Discussion. COMMONWEAL 97:358-359, January 19, 1973.

"First trimester abortions induced by the extraovular infusion of prostaglandin F2a," by A. I. Csapo, et al. PROSTAGLANDINS 1:295-303, 1972.

"First trimester abortions induced by a single extraovular injection of prostaglandin F2a," by A. I. Csapo, et al. PROSTAGLANDINS 1:365-371, 1972.

"Five popular myths about abortion," by T. Jermann. OSV 62:1 plus, May 27, 1973.

"Five thousand consecutive saline inductions," by T. D. Kerenyi, et al. AM J OBSTET GYNECOL 116:593-600, July 1, 1973.

"Foes of abortion vow to continue efforts." AMER MED NEWS 16:7, January 29, 1973.

"Follow-up after therapeutic abortion in early adolescence," by M. G. Perez-Reyes, et al. ARCH GEN PSYCHIATRY 28:120-126, January, 1973.

"A follow-up study of women who request abortion," by E. M. Smith. AM J ORTHOPSYCHIATRY 43:574-585, July, 1973.

"For American Catholics: end of an illusion," by T. O'Connell. AMERICA 128:514-517, June 2, 1973.

"Forest and the trees: Roe v. Wade (93 Sup Ct 705) and its critics," by P. B. Heymann, et al. BU L REV 53:765-784, July, 1973.

"Former NAL member hits abortion statement." NAT CATH REP 9:3, February 16, 1973.

"Forensic problems in abortion caused by gunshot," by G. Lins, et al. Z RECHTSMED 71:108-113, November 28, 1972.

"480,000 legal abortions in 1971." HOSP PROGRESS 54:96b, March, 1973.

"France: abortion, oul!" NEWSWEEK 81:46 plus, June 11, 1973.

"France; the power to start and end a life." ECONOMIST 245:45, December 2, 1972.

"Free abortion in Denmark?" by M. Johansson. NORD MED 88:13, January, 1973.

"Free standing abortion clinics: a new phenomenon," by R. U. Hausknecht. BULL NY ACAD MED 49:985-991, November, 1973.

"The French Episcopate, firm and clear against revision of abortion law." OR 33,28:3 plus, August 16, 1973.

"French manifesto." TIME 101:76, February 19, 1973 .

"French medicine: the abortion battle." MED WORLD NEWS 14:4-5, March 2, 1973.

"Frequency of chromosome abnormalities in abortions," by H. Pawlowitzki. HUMANGENETIK 16:131-136, 1972.

"Frequency of criminal abortion. Elucidated in interviews of women hospitalized for abortion," by J. G. Lauritsen. UGESKR LAEGER 135: 770-771, April 23, 1973.

"From abortion to sex education," by K. Whitehead. HPR 74:60-69, November, 1973.

"The functional state of the thyroid gland and iodine metabolism in habitual abortion," by E. A. Danilova. ZH EKSP KLIN MED 11:60-65, 1971.

"Further experience with intrauterine prostaglandin administration," by M. Bygdeman, et al. J REPROD MED 9:392-396, December, 1972.

"Further experience with laparoscopic sterilization concomitant with vacuum curettage for abortion," by H. K. Amin, et al. FERTIL STERIL 24:592-594, August, 1973.

"Future of abortion; alternatives," by C. Behrens. CURRENT 154:28-31, September, 1973.

"Gangrene of the uterus and its sequelae," by R. A. Jones. S AFR MED J 47:1327-1330, July 28, 1973.

"Generative activity in some groups of women and its reflection on the state of the uterine cervix," by T. Pipetkov. AKUSH GINEKOL 11:251-258, 1972.

"Georgetown University statement on abortion," by R. Henle. C MIND 71:9-10, September, 1973.

"Georgia, Texas file appeals." NAT CATH REP 9:3, February 23, 1973.

"Giemsa banding in the t(13q13q) carrier mother of a translocation trisomy 13 abortus," by M. I. Parslow, et al. HUMANGENETIK 18: 183-184, April 16, 1973.

" 'Glioma' of the uterus: a fetal homograft," by P. A. Niven, et al. AM J OBSTET GYNECOL 115:534-538, February 15, 1973.

"Gonorrhea in women prior to pregnancy interruption," by M. Mesko, et al. ZENTRALBL GYNAEKOL 94:169-172, February 5, 1972.

"Goodbye to the Judeo-Christian era in law," by R. Byrn. AMERICA 128:511-514, June 3, 1973.

"Government, providers urged to develop abortion program: John H. Knowles, MD." HOSPITALS 47:19, April 16, 1973.

"Gram negative bacterial septicemia after abortion," by M. Vitse, et al. BULL FED SOC GYNECOL OBSTET LANG FR 23:603, November-December, 1971.

"The growing scandal of abortion," by K. Mitzner. C ECON p 33,

October, 1972.

"Guidelines for physician performance of induced abortions." MARYLAND STATE MED J 22:68, September, 1973.

"Guidelines on abortion published: American College of Obstetricians and Gynecologists." US MED 9:6, March 1, 1973.

"Haemophilus influenzae in septic abortion," by J. Berczy, et al. LANCET 1:1197, May 26, 1973.

"Hazards in the operating theatre. Contamination of air by anaesthetics," by A. A. Spence. ANN R COLL SURG ENGL 52:360-361, June, 1973.

"Health education for prevention of abortion," by S. L. Polchanova. FELDSHER AKUSH 37:28-32, November, 1972.

"The health system and the Supreme Court decision. An affirmative response," by J. H. Knowles. FAMILY PLANN PERSPECT 5:113-116, Spring, 1973.

"High court lifts restrictions on abortions: Catholic hospitals will resist, others move cautiously." MOD HOSP 120:31-32, February, 1973.

"High court rates privacy over fetus," by R. Casey. NAT CATH REP 9:1 plus, February 2, 1973.

"High court's abortion decision raises problems for Rxmen." AM DRUGGIST MERCH 167:26, May 15, 1973.

"Histological analysis of spontaneous abortions with triploidy," by M. Geisler, et al. HUMANGENETIK 16:283-294, 1972.

"Histological study of the placenta and basal decidua in habitual abortion caused by hyperandrogenism. Spontaneously interrupted pregnancies during the 1st 6 months and pregnancies treated successfully by corticotherapy," by L. Badarau, et al. REV FR GYNECOL OBSTET 67:685-697, December, 1972.

"Histopathologic changes associated with prostaglandin induced abortion," by P. D. Bullard, Jr., et al. CONTRACEPTION 7:133-144, 1973.

"History and evolution of abortion laws in the United States," by D. L. Brown. SOUTHERN MED 61:11-14, August, 1973.

"Hormonal changes during induction of midtrimester abortion by prostaglandin F 2," by B .Cantor, et al. AM J OBSTET GYNECOL 113:607-615, July 1, 1972.

"Hormonal therapy of spontaneous abortion and premature labor in women with menstrual disorders," by P. G. Shushaniia, et al. AKUSH GINEKOL 47:54-58, October, 1971.

"Hormone therapy of threatened abortion during the early stages of pregnancy," by S. Trepechov, et al. AKUSH GINEKOL 11:152-160, 1972.

"Hospital statistics of births, abortions, still births, premature births and neonatal deaths from Army hospitals in Western Command 1967-70," by M. C. Sanyal. ARMED FORCES MED J INDIA 28:226-230, 1972.

"Hospitals and the abortion ruling." NEWSLETTER 6:2, March, 1973.

"Hot rhetoric: abortion issue in Catholic diocesan press," by S. J. Adamo. AMERICA 128:375-376 plus, April 21, 1973.

"Human chorionic gonadotropin (HCG) excretion in the urine in habitual threatened abortion treated with gestanon," by R. Wawryk, et al. GINEKOL POL 44:665-670, June, 1973.

"Human chorionic gonadotropin (HCG) in threatened abortion," by P. Baillie, et al. S AFR MED J 47:1293-1296, July 28, 1973.

"Hyperosmolal crisis following infusion of hypertonic sodium chloride for purposes of therapeutic abortion," by E. D. De Villota, et al. AM J MED 55:116-122, July, 1973.

"Hypertonic saline-induced abortion complicated by consumptive coagulopathy: a case report," by J. C. Morrison, et al .SOUTH MED J 66:561-562, May, 1973.

"Hypertonic saline-induced abortion. Correlation of fetal death with disseminated intravascular coagulation," by H. I. Glueck, et al. JAMA 225:28-31, July 2, 1973.

"Hysterectomy by septic processes during pregnancy," by J. Rosas Arceo, et al. GINECOL OBSTET MEX 33:559-568, June, 1973.

"IBR abortion and its control," by F. E. Steves, et al. VET MED SMALL ANIM CLIN 68:164-166, February, 1973.

"The identification of Mortierella wolfii isolated from cases of abortion and pneumonia in cattle and a search for its infection source," by M. E. Di Menna, et al. RES VET SCI 13:439-442, September, 1972.

"IgG cold agglutinins and first trimester abortion," by K. Mygind, et al. VOX SANG 22:552-560, December, 1972.

"Illinois, Massachusetts enact conscience clause legislation." HOSPITALS 47:85, August 16, 1973.

"Imminent abortion," by H. J. Wallner. MED KLIN 68:497-500, April 20, 1973.

"The impact of the Abortion Act," by P. D. John. BR J PSYCHIATRY 122:115-116, January, 1973.

"Impact of the liberalized abortion law in New York City on deaths associated with pregnancy: a two-year experience," by J. Pakter, et al. BULL NY ACAD MED 49:804-818, September, 1973.

"Impact of a permissive abortion statute on community health care," by J. J. Rovinsky. OBSTET GYNECOL 41:781-788, May, 1973.

"In defense of liberty: a look at the abortion decisions." GEO L J 61:1559-1575, July, 1973.

"In defense of the unborn," by V. Gager. MARRIAGE 55:38-45, July, 1973.

"In defense of the unborn," by N. Walsh. STUDIES 61:303-314, Winter, 1972.

"Incidence of Rh immunization following abortion: possible detection of lymphocyte priming to Rh antigen," by J. Katz, et al. AM J OBSTET GYNECOL 117:261-267, September 15, 1973.

"Increased frequency of chromosomal anomalies in abortions after induced ovulation," by J. G. Boue, et al. LANCET 1:679-680, March

24, 1973.

"Indices of the coagulant and anticoagulant systems of the blood in threatened and incipient abortion," by A. I. Zherzhov. VOPR OKHR MATERIN DET 17:85-86, August, 1972.

"Induced abortion," by L. B. Davis. J AM OSTEOPATH ASSOC 73:74-76, September, 1973.

"Induced abortion and ectopic pregnancy," by P. P. Panayotou, et al. AM J OBSTET GYNECOL 114:507-510, October 15, 1972.

"The induced abortion and the gynecologist," by Z. Polishok. HAREFUAH 83:264-265, September 15, 1972.

"Induced abortion: source of guilt or growth?" by F. Addelson. AM J ORTHOPSYCHIATRY 43:815-823, October, 1973.

"Induced Maude abortion charged." NAT CATH REP 10:12, November 9, 1973.

"The induction of abortion and menstruation by the intravaginal administration of prostaglandin F 2a," by T. Sato, et al. AM J OBSTET GYNECOL 116:287-289, May 15, 1973.

"Induction of abortion by combined intra-amniotic urea and prostaglandin E 2 or prostaglandin E 2 alone," by I. Craft. LANCET 1:1344-1346, June 16, 1973.

"Induction of abortion by extra-amniotic administration of prostaglandin F2a: a preliminary report," by V. Hingorani, et al. CONTRACEPTION 6:353-359, 1972.

"Induction of abortion by intra- and extra-amniotic prostaglandin F2 administration," by P. A. Jarvinen, et al. PROSTAGLANDINS 3:491-504, April, 1973.

"Induction of abortion by intravenous and intra-uterine administration of prostaglandin F 2," by A. A. Haspels, et al. J REPROD MED 9:442-447, December, 1972.

"Induction of abortion by intravenous infusions of prostaglandin F 2," by E. Dreher, et al. ARCH GYNAEKOL 213:48-53, 1972.

"Induction of embryonic death in sheep by intrauterine injection of a small volume of normal saline," by M. M. Bryden, et al. J REPROD FERTIL 32:133-135, January, 1973.

"Induction of midtrimester abortion by increasing intra-uterine volume," by M. O. Pulkkinen, et al. ACTA OBSTET GYNECOL SCAND 52:9-12, 1973.

"Induction of mid-trimester abortion with intrauterine alcohol," by V. Gomel, et al. OBSTET GYNECOL 41:455-458, March, 1973.

"The induction of second trimester abortions using an intra-amniotic injection of urea and prostaglandin E2," by P. Bowen-Simpkins. J OBSTET GYNAECOL BR COMMONW 80:824-826, September, 1973.

"Induction of therapeutic abortion with intra-amniotically administered prostaglandin F 2. A comparison of three repeated-injection dose schedules," by W. E. Brenner, et al. AM J OBSTET GYNECOL 116: 923-930, August 1, 1973.

"Infection as a complication of therapeutic abortion," by A. H. De Cherney, et al. PA MED 75:49-52, December, 1972.

"Infectious complications following legal abortion," by E. Gaziano, et al. MINN MED 56:269-272, April, 1973.

"Influence of induced and spontaneous abortions on the outcome of subsequent pregnancies," by S. N. Pantelakis, et al. AM J OBSTET GYNECOL 116:799-805, July 15, 1973.

"The influence of recent use of an oral contraceptive on early intrauterine development," by B. J. Poland, et al. AM J OBSTET GYNECOL 116:1138-1142, August 15, 1973.

"Inhibition of abortion and fetal death produced by endotoxin or prostaglandin F2alpha," by M. J. Harper, et al. PROSTAGLANDINS 2:295-309, October, 1972.

"Initial experiences with prostaglandin F2 in induced abortion," by H. Igel, et al. ZENTRALBL GYNAEKOL 95:353-357, March 16, 1973.

"Injuries of the cervix after induced midtrimester abortion," by P. J. Bradley-Watson, et al. J OBSTET GYNAECOL BR COMMONW

80:284-285, March, 1973.

"Interrupting late-term pregnancy by means of an intra-amniotic introduction of hypertonic solutions," by K. I. Braginskii. AKUSH GINEKOL 48:61-62, 1972.

"Interrupting late-term pregnancy with an intra-amniotic administration of a hypertonic solution of sodium chloride," by G. A. Palladi, et al. AKUSH GINEKOL 48:58-61, 1972.

"Intra-amniotic administration of prostaglandin F 2 for induction of therapeutic abortion. A comparison of four dosage schedules," by W. E. Brenner, et al. J REPROD MED 9:456-463, December, 1972.

"Intra-amniotic administration of prostaglandin F 2 to induce therapeutic abortion. Efficacy and tolerance of two dosage schedules," by W. E. Brenner, et al. AM J OBSTET GYNECOL 114:781-787, November 15, 1972.

"Intra-amniotic prostaglandin E 2 and F 2 for induction of abortion: a dose response study," by I. Craft. J OBSTET GYNAECOL BR COMMONW 80:46-47, January, 1973.

"Intra-amniotic prostaglandin E 2 and urea for abortion," by I. Craft. LANCET 1:779, April 7, 1973.

"Intra-amniotic prostaglandin F2 alpha to induce midtrimester abortion," by S. L. Corson, et al. AM J OBSTET GYNECOL 117:27-34, September 1, 1973.

"Intraamniotic prostaglandin F2-alpha dose--twenty-four-hour abortifacient response," by W. E. Brenner, et al. J PHARM SCI 62:1278-1282, August, 1973.

"Intra-amniotic prostaglandins and urea for abortion," by I. Craft. LANCET 2:207 passim, July, 1973.

"Intraamniotic urea for induction of mid-trimester abortion," by P. C. Weinberg, et al. OBSTET GYNECOL 41:451-454, March, 1973.

"Intra-uterine administration of prostaglandin F 2 during the second trimester of pregnancy; clinical and hormonal results," by R. Shearman, et al. J REPROD FERTIL 32:321-322, February, 1973.

"Intrauterine extra-amniotic administration of prostaglandin F 2 for therapeutic abortion. Early myometrial effects," by J. T. Braaksma, et al. AM J OBSTET GYNECOL 114:511-515, October 15, 1972.

"Intra-uterine suction for evacuation of the uterus in early pregnancy," by A. K. Ghosh. J INDIAN MED ASSOC 59:366-368, October 16, 1972.

"Investigation of women admitted to hospital with abortion," by L. Freundt. ACTA PSYCHIATR SCAND 242:1-221, 1973.

"Is abortion advertising ethical?" MED WORLD NEWS 14:53-54, September 7, 1973.

"Is 'liberalized' abortion lawful?" by L. L. McNamara. SOUTHERN MED 61:27-31, August, 1973.

"Is the unborn child a person at law?" by J. P. Wadsworth. QUIS CUSTODIET 36:88-92, 1972.

"Isoimmunization of women during pregnancy," by G. S. Aleskerov. AKUSH GINEKOL 48:65-67, November, 1972.

"Italian abortion law faces opposition." NAT CATH REP 9:5, February 9, 1973.

"It's time to speak out for all life," by K. Katafiasz. ST ANTH 81:26-27, October, 1973.

"Jane Roe and Mary Doe; abortion ruling." NATION 216:165, February 5, 1973.

"Jewish religious tradition and the issue of abortion," by S. Freedman. DIMENSION 5:90-93, Summer, 1973.

"Judicial power and public conscience; symposium," by J. Kennedy, et al. SIGN 52:26-27, March, 1973.

"Judicial power and the right to life," by J. Noonan. TABLET 227:323-326, April 7, 1973.

"The Karman catheter," by P. Fairbrother. AM J OBSTET GYNECOL 116:293, May 15, 1973.

"Karman catheter," by A. J. Margolis, et al. AM J OBSTET GYNECOL 115:589, February 15, 1973.

"Krol, Cooke, and McHugh denounce Supreme Court abortion ruling." HOSP PROGRESS 54:22a-b, February, 1973.

"Laboratory findings from ovine abortion and perinatal mortality," by J. W. Plant, et al. AUST VET J 48:558-561, October, 1972.

"Lack of coagulation defect after terminating second-trimester pregnancy by the catheter technique," by F. K. Beller, et al. AM J OBSTET GYNECOL 115:822-826, March 15, 1973.

"Laminaria augmentation of intra-amniotic prostaglandin F2 alpha for the induction of mid-trimester abortion," by W. E. Brenner, et al. PROSTAGLANDINS 3:879-894, June, 1973.

"Laminaria: an underutilized clinical adjunct," by R. W. Hale, et al. CLIN OBSTET GYNECOL 15:829-850, September, 1972.

"Landmark abortion decisions: justifiable termination or miscarriage of justice?--proposals for legislative response." PACIFIC L J 4:821-860, July, 1973.

"Landmark decision: three Texas women who fought the abortion issue," by J. N. Bell. GOOD H 176:77-79 plus, June, 1973.

"Laparoscopic tubal sterilization coincident with therapeutic abortion by suction curettage," by L. G. Whitson, et al. OBSTET GYNECOL 41:677-680, May, 1973.

"Laparotomy during pregnancy: an assessment of diagnostic accuracy and fetal wastage," by P. Saunders, et al. BR MED J 3:165-167, July 21, 1973.

"Latent morbidity after abortion." BR MED J 1:506, March 3, 1973.

"Latent morbidity after abortion." BR MED J 1:739-740, March 24, 1973.

"Latent morbidity after abortion." BR MED J 2:51, April 7, 1973.

"Latent morbidity after abortion." BR MED J 2:611, June 9, 1973.

"Latent morbidity after abortion," by C. Buck, et al. BR MED J 3:292-293, August 4, 1973.

"Latent morbidity after abortion," by A. Hordern. BR MED J 2:368, May 12, 1973.

"Latent morbidity after abortion," by A. Ogborn. BR MED J 2:114-115, April 14, 1973.

"Latent toxoplasomosis and pregnancy," by M. Sharf, et al. OBSTET GYNECOL 42:349-354, September, 1973.

"Law of consent and abortion in California," by A. H. Bernstein. HOSPITALS 47:132 passim, February 1, 1973.

"The law on abortion and the defence of life; a declaration of the Belgian bishops." OR 24,272:9, June 14, 1973.

"Law on abortion and sterilization, 1973," by G. H. Roux. S AFR MED J 47:596, April 14, 1973.

"Law to protect the unborn; New Orleans, Louisiana." OR 30,278:3, July 26, 1973.

"Learning abortion care," by A. Goldmann. NURS J INDIA 63:153-154 plus, May, 1972.

"Legal abortion and the attitude of hospital staff," by L. Jacobsson, et al. LAKARTIDNINGEN 70:273-275, January 24, 1973.

"Legal abortion as a positive mental health measure in family planning," by Z. M. Lebensohn. COMPR PSYCHIATRY 14:95-98, March-April, 1973.

"Legal abortion..An assessment following the Danish abortion law of 1.IV.1970," by E. Gregersen. UGESKR LAEGER 135:417-420, February 19, 1973.

"Legal abortion by extra-amniotic instillation of Rivanol in combination with rubber catheter insertion into the uterus after the twelfth week of pregnancy," by C. A. Ingemanson. AM J OBSTET GYNECOL 115: 211-215, January 15, 1973.

"Legal abortion in a day-ward," by E. Gregersen. UGESKR LAEGER 135:429-431, February 19, 1973.

"Legal abortion 1970-1971--the New York City experience," by D. Harris, et al. AM J PUBLIC HEALTH 63:409-418, May, 1973.

"Legal abortion, the South Australian experience." MED J AUST 1:821-823, April 28, 1973.

"Legal counsel analyzes abortion ruling," by F. Speaker. PA MED 76:21-22, April, 1973.

"Legal interruption of pregnancy by the aspiration method and the pericervical block with Gynesthesin," by M. Beric. SCHWEIZ Z GYNAEKOL GEBURTSHILFE 3:151-159, 1972.

"Lesions of blood vessels in the uterine cervix as a cause of bleedings following interruption of pregnancy," by M. Cislo, et al. POL TYG LEK 27:2066-2068, December 25, 1972.

"Letter: interruption of pregnancy because of embryonal damage," by H. J. Rieger. DTSCH MED WOCHENSCHR 98:1782, September 21, 1973.

"Letter: intrauterine prostaglandins for outpatient termination of very early pregnancy," by S. M. Karim. LANCET 2:794, October 6, 1973.

"Letter: orgasm-induced abortion," by J. P. Keeve. LANCET 2:970, October 27, 1973.

"Letter: prenatal treatment of hereditary diseases?" by C. Valenti. LANCET 2:797-798, October 6, 1973.

"Letter: Trisomy in abortion material," by H. R. McCreanor, et al. LANCET 2:972-973, October 27, 1973.

"Lib and let live," by N. Roberts. GUARDIAN p 12, February 15, 1973.

"Liberal thinking on abortion: not a solution in itself," by D. Laulicht. TIMES p 13, May 2, 1973.

"Liberalized abortion and birth rates changes in Baltimore," by W. Oppel, et al. AM J PUBLIC HEALTH 63:405-408, May, 1973.

"Liberal abortion laws are worldwide trend," by M. Ostro. NAT CATH REP 10:3-4, November 9, 1973.

"Listeria as a cause of abortion and neonatal mortality in sheep," by D. W. Broadbent. AUST VET J 48:391-394, July, 1972.

"Listeric abortion in sheep. II. Feto-placental changes," by C. O. Njoku, et al. CORNELL VET 63:171-192, April, 1973.

--III. Feto-placental-myometrial interaction," by C. O. Njoku, et al. CORNELL VET 63:193-210, April, 1973.

--IV. Histopathologic comparison of natural and experimental infection," by C. O. Njoku, et al. CORNELL VET 63:211-219, April, 1973.

"Listeriosis. Occurrence in spontaneous interruptions of pregnancy," by J. R. Giraud, et al. NOUV PRESSE MED 2:215-218, January 27, 1973.

"Litigation: preparation and response," by S. M. Blaes. HOSP PROG 54:70-72 passim, August, 1973.

"Lobbying for the unborn." CHR TODAY 17:44, July 20, 1973.

"Local potentiated anesthesia in artificial abortions," by E. I. Gorobets. PEDIATR AKUSH GINEKOL 1:55-56, 1973.

"Locus of control, latitude of acceptance and attitudes toward abortion," by B. Corenblum. PSYCHOL REP 32:753-754, June, 1973.

"Making abortion an accepted right of women," by P. C. Newman. MACLEAN'S 86:3, February, 1973.

"Making abortion consultation therapeutic," by C. M. Friedman. AM J PSYCHIATRY 130:1257-1261, November, 1973.

"Male factor as a possible cause of habitual abortion and infertility," by C. A. Joel. SCHWEIZ MED WOCHENSCHR 102:1377-1383, September 30, 1972.

"Malnutrition of the foetus as a cause of abortion," by S. J. van Rensburg. J S AFR VET MED ASSOC 42:305-308, December, 1971.

"The management of abruptio placentae," by C. B. Lunan. J OBSTET

GYNAECOL BR COMMONW 80:120-124, February, 1973.

"Management of premature detachment of the normally implanted placenta," by R. Ortiz Arroyo, et al. GINECOL OBSTET MEX 33:209-215, February, 1973.

"Maori attitudes toward abortion," by L. Gluckman. LINACRE 40:44-48, February, 1973.

"The March of Dimes and abortion," by B. Williams. HPR 74:48-58, October, 1973.

"Marjory Mecklenburg is for life; pro-life movement," by J. Mahowald. C DGST 37:39-44, June, 1973.

"Maryland's 'hospital only' provision in abortion law declared unconstitutional." HOSPITALS 47:17, September 1, 1973.

"Maternal death due to DIC after saline abortion," by S. R. Lemkin, et al. OBSTET GYNECOL 42:233-235, August, 1973.

"Maternal deaths in Australia compared with England and Wales in 1964-1966," by J. R. Neil, et al. MED J AUST 59:682-685, 1972.

"Maternal plasma oestrogen and progesterone levels during therapeutic abortion induced by intra-amniotic injection of prostaglandin F 2," by E. M. Symonds, et al. J OBSTET GYNAECOL BR COMMONW 79:976-980, November, 1972.

"Maternal x-radiation and chromosome abnormalities in subsequent conceptions," by E. D. Alberman. BR J PREV SOC MED 27:67-68, February, 1973.

"Maude dropouts threatened by boycott." BROADCASTING 85:74, August 20, 1973.

"Measles virus-associated endometritis, cervicitis, and abortion in a rhesus monkey," by R. A. Renne, et al. J AM VET MED ASSOC 163:639-641, September 15, 1973.

"Measure of attitudes toward abortion," by H. S. Lackey, Jr., et al. J COMMUNITY PSYCHOL 1:31-33, January, 1973.

"MED-CHI guidelines for physician performance of induced abortions." MD STATE MED J 22:68, September, 1973.

"Medical abortion in South Australia. A critical assessment of early complications," by J. M. Miller. MED J AUST 1:825-830, April 28, 1973.

"The medical profession and the 1967 Abortion Act in Britain," by S. J. Macintyre. SOC SCI MED 7:121-134, February, 1973.

"Medical termination of pregnancy Act, 1971 (34 of 1971)." INDIAN J PUBLIC HEALTH 16:37-38, April, 1972.

"Medicine and abortion; interview by Vatican Radio," by A. Bompiani. OR 13,261:4, March 29, 1973.

"Medicolegal forum," by D. H. Mills. J AM OSTEOPATH ASSOC 72:957-958, June, 1973.

"The mental health of the prospective father: a new indication for therapeutic abortion?" by R. Lacoursiere. BULL MENNINGER CLIN 36: 645-650, November, 1972.

"A methodology for the planning of therapeutic abortion services," by S. J. Williams. HEALTH SERV REP 87:983-991, December, 1972.

"Mid-term abortion induced in sheep by synthetic corticoids," by P. Fylling, et al. J REPROD FERTIL 32:305-306, February, 1973.

"Mid-trimester abortion," by A. A. Finks. LANCET 1:263-264, February 3, 1973.

"Midtrimester abortion produced by intra-amniotic prostaglandin F2a augmented with intravenous oxytocin," by N. Kochenour, et al. AM J OBSTET GYNECOL 114:516-519, 1972.

"Midtrimester abortion using intra-amniotic prostaglandin F2 alpha with intravenous Syntocinon," by G. G. Anderson, et al. J REPROD MED 9:434-436, December, 1972.

"Midtrimester abortion using prostaglandin F2alpha, oxytocin, and laminaria," by T. Engel, et al. FERTIL STERIL 24:565-568, August, 1973.

"Mid-trimester abortion with intraamniotic saline and intravenous oxytocin," by C. A. Ballard, et al. OBSTET GYNECOL 41:447-450, March, 1973.

"Mid-trimester hypertonic saline--induced abortion: effect of indomethacin on induction-abortion time," by R. Waltman, et al. AM J OBSTET GYNECOL 114:829-831, November 15, 1972.

"A midtrimester procedure, not without its risks...Saline abortion: a review of the experience at Kapiolani hospital," by T. I. Hooper, et al. HAWAII MED J 32:222-225, July-August, 1973.

"Minor cannot be compelled to have abortion: Maryland." NEWSLETTER 6:5, January, 1973.

"Misplaced allegiance," by E. Glynn. AMERICA 128:177, March 3, 1973.

"Moccasins and abortion; reprint from The Camillan," by M. Flynn. C CHAR 57:16-23, June, 1973.

"Model 'conscience clause' legislation proposed by Executive Committee of Catholic Hospital Association Board." HOSP PROGRESS 54:20, April, 1973.

"Modified cervical block for elective abortion procedures," by W. D. Walden. OBSTET GYNECOL 41:473-474, March, 1973.

"Monkey anti-placental serum as an abortifacient," by S. J. Behrman, et al. CONTRACEPTION 5:357-368, 1972.

"Moral and medical problems concerning abortion," by M. Bermejillo. AN R ACAD NACL MED 90:307-326, 1973.

"Moral consideration of abortion from the viewpoint of the Christian value of human life," by J. M. Diaz Moreno. AN R ACAD NACL MED 90:235-261, 1973.

"The morality of abortion," by R. B. Brandt. MONIST 56:503-526, October, 1972.

"The mortality of human XO embryos," by B. Santesson, et al. J REPROD FERTIL 34:51-55, July, 1973.

"Mortality with legal abortion in New York City, 1970-1972: a preliminary report," by C. Tietze, et al. J AMER MED ASS 225:507-509, July 30, 1973.

"More on abortion." CALIF MED 118:52-54, March, 1973.

"Morphological, autoradiographic, immunochemical and cytochemical investigation of a cell strain with trisomy 7 from a spontaneous abortus," by A. M. Kuliev, et al. HUMANGENETIK 17:285-296, 1973.

"Most insurers are paying for abortions: legality still the key question." AMER MED NEWS 16:7, March 26, 1973.

"Motivational factors in abortion patients," by R. J. Kane, Jr., et al. AM J PSYCHIATRY 130:290-293, March, 1973.

"Multiple sclerosis and zoonoses. Importance of the role of the bovine abortion virus (pararickettsia X-14) in the etiopathogenesis of multiple sclerosis," by P. Le Gac. C R ACAD SCI 275:147-148, July 3, 1972 .

"Must the Church eliminate morality?" by D. Barsotti. OR 14,262:8, April 5, 1973.

"NAL applauds Court for abortion ruling," by D. Gibeau. NAT CATH REP 9:3, February 9, 1973.

"National Conference of Catholic Bishops Administrative Committee rejects abortion ruling." HOSP PROGRESS 54:83 plus, March, 1973.

"NCCB backs antiabortion step." NAT CATH REP 9:20, September 28, 1973.

"Need for an expanded abortion service: problems encountered, solutions," by M. B. Sell. SOUTHERN MED 61:22-26, August, 1973.

"Neonatal intravascular coagulation associated with abruptio placentae," by F. L. al-Salihi. J MED SOC NJ 70:381-383, May, 1973.

"Neuroleptanalgesia using innovar in minor gynecological procedures," by L. D. McLaughlin, Jr., et al. J AM ASSOC NURSE ANESTH 41:211-215, June, 1973.

"The new abortion law--some salient features," by I. B. Rao. J INDIAN

MED ASSOC 59:332-336, October 16, 1972.

"The new abortion ruling," by H. Creighton. SUPERV NURSE 4:8 plus, July, 1973.

"A new approach to the abortion problem," by L. Durpe. THEOL STDS 34:481-488, September, 1973.

"A new Catholic strategy on abortion." MONTH 6:163-171, May, 1973.

"A new cause: many Americans join move to ban abortion; legislators take note," by J. A. Tannenbaum. WALL ST J 182:1 plus, August 2, 1973.

"New etiopathogenetic and therapeutic studies in threatened abortion," by M. Golsis, et al. MINERVA GINECOL 25:481-492, August, 1973.

"The new Georgia abortion law," by J. W. Huff. J MED ASSOC GA 62:241-242, June, 1973.

"New Law gives rights to fetus." NAT CATH REP 9:1, March 23, 1973.

"New methods for interruption of very early pregnancy," by J. Presl. CESK GYNEKOL 38:474-475, July, 1973.

"New York State physicians and the social context of abortion," by S. Wassertheil-Smoller, et al. AM J PUBLIC HEALTH 63:144-149, February, 1973.

"1970-1972. A preliminary report," by C. Tietze, et al. JAMA 225:507-509, July 30, 1973.

"Nixon signs hospital law." NAT CATH REP 9:15, July 6, 1973.

"A note on the effects of maternal or fetal injection of flumethasone and of thyroidectomy on the termination of pregnancy," by J. M. Van Der Westhuysen. S AFR J ANIM SCI 1:67, 1971.

"Now that abortion is legal; unforeseen emotions that follow," by B. G. Harrison. MC CALLS 101:64 plus, November, 1973.

"Numbers go on rising." ECONOMIST 247:30, May 26, 1973.

"The nurse and the abortion patient," by B. Clancy. NURS CLIN NORTH AM 8:469-478, September, 1973.

"A nurse's biography of an abortion," by S. Kilby-Kelberg, et al. US CATH 38:19-21, February, 1973.

"Nurses' rights regarding abortion: Association of Operating Room Nurses policy statement." AORN 17:191, April, 1973.

"Nursing care in placenta previa and abruptio placentae," by R. C. Kilker, et al. NURS CLIN NORTH AM 8:479-487, September, 1973.

"Nursing home abortions may be permitted under Supreme Court rulings." MOD NURSING HOME 30:72-73, March, 1973.

"Objectifs de morale chretienne," by H. de Lavalette. ETUDES 338: 499-509, April, 1973.

"Objections aim at wrong target," by W. VanderMarck. NAT CATH REP 9:11, March 16, 1973.

"Of life and death," by J. Noble. PRES J p 7, February 14, 1973.

"Of many things; constitutional right and abortion legislation," by C. M. Whelan. AMERICA 128:inside cover, February 10, 1973.

"Offers pro-life amendment." NAT CATH REP 9:18, February 9, 1973.

"On abortion and the college woman," by K. J. Monsour. MADEMOISELLE 78:64 plus, November, 1973.

"On the incidence of illegal abortion (Great Britain); with a reply to Dr. W. H. James," by C. B. Goodhart. POPULATION STUDIES 27:207-233, July, 1973.

"On killing inconvenient people," by A. Roche. SAT N 88:29-31, September, 1973.

"On the mechanism of the abortifacient action of prostaglandin F 2," by A. I. Csapo. J REPROD MED 9:400-412, December, 1972; also in PROSTAGLANDINS 1:157-165, 1972.

"On the mechanism of midtrimester abortions induced by prostaglandin 'impact'," by L. Saldana, et al. PROSTAGLANDINS 3:847-858, June, 1973.

"On the moral and legal status of abortion," by M. A. Warren. THE MONIST 57:43-61, January, 1973.

"On the pathomorphism of threatened abortion (labor complications and fetal diseases)," by A. Weidenbach. MINERVA GINECOL 25:457-461, August, 1973.

"On the question of the liberalization of abortion," by M. Mall-Haefeli. SCHWEIZ Z GYNAEKOL GEBURTSHILFE 3:69-91, 1972.

"On the topic of abortion: embryonal anthropology," by H. Scheck. PRAXIS 62:1068-1071, August 28, 1973.

"One death and a cluster of febrile complications related to saline abortions," by G. S. Berger, et al. OBSTET GYNECOL 42:121-126, July, 1973.

"101 femmes," by J. Pare. LE MACLEAN 13:15, 32 plus, February, 1973.

"100,000 sign OSV pro-life petition." OSV 62:1 plus, May 20, 1973.

"One man's love for life," by L. Lueras. COLUMBIA 53:20-27, April, 1973.

"Only a constitutional amendment can stop the flood of abortion," by J. Noonan, Jr. NAT CATH REP 9:9, February 16, 1973.

"Operating room nurses face decision in abortion procedures," by E. S. Schrader. AORN J 17:13 plus, May, 1973.

"Operation on demand?" by C. O. Rice. MINN MED 56:412, May, 1973.

"Opinion towards induced abortion among urban women in Delhi, India," by S. B. Kar. SOC SCI MED 6:731-736, December, 1972.

"OR nurses face decision in abortion procedures," by E. S. Schrader. AORN J 17:13-16, May, 1973.

"Organization of dispensary care women with habitual abortions," by G. P. Koreneva, et al. PEDIATR AKUSH GINEKOL 6:39-43, 1972.

"Organizing on abortion service," by A. H. Danon. NURS OUTLOOK 21:460-464, July, 1973.

"Our experience in the premature detachment of the normally inserted placenta," by R. M. Nava y Sanchez, et al. GINECOL OBSTET MEX 33:269-284, March, 1973.

"Outcome of pregnancies following a spontaneous abortion with chromosomal anomalies," by J. G. Boue, et al. AM J OBSTET GYNECOL 116:806-812, July 15, 1973.

"Outcome of pregnancy in women denied legal abortion in several subregions of the Croatian republic," by D. Stampar. NAR ZDRAV 28:205-211, June, 1972.

"Outpatient termination of pregnancy by vacuum aspiration," by A. Y. Ng, et al. SINGAPORE MED J 14:23-25, March, 1973.

"Ovarian function in women with habitual abortion," by M. A. Petrov-Maslakov, et al. AKUSH GINEKOL 48:27-30, September, 1972.

"Oxytocin administration in mid-trimester saline abortions," by N. H. Lauersen, et al. AM J OBSTET GYNECOL 115:420-430, February 1, 1973.

"Oxytocin augmentation of saline abortion," by F. W. Hanson, et al. OBSTET GYNECOL 41:608-610, April, 1973.

"Paracervical block anaesthesia for minor gynaecological operations," by I. S. Jones. NZ MED J 78:15-18, July 11, 1973.

"Parainfluenza-3 and bovine enteroviruses as possible important causative factors in bovine abortion," by H. W. Dunne, et al. AM J VET RES 34:1121-1126, September, 1973.

"Parallels in treachery," by D. DeMarco. SISTERS 45:82-89, October, 1973.

"The paramedic abortionist," by R. F. Mattingly. OBSTET GYNECOL 41:929-930, June, 1973.

"Parental x-irradiation and chromosomes constitution in their spontaneously aborted foetuses," by E. Alberman, et al. ANN HUM GENET

36:185-194, November, 1972.

"Passive hemagglutination test for bovine chlamydial abortion," by E. L. Belden, et al. INFECT IMMUN 7:141-146, February, 1973.

"A pastoral approach to the abortion dilemma," by F. Meehan, et al. DIMENSION 4:131-143, Winter, 1972.

"Pastoral guidelines for the Catholic hospitals and health care personnel in the United States." OR 25,273:11-12, June 21, 1973.

"Pastoral message on abortion." C MIND 71:7-9, September, 1973.

"The pathogenesis and prevention of habitual abortion," by V. I. Bodiazhina. AKUSH GINEKOL 48:12-18, September, 1972.

"Pathohistologic changes of the fetus in enzootic virus abortion of sheep," by A. Djurov. ZENTRALBL VETERINAERMED 19:578-587, August, 1972.

"Pelvic venography," by P. W. Silverberg, et al. RADIOLOGY 107:523-526, June, 1973.

"Personal experience in the premature detachment of a normally implanted placenta," by R. M. Nava y Sanchez, et al. GINECOL OBSTET 33:269-284, March, 1973.

"The physician and family planning," by A. Alvarez-Bravo. GAC MED MEX 105:498-507, May, 1973.

"A physician looks at the abortion problem," by J. Finn. DIMENSION 5:14-24, Spring, 1973.

"A physician's right to practice." J LA STATE MED SOC 125:288-290, August, 1973.

"Physiology and pathology of female reproductive functions," by M. A. Petrov-Maslakov. VESTN AKAD MED NAUK SSSR 28:53-61, 1973.

"Placenta previa: a rare complication of midtrimester abortion by amnioinfusion," by J. A. Goldman, et al. INT SURG 58:707, October, 1973.

"Placental lactogen levels in threatened abortion," by P. A. Niven, et al. PROC R SOC MED 66:188, February, 1973.

"Plasma progesterone and prostaglandin F2 levels during the insertion of prostaglandin F2 vaginal tablet," by T. Sato, et al. PROSTAGLANDINS 4:107-113, July, 1973.

"Plasma progesterone changes in abortion induced by hypertonic saline in the second trimester of pregnancy," by A. J. Tyack, et al. J OBSTET GYNAECOL BR COMMONW 80:548-552, June, 1973.

"Pleasure without trouble," by A. Vogl. THER GGW 111:1352-1354 passim, September, 1972.

"Politicians' and physicians' responsibility in abortion matters," by H. Lefevre. UGESKR LAEGER 135:723-726, March 26, 1973.

"Politics of abortion," by S. Alexander. READ DIGEST 102:69-71, March, 1973.

"Poll finds physicians endorse Supreme Court abortion rule." PSYCHIAT NEWS 8:10 plus, June 20, 1973.

"Poor legislative response to Walsingham v. State (Fla) 250 S 2d 857 ," by J. M. Ellis. FLA B J 47:18, January, 1973.

"Population-political aspects of induced abortion," by D. Klessen, et al. Z AERZTL FORTBILD 67:57-63, January 15, 1973.

"Population, rhythm, contraception and abortion policy questions," by A. Hellegers. LINACRE 40:91-96, May, 1973.

"Possible mode of action of prostaglandins: V. Differential effects of prostaglandin F2a before and after the establishment of placental physiology in pregnant rats," by A. Chatterjee. PROSTAGLANDINS 3:189-199, 1973.

"Postabortal metastatic panophthalmia," by F. Deodati, et al. BULL SOC OPHTALMOL FR 72:729-730, July-August, 1972.

"The postabortal pain syndrome: a new entity," by B. N. Nathanson. OBSTET GYNECOL 41:739-742, May, 1973.

61

"Postabortal posterior colpotomy and sterilization," by S. S. Sheth, et al. J OBSTET GYNAECOL BR COMMONW 80:274-275, March, 1973.

"Post-abortion and post-partum septico-pyemia. Apropos of 27 cases," by V. Vic-Dupont, et al. ANN MED INTERNE 124:291-302, April, 1973.

"Postabortion attitudes," by D. A. Evans, et al. NC MED J 34:271-273, April, 1973.

"The postabortive ovarian disfunction (clinical, pathological and endocrine study)," by J. Botella-Llusia. GYNECOL PRAT 23:117-123, 1972.

"Post-abortum cervical spondylodiscitis," by A. J. Chaumont, et al. MED LEG DOMM CORPOR 5:155-156, April-June, 1972.

"Posterior cervical rupture following prostaglandin-induced mid-trimester abortion," by A. C. Wentz, et al. AM J OBSTET GYNECOL 115:1107-1110, April 15, 1973.

"Potentiation of ovarian response to H.C.G. with Clomiphene. Application to the treatment of luteal deficiency," by S. Geller, et al. J GYNECOL OBSTET BIOL REPROD 1:417-434, July-August, 1972.

"Pour une reforme de la legislation francaise relative a l'avortement," by D. Albe-Fessard, et al. ETUDES 338:55-84, January, 1973.

"Preconception surgical treatment of uterine insufficiency in women with habitual abortions," by A. Zwinger, et al. CESK GYNEKOL 38:256-258, May, 1973.

"Pregnancy and abortion: implications for career development of professional women," by M. T. Notman. ANN NY ACAD SCI 208:205-210, March 15, 1973.

"Pregnancy after hysterotomy," by R. F. Heys. BR MED J 1:681-682, March 17, 1973.

"Pregnancy counseling and the request for abortion: tentative suggestions for Catholic Charities agencies," by E. Ryle. C CHAR 57:8-15, June, 1973.

"Pregnancy interruption with Prostaglandins F2a," by T. Brat, et al. J GYNECOL OBSTET BIOL REPROD 1:385-387, 1972.

"Pregnancy loss among British Columbia mothers." CANAD J PUBLIC HEALTH 64:25-35, January-February, 1973.

"Pregnancy outcome with removal of intrauterine device," by G. T. Alvior, Jr. OBSTET GYNECOL 41:894-896, June, 1973.

"Pregnancy termination and infectious diseases," by J. E. Hodgson. MINN MED 56:698-699, August, 1973.

"Pregnancy wastage in operating room personnel," by I. H. Kaiser. OBSTET GYNECOL 41:930-932, June, 1973.

"A preliminary report: Abortion in Hawaii--present and future trends," by P. I. McNamee, et al. HAWAII MED J 32:220-221, July-August, 1973.

"Premature abruptio placentae in the last 12 years in patients of the Medical Center in Mostar," by V. Martinovic. MED ARH 26:247-250, July-August, 1972.

"Prenatal diagnosis and selective abortion," by K. Lebacqz. LINACRE 40:109-127, May, 1973.

"Prenatal mortality in Iowa, 1963," by M. Mackeprang, et al. J IOWA MED SOC 63:16-18, January, 1973.

"Present concepts of abortion," by E. C. Smith. SOUTHERN MED 61:15-19, August, 1973.

"Prevention and abortion," by B. Grunfeld. TIDSSKR NOR LAEGEFOREN 93:324-325, February 20, 1973.

"Prevention of abortion in the presence of developmental anomalies of the uterus," by N. L. Piganova. AKUSH GINEKOL 48:38-42, September, 1972.

"Prevention of mortality from abortions," by G. D. Safronenko, et al. PEDIATR AKUSH GINEKOL 5:57-59, October, 1972.

"Prevention of premature labor with beta receptor stimulants," by

L. Kovacs, et al. ORV HETIL 114:2537-2538, October 21, 1973.

"Prevention of Rh immunization by anti-D globulin injection after birth and abortion," by J. Vardy, et al. HAREFUAH 83:115-120, August 1, 1972.

"Prevention of Rh immunization following abortion," by J. A. Goldman, et al. HAREFUAH 83:100-101, August 1, 1972.

"The problem of legal pregnancy interruption," by C. Zwahr. ZENTRALBL GYNAEKOL 94:156-163, February 5, 1972.

"Problem of pregnancy interruption as a question for the physician," by R. Reimann-Hunziker. PRAXIS 62:397-399, March 27, 1973.

"Le probleme de l'avortement; lettre pastorale des eveques allemands." DOC CATH 70:626-629, July 1, 1973.

"Problems of reproduction in adolescence," by J. A. Grant, et al. WORLD MED J 20:57, May-June, 1973.

"Products of late abortion. Occurrence of chromosome aberrations," by S. Foussereau, et al. J GYNECOL OBSTET BIOL REPROD 1:651-656, October-November, 1972.

"Professional nursing and the abortion decisions." REGAN REP NURS LAW 13:1, February, 1973.

"Prognostic value of immunologic determinations of chorionic gonado-tropins (C.G.H.) in threatened abortion," by D. Chouvacovic, et al. BULL FED SOC GYNECOL OBSTET LANG FR 23:629-630, November-December, 1971.

"The pro-life movement at the crossroads," by M. Lawrence. TRIUMPH 8:11-15, June, 1973.

"Prolonged gestation in the blue fox after treatment with choriongonado-tropins," by O. M. Moller. NORD VET MED 24:492-500, October, 1972.

"The prospects of PGs in postconceptional therapy," by A. I. Csapo. PROSTAGLANDINS 3:245-289, March, 1973.

"Prostaglandin administration for induction of mid-trimester abortion in complicated pregnancies," by M. Toppozada, et al. LANCET 2:1420-1421, December 30, 1972.

"Prostaglandin developments in Uganda," by S. M. Karim. J REPROD MED 9:255-257, December, 1972.

"Prostaglandin effects on rat pregnancy. II. Interruption of pregnancy," by A. R. Fuchs, et al. FERTIL STERIL 24:275-283, April, 1973.

"Prostaglandin-oxytocin abortion: a clinical trial of intra-amniotic prostaglandin F2alpha in combination with intravenous oxytocin," by M. Seppala, et al. PROSTAGLANDINS 2:311-319, October, 1972.

"Prostaglandins," by R. K. Laros, Jr., et al. AM J NURS 73:1001-1003, June, 1973.

"Prostaglandins and their clinical applications in human reproduction," by E. M. Southern, et al. J REPROD MED 9:472-477, December, 1972.

"Prostaglandins and therapeutic abortion: summary of present status," by C. H. Hendricks. J REPROD MED 9:466-468, December, 1972.

"Prostaglandins as therapeutic agents," by J. Lee, et al. ARCH INTERN MED 131:294-300, 1973.

"Prostaglandins for inducing labor and abortion." DRUG THER BULL 11:41-43, May 25, 1973.

"Prostaglandins in gynecology," by M. Breckwoldt, et al. HIPPOKRATES 43:494-495, December, 1972.

"Prostaglandins: a panacea in reproduction physiology?" by C. Revaz. SCHWEIZ Z GYNAEKOL GEBURTSHILFE 3:95-102, 1972.

"Prostaglandins: a synoptic study," by H. J. S. Rall. S AFR MED J 46:468-471, 1972.

"Protestant theologians debate court ruling on abortion," by E. Wright. CH HER p 12, March 22, 1973.

"A primigravida in preparation for a therapeutic abortion," by D. M. Waselefsky. MATERNAL-CHILD NURS J 2:67-77, Spring, 1973.

"A private matter." ECONOMIST 246:43, 45, January 27, 1973.

"Psychiatric sequelae to legal abortion in South Australia," by F. Weston. MED J AUST 1:350-354, February 17, 1973.

"Psychological factors in mid-trimester abortion," by N. B. Kaltreider. PSYCHIATRY MED 4:129-134, Spring, 1973.

"The psychological impact of abortion," by N. D. West. AORN J 17:132 plus, March, 1973.

"Psychological problems of abortion for the unwed teenage girl," by C. D. Martin. GENET PSYCHOL MONOGR 88:23-110, August, 1973.

"Psychological sequelae of abortion: anxiety and depression," by M. E. Fingerer. J COMMUNITY PSYCHOL 1:221-225, April, 1973.

"Public policy on abortion: John H. Knowles, M. D. urges affirmative response...to Supreme Court decision (No. 9329/373) (News release and Speech)." PLANN PARENTHOOD-FED AM :1-4; 1-14, March 14, 1973.

"Quelques reflexions sur le droit a l'avortement dans le monde anglo-saxon," by M. Rivet. C DE D 13:591-597, 1972.

"A question of credibility," by L. R. McEvoy. POSTGRAD MED 54:33, October, 1973.

"RANF policy on abortion law." RANF REV 4:3, January, 1973.

"Raw judicial power," by J. T. Noonan, Jr. NAT R 25:260-264, March 2, 1973.

"Reaction to abortion ruling: physicians urged to await legal guidelines." AMER MED NEWS 16:3, February 12, 1973.

"Reactions against the bill for the liberalization of abortion; in Germany. " OR 22,270:10, May 31, 1973.

"Reasons for delayed abortion: results of four hundred interviews," by T. D. Kerenyi, et al. AM J OBSTET GYNECOL 117:299-311, October 1, 1973.

"Recent aspects on systemic administration of prostaglandin," by N. Wiqvist, et al. J REPROD MED 9:378-382, December, 1972.

"Recent United States court decisions concerning abortion," by M. A. Olea. AN R ACAD NACL MED 90:327-335, 1973.

"Recommended program guide for abortion services: American Public Health Association." AMER J PUBLIC HEALTH 63:639-644, July, 1973.

"Recurrent abortions and chromosome abnormalities," by M. Lucas, et al. J OBSTET GYNAECOL BR COMMONW 79:1119-1127, December, 1972.

"Reducing the need for abortions," by M. Mead. REDBOOK 141:62 plus, September, 1973.

"Reflections on the Supreme Court's ruling on abortion," by Haines, et al. UC HER p 59, April, 1973.

"Regulating abortions," by S. Shapiro. N ENGL J MED 288:1027-1028, May 10, 1973.

"Regulation of menstrual cycle and termination of pregnancy in the monkey by estradiol and PGF2o," by A. A. Shaikh. PROSTAGLANDINS 2:227-233, 1972.

"Rehnquist: ruling confuses privacy," by W. Rehnquist. NAT CATH REP 9:14, February 2, 1973.

"Remarks on abortion." SEM HOP PARIS 49:123-127, April 8, 1973.

"Repeat abortions in New York city: 1970-1972," by E. F. Daily, et al. FAMILY PLANNING PERSPECTIVES 5:89-93, Spring, 1973.

"Repeated abortive pregnancy," by J. L. Mastboom. NED TIJDSCHR GENEESKD 117:740-743, May 12, 1973.

"Repeated pregnancy loss," by J. Schneider. CLIN OBSTET GYNECOL 16:120-133, March, 1973.

"Report of the Swedish Abortion Committee," by C. Tietze. STUD FAM PLANN 3:28, February, 1972.

"Response of the midpregnant human uterus to systemic administration of 15(S)-15-methyl-prostaglandin F2a," by M. Toppozada, et al. PROSTAGLANDINS 2:239-249, 1972.

"Responsible and demanding part of the work of National Commitees: decisions on legal abortion," by B. Stipal. CESK ZDRAV 21:353-356, September, 1973.

"Resumption of ovulation after incomplete abortion," by G. J. Ratten. AUST NZ J OBSTET GYNAECOL 12:217-219, November, 1972.

"Retinal detachment and interruption of pregnancy," by C. Legerlotz. KLIN MONATSBL AUGENHEILKD 159:827-832, 1971.

"A review of one thousand uncomplicated vaginal operations for abortion," by D. G. Bluett. CONTRACEPTION 7:11-25, 1973.

"Rh immunization in induced abortion," by J. A. Goldman, et al. MINERVA GINECOL 25:100-102, February, 1973.

"The right to be born," by D. DeMarco. SISTERS 44:490-495, April, 1973.

"The right to life debate; excerpt from What a modern Catholic believes about the right to life," by R. Westley. CRITIC 31:50-59, July-August, 1973.

"The right to life; pastoral letter," by J. Camey. OR 32,280:4 plus, August 9, 1973.

"The right to life vs the right to privacy," by C. Dozier. OSV 61:1 plus, April 8, 1973.

"The right to privacy," by J. Connery. LINACRE 40:138-143, May, 1973.

"Right to refuse to perform abortions remains intact: American Hospital Association." AMER MED NEWS 16:3, February 12, 1973.

" 'Right to' what? editorial," by D. Anderson. CHATELAINE 46:1, June, 1973.

"Rights affecting human reproduction," by A. W. Diddle. OBSTET GYNECOL 41:789-794, May, 1973.

"Rights and deaths," by J. J. Thomson. PHILOSOPHY & PUBLIC AFFAIRS 2:146-160, Winter, 1973.

"The rights and wrongs of abortion: a reply to Judith Thomson." PHILOSOPHY & PUBLIC AFFAIRS 2:117-146, Winter, 1973.

"Rights before birth," by L. E. Rozovsky. CAN HOSP 50:17-18, March, 1973.

"The rights of the unborn," by T. Glenister. TABLET 227:557-559, June 16, 1973; Reply 227:603, June 30, 1973.

"The rights to abortion: expansion of the privacy through the fourteenth amendment," by D. Goldenberg. C LAWYER 19:36-57, Winter, 1973.

"RNA concentration in the endometrium of women with habitual abortion," by R. K. Ryzhova. AKUSH GINEKOL 48:23-27, September, 1972.

"Roe v. Wade - the abortion case," by B. White. C MIND 71:11-12, April, 1973.

"Roe v. Wade (93 Sup Ct 705)--the abortion decision--an analysis and its implications." SAN DIEGO L REV 10:844-856, June, 1973.

"Roe v. Wade (93 Sup Ct 705) and Doe v. Bolton (93 Sup Ct 739): compelling state interest test in substantive due process." WASH & LEE L REV 30:628-646, Fall, 1973.

"Roe vs. Wade: the new class warfare," by P. Riga. PRIEST 29:13-16 plus, September, 1973.

"Role of abortion in the etiology of iso-immunization in Rh-incompatibility pregnancies," by P. F. Bolis, et al. ARCH OSTET GINECOL 77:44-49, February, 1972.

"Role of histoclinical studies in the prophylaxis of spontaneous abortions," by W. Waronski, et al. GINEKOL POL 44:425-429, April, 1973.

"The role of infection in spontaneous abortion," by A. P. Egorova, et al. VOPF OKHR MATERIN DET 17:65-70, September, 1972.

"Role of listeriosis in abortions, in utero fetal deaths and premature labor," by J. R. Giraud, et al. BULL FED SOC GYNECOL OBSTET

LANG FR 23:593-594, November-December, 1971.

"The role of the placenta in fetal and perinatal pathology. Highlights of an eight months' study," by G. Altshuler, et al. AM J OBSTET GYNECOL 113:616-626, July 1, 1972.

"Round table discussion on abortions of chromosomal origin." CAH MED 14:191-203, March, 1973.

"Rubella vaccination and the termination of pregnancy." BR MED J 4:666, December 16, 1972.

"A ruptured dermoid cyst in labor simulating abruptio placentae. A possible complication of amniocentesis," by F. H. Boehm, et al. J REPROD MED 4:229-230, June, 1970.

"A safer cervical dilator," by C. Michael. MED J AUST 1:1254, June 23, 1973.

"Le Saint-Siege et l'avortement," by S. Luoni. DOC CATH 70:574-575, June 17, 1973.

"Saline instillation with oxytocin administration in midtrimester abortion," by L. I. Mann, et al. OBSTET GYNECOL 41:748-752, May, 1973.

"Salmonella anatum from an aborted foal," by S. Kumar, et al. BR VET J 128:ixiv, November, 1972.

"Salmonella dublin abortion in a New South Wales dairy herd," by K. R. Davidson. AUST VET J 49:174, March, 1973.

"San Miguel sea lion virus isolation, preliminary characterization and relationship to vesicular exanthema of swine virus," by A. W. Smith, et al. NATURE 244:108-110, July 13, 1973.

"The sanctity of human life." CH HER p 8, October 20, 1972.

"Says no doctor or hospital can be forced to perform abortion: New Jersey's Attorney General." HOSP PROGRESS 54:96d, March, 1973.

"Science and the citizen." SCI AM 228:44-46 plus, March, 1973.

"Scintiphotographic diagnosis of abruptio placentae," by M. L. Moss, et al. J NUCL MED 14:297-298, May, 1973.

"Scottish abortion statistics -1971." HEALTH BULL 31:39-50, January, 1973.

"A second look at 'Humane Vitae'," by H. Klaus. HPR 74:59-67, October, 1973.

"Second trimester termination by intra-uterine prostaglandin F2. Clinical and hormonal results with observations on induced lactation and chronoperiodicity," by R. Shearman, et al. J REPROD MED 9:448-452, December, 1972.

"The selective effect of therapeutic abortion when children thus eliminated are carriers of a recessive autosomic or x-chromosome-linked defect," by U. Pfandler, et al. J GENET HUM 20:135-150, June, 1972.

"Senate OKs fetal experiments ban." NAT CATH REP 9:20, September 28, 1973.

"Septic abortion," by F. Kubli. MED KLIN 68:500-504, April 20, 1973.

"Septic abortion and septic shock," by M. Botes. S AFR MED J 47:432-435, March 10, 1973.

"Septic abortion and septic shock," by W. H. Utian. S AFR MED J 47:639, April 21, 1973.

"Septic induced abortion," by J. F. Jewett. N ENGL J MED 289:748-749, October 4, 1973.

"Septicemia with Listeria monocytogenes following abortion induced after 2 and one-half months," by J. F. Lemeland, et al. NOUV PRESSE MED 2:1616, June 9, 1973.

"The serological response to Aspergillus fumigatus antigens in bovine mycotic abortion," by M. J. Corbel. BR VET J 128:73-75, December, 1972.

"Severe postabortal Clostridium welchii infection: trends in management," by J. P. O'Neill, et al. AUST NZ J OBSTET GYNAECOL 12:157-165, August, 1972.

"Sexuality, birth control and abortion: a decision-making sequence," by M. Diamond, et al. J BIOSOC SCI 5:347-361, July, 1973.

"The significance of urogenital trichomoniasis in the etiology of abortion," by S. S. Zakharchuk, et al. AKUSH GINEKOL 48:44-45, September, 1972.

"Social hygiene and social politics," by D. Klessen, et al. Z AERZTL FORTBILD 66:1148-1150, November 15, 1972.

"The social indications for abortion," by W. Becker. THER GGW 111: 587-604, 1972.

"Social indications for interruption of pregnancy," by W. Kokoszka, et al. POL TYG LEK 28:139-140, January 22, 1973.

"Sociologist calls U. S. abortion law 'worst law in world'." HOSP PROGRESS 54:21-22, April, 1973.

"La solution du voisin," by L. Martin. LE MACLEAN 13:18-19, 38 plus, February, 1973.

"Somatic complications after legal abortion by vacuum aspiration combined with oxytocin infusion," by E. D. Johansson, et al. LAKARTID-NINGEN 69:6045-6048, December 13, 1972.

"Some abortions may lead to murder charges." NAT CATH REP 9:3, April 3, 1973.

"Some additional arguments against abortion," by O. Bennett. HPR 73: 50-53, January, 1973.

"Some aspects of implementation of legal abortion," by A. Chatterjee. J INDIAN MED ASSOC 59:342-343, October 16, 1972.

"Some implications of self-selection for pregnancy," by W. Z. Billewicz. BR J PREV SOC MED 27:49-52, February, 1973.

"Some observations on the aetiology and management of coagulation failure complicating abruptio placentae," by H. K. Basu. J INDIAN MED ASSOC 58:409-416, June 1, 1972.

"Some psychiatric problems related to therapeutic abortion," by

D. S. Werman, et al. NC MED J 34:274-275, April, 1973.

"Some recent world events in relation to pregnancy termination." WORLD MED J 20:72-75, July-August, 1973.

"Spontaneous abortion: the most common complication in pregnancy," by D. A. Aiken. NURS TIMES 69:898-899, July 12, 1973.

"Spontaneous abortions and triploidy," by J. Levy, et al. REV FR GYNE-COL OBSTET 67:327-342, May, 1972.

"Spontaneous premature interruption of pregnancy and its causes," by M. A. Petrov-Maslakov. AKUSH GINEKOL 48:7-11, September, 1972.

"Standards for outpatient facilities for abortion service." MARYLAND STATE MED J 22:69-70, September, 1973.

"Staphylococcal lung abscesses following septic abortion," by A. Singh, et al. INDIAN J CHEST DIS 14:274-276, October, 1972.

"State legislation can lessen impact of Court's abortion decision," by R. W. Stratton. HOSP PROG 54:8-9, October, 1973.

"Statement by Sisters of Charity of the Incarnate Word." HOSP PROGRESS 54:96b, March, 1973.

"Statement on abortion: the American College of Obstetricians and Gynecologists." J MED ASS STATE ALA 42:736, April, 1973.

"Statements of national conference of Catholic bishops; pastoral message." C LAWYER 19:29-35, Winter, 1973.

"Statistical analysis of 1021 abortions. Treatment of abortus imminens," by T. J. Horvath. MED WELT 23:1929-1930, December 16, 1972.

"Status of abortions, fertility and family planning in the Rostock region during 1962-1971," by K. H. Mehlan, et al. Z AERZTL FORTBILD 67:539-545, June, 1973.

"Sterilization and therapeutic abortion counselling for the mentally retarded," by C. W. Smiley. CURR THER RES 15:78-81, February, 1973.

"Sterilization associated with induced abortion: JPSA findings (based on a Joint program for the study of abortion examination of the abortion experience of 72,988 American women who had legal abortions, 1970-1971)," by S. Lewit. FAMILY PLANNING PERSPECTIVES 5:177-182, Summer, 1973.

"Storm rages over abortion in Australia," by R. Mathias. CHR CENT 90:810-811, August 15, 1973.

"Student opinion on legalized abortion at the University of Toronto," by F. M. Barrett. CANAD J PUBLIC HEALTH 64:294-299, May-June, 1973.

"Studies of early modifications of maternal coagulation-fibrinolysis balance in intrauterine death of the fetus," by P. Capetta, et al. MINERVA GINECOL 25:492-495, August, 1973.

"Studies of prostaglandin F2 in the cow," by D. R. Lamond, et al. PROSTAGLANDINS 4:269-284, August, 1973.

"Studies of the role of Dermacentor occidentalis in the transmission of bovine chlamydial abortion," by H. D. Caldwell, et al. INFECT IMMUN 7:147-151, February, 1973.

"Studies of serological reactions in ovine toxoplasmosis encountered in intensively-bred sheep," by G. A. Sharman, et al. VET REC 91:670-675, December 30, 1972.

"Studies on accidental intravascular injection in extra-amniotic saline induced abortion and a method for reducing this risk," by B. Gustavii. J REPROD MED 8:70-74, February, 1972.

"Studies on the pathogenesis of clotting defects during salt-induced abortions," by L. M. Talbert, et al. AM J OBSTET GYNECOL 115:656-662, March 1, 1973.

"Stunning approval for abortion: decision blow by blow." TIME 101:50-51, February 5, 1973.

"Suffer, little children," by E. Figes. NEW HUMANIST 89:521, May, 1973.

"Supreme Court abortion decisions," by W. A. Regan. HOSP PROGRESS 54:12 plus, April, 1973.

"Supreme court abortion opinions," by J. H. Hedgepeth. HOSP MED

STAFF 2:10-17, April, 1973; 33-39, May, 1973; 44-48, June, 1973.

"The Supreme court and legitimate state interest (commenting on the U.S. Supreme court's decision in Roe v. Wade, as it pertains to the right of a state to prohibit abortion), by Robert G. Stewart; The abortion decision, by John C. Robbins." RIPON FORUM 9:8-11, April, 1973.

"The Supreme Court decision on abortion," by R. E. Hall. AM J OBSTET GYNECOL 116:1-8, May 1, 1973.

"Supreme court eases rules on abortion." U. S. NEWS 74:36, February 5, 1973.

"Supreme Court issues broad pronouncements on constitutionality of State abortion laws." HOSPITALS 47:108, February 16, 1973.

"Supreme court on abortion." AMERICA 128:81, February 3, 1973.

"The Supreme Court on abortion: a dissenting opinion," by P. Conley, et al. C LAWYER 19:19-28, Winter, 1973.

"The Supreme Court on abortion: a dissenting opinion," by P. Conley, et al. R REL 32:473-481, May, 1973.

"Supreme Court refuses abortion review." AMER MED NEWS 16:1, March 5, 1973.

"Supreme Court: right of privacy includes abortion; excerpts from abortion decision." NAT CATH REP 9:8 plus, February 2, 1973.

"The syndrome of chronic abruptio placentae, hydrorrhea, and circumvallate placenta," by F. Naftolin, et al. AM J OBSTET GYNECOL 116:347-350, June 1, 1973.

"Telling it like it is about abortion," by J. Breig. OSV 62:1 plus, August 26, 1973.

"Tennessee's new abortion law," by H. Williams. J TENN MED ASSOC 66:651-652, June, 1973.

"The termination of adolescent out-of-wedlock pregnancies and the prospects for their primary prevention," by W. G. Cobliner, et al. AM J OBSTET GYNECOL 115:432-444, February 1, 1973.

"Termination of early gestation with vaginal prostaglandin F2 alpha tablets," by R. C. Corlett, et al. PROSTAGLANDINS 2:453-464, December, 1972.

"Termination of early pregnancy in rats after ovariectomy is due to immediate collapse of the progesterone-dependent decidua," by R. Deanesly. J REPROD FERTIL 35:183-186, October, 1973.

"Termination of pregnancy." J IOWA MED SOC 63:248 passim, June, 1973.

"Termination of pregnancy," by D. Bluett. BR MED J 3:700, September 16, 1972.

"Termination of pregnancy by abdominal hysterotomy," by J. Higginbottom. LANCET 1:937-938, April 28, 1973.

"Termination of pregnancy by intra-uterine prostaglandin F 2," by A. Korda, et al. AUST NZ J OBSTET GYNAECOL 12:166-169, August, 1972.

"The termination of pregnancy by intravenous infusion of a synthetic prostaglandin F2 analogue," by D. S. Sharp, et al. J OBSTET GYNAECOL BR COMMONW 80:138-141, February, 1973.

"Termination of pregnancy by 'super coils': morbidity associated with a new method of second-trimester abortion," by G. S. Berger, et al. AM J OBSTET GYNECOL 116:297-304, June 1, 1973.

"Termination of pregnancy: guideline statement of the Iowa Medical Society." J IOWA MED SOC 63:248 plus, June, 1973.

"Termination of pregnancy, Sydney, 1972," by D. Pfanner, et al. MED J AUST 1:710-711, April 7, 1973.

"Termination of pregnancy with 15 methyl analogues of prostaglandins E 2 and F 2," by S. M. Karim, et al. J REPROD MED 9:383-391, December, 1972.

"Termination of pregnancy with intrauterine devices. A comparative study of coils, coils and balsa, and catheters," by B. Mullick, et al. AM J OBSTET GYNECOL 116:305-308, June 1, 1973.

"Termination of second trimester pregnancy with intra-amniotic administration of prostaglandins E 2 and F 2," by S. M. Karim, et al. J REPROD MED 9:427-433, December, 1972.

"Theological reasons for the sanctity of life. A review," by K. D. O'Rourke. HOSP PROGRESS 54:73-77, August, 1973.

"Therapeutic abortion," by R. H. Christie. CENT AFR J MED 19:54-58, March, 1973.

"Therapeutic abortion," by A. Eistetter. CATH HOSP p 3-4, January-February, 1973.

"Therapeutic abortion and its complications in Halifax, N. S.," by C. Resch, et al. NS MED BULL 52:67-70, April, 1973.

"Therapeutic abortion and a prior psychiatric history," by J. A. Ewing, et al. AM J PSYCHIATRY 130:37-40, January, 1973.

"Therapeutic abortion by extra-amniotic administration of prostaglandins," by M. P. Embrey, et al. J REPROD MED 9:420-424, December, 1972.

"Therapeutic abortion by intrauterine infusion of prostaglandin F 2," by T. H. Lippert, et al. ARCH GYNAEKOL 213:197-201, 1973.

"Therapeutic abortion employing the synergistic action of extra-amniotic prostaglandin E 2 and an intravenous infusion of oxytocin," by G. A. Morewood. J OBSTET GYNAECOL BR COMMONW 80:473-475, May, 1973.

"Therapeutic abortion in the second trimester by intra-amniotic prostaglandin F 2," by C. A. Ballard, et al. J REPROD MED 9:397-399, December, 1972.

"Therapeutic abortion: a multidisciplined approach to patient care from a social work perspective," by J. M. Rogers, et al. CANAD J PUBLIC HEALTH 64:254-259, May/June, 1973.

"Therapeutic abortion of early human gestation with vaginal suppositories of prostaglandin (F 2)," by D. R. Tredway, et al. AM J OBSTET GYNECOL 116:795-798, July 15, 1973.

"Therapeutic abortion on psychiatric grounds. A follow-up study," by J. A. Ewing, et al. NC MED J 34:265-270, April, 1973.

"Therapeutic abortion: a prospective study. II," by S. Meikle, et al. AM J OBSTET GYNECOL 115:339-346, February 1, 1973.

"Therapeutic abortion utilizing local application of prostaglandin F2 alpha," by F. Naftolin, et al. J REPROD MED 9:437-441, December, 1972.

"Therapeutic abortions in Siriraj Hospital," by S. Toongsuwan, et al. J MED ASSOC THAI 56:237-240, April, 1973.

"Therapeutic termination of pregnancy in private practice," by J. M. Miller. MED J AUST 1:831-834, April 28, 1973.

"Three abortion amendments in Congress." NAT CATH REP 9:16, June 22, 1973.

"Thrombocytopenia indicating gram-negative infection and endotoxemia," by F. K. Beller, et al. OBSTET GYNECOL 41:521-524, April, 1973.

"Thrombotic thrombocytopenic purpura and gynaecological manifestations," by M. Yudis. LANCET 1:1445, June 25, 1973.

"To respect human life," by N. Pole. PHIL CONTEXT 2:16-22, 1973.

"Toward a sound moral policy on abortion," by P. Coffey. NEW SCHOL 47:105-112, Winter, 1973.

"Transplantation in a system of complex treatment of habitually aborted pregnancy," by O. V. Nadeina, et al. AKUSH GINEKOL 48:35-38, September, 1972.

"Traumatic rupture of the placenta," by R. Schuhmann, et al. ZENTRALBL GYNAEKOL 94:1239-1243, September 23, 1972.

"Treatment with synthetic ACTH of threatened abortion in women with secondary hypophyseal insufficiency," by R. Klimek, et al. GINEKOL POL 44:25-29, January, 1973.

"Trends in legalized abortion in South Australia," by A. F. Connon. MED J AUST 1:231-234, February 3, 1973.

"Trends in therapeutic abortion in San Francisco," by P. Goldstein, et al. AM J PUBLIC HEALTH 62:695-699, 1972.

"The triad of polyptychencephaly, embryonal resorption and spontaneous abortion," by J. Dankmeijer. NED TIJDSCHR GENEESKD 117:519-524, March 31, 1973.

"Two essays on abortion," by D. DeMarco. R REL 32:1064-1069, September, 1973.

"The two separate issues in the abortion debate," by M. Dobbin. MED J AUST 1:1165-1166, June 9, 1973.

"Two years experience in New York City with the liberalized abortion law--progress and problems," by J. Pakter, et al. AM J PUBLIC HEALTH 63:524-535, June, 1973.

"Two years' experience with a liberal abortion law: Its impact on fertility trends in New York City," by C. Tietze. FAMILY PLANN PERSPECT 5:36-41, Winter, 1973.

"The tuskegee syphilis study," by W. J. Curran. N ENGL J MED 289:730-731, October 4, 1973.

"Ultrasonographic examination in hemorrhages in the 3d trimester," by A. Zacutti, et al. MINERVA GINECOL 25:468-475, August, 1973.

"Ultrasonography in abortion diagnosis," by H. Meyenberg. GEBURTSHILFE FRAUENHEILKD 33:272-276, April, 1973.

"The unborn." BANNER p 13, April 13, 1973.

"Unfavorable outcome of pregnancy: repeated losses," by R. L. Naeye, et al. AM J OBSTET GYNECOL 116:1133-1137, August 15, 1973.

"The unwilling dead," by S. M. Harrison. PROC CATH PHIL ASS 46:199-208, 1972.

"U. S. bishops oppose Supreme Court decision." OR 7,255:6-7, February 15, 1973.

"U. S. bishops' pastoral on abortion." OSV 61:4, March 11, 1973.

"U. S. Supreme Court lifts curbs on abortion." AMER MED NEWS 16:1 plus, January 29, 1973.

"U. S. Supreme Court on abortion." SOC JUST 65:359 plus, February, 1973.

"U. S. Supreme Court on abortion," by C. B. Goodhart. LANCET 1:429, February 24, 1973.

"U. S. Supreme Court on abortion," by M. Simms. LANCET 1:544, March 10, 1973.

"U. S. Supreme Court on abortion. Roe v. Wade, 41 U.S.L.W. 4213(1973)." CONN MED 37:279-289, June, 1973.

"United States' Cardinals protest Court's decision; abortion." OR 5,253: 5, February 1, 1973.

"United States Supreme Court and abortion. 1," by E. J. Holman. JAMA 225:215-216, July 9, 1973.

--3," by E. J. Holman. JAMA 225:447-448, July, 1973.

"United States Supreme Court and abortion," by E. J. Holman. J AMER MED ASS 225:215-216, July 9, 1973; 343-344, July 16, 1973; 447-448, July 23, 1973.

"An unusual surgical injury to the ureter," by M. P. Gangai. J UROL 109:32, January, 1973.

"Urinary excretion of various steroid hormones during the physiological course of pregnancy and in threatened spontaneous premature interruption," by L. V. Timoshenko, et al. .PEDIATR AKUSH GINEKOL 5:38-40, October, 1972.

"Use of Alupent in obstetrics. Our personal experiences," by G. Di Terlizzi. MINERVA GINECOL 25:225-245, April, 1973.

"Use of cephalothin in septic abortion," by C. H. Dahm, Jr., et al. OBSTET GYNECOL 41:693-696, May, 1973.

"Use of combined premedication in induced abortion," by E. I. Gorobets. AKUSH GINEKOL 48:67-68, November, 1972.

"Use of isoxsuprine in the obstetrical pathology," by I. Signorelli, et al. ARCH OSTET GINECOL 77:115-128, April, 1972.

"Use of laminaria tents with hypertonic saline amnioinfusion," by J. H. Lischke, et al. AM J OBSTET GYNECOL 116:586-587, June 15, 1973.

"Use of prostaglandin F 2 alpha for interruption of pregnancy in 1st and 2d trimester," by F. Havranek, et al. CESK GYNEKOL 38:432-435, July, 1973.

"The use of prostaglandin pessaries prior to vaginal termination," by I. Craft. PROSTAGLANDINS 3:377-381, March, 1973.

"Use of vaginal wall cytologic smears to predict abortion in high-risk pregnancies," by M. T. McLennan, et al. AM J OBSTET GYNECOL 114:857-860, December 1, 1972.

"Use of vitamin preparations of reduce calf loss as well as to stabilise and normalise puerperium of cattle," by R. Liebetrau, et al. MONATSH VET MED 27:695-697, September 15, 1972.

" 'Uterine' and 'luteal' effects of prostaglandins (PG) in rats and guinea pigs as potential abortifacient mechanisms," by W. Elger, et al. ACTA ENDOCRINOL 173:46, 1973.

"Uterine contractility and placental histology in abortion by laminaria and metreurynter," by Y. Manabe, et al. OBSTET GYNECOL 41:753-759, May, 1973.

"Uterine evacuation by aspiration," by J. Delgado Urdapilleta, et al. GINECOL OBSTET MEX 32:607-609, December, 1972.

"Vaccination against vibrionic abortion in sheep with a cell-disrupted adjuvant vaccine," by N. J. Gilmour, et al. RES VET SCI 13:601-602, November, 1972.

"Vaccination of a large cattle herd against infectious pustular vulvovaginitis and rhinotracheitis," by O. C. Straub, et al. DTSCH TIERAERZTL WOCHENSCHR 80:73-77, February 15, 1973.

"Vacuum extraction of hydrocephalic fetus," by T. G. Price. J OBSTET GYNAECOL BR COMMONW 79:1053, November, 1972.

"Vaginal adenocarcinoma as a late result of treatment of threatened abortion with diethylstilbestrol," by J. Presl. CESK GYNEKOL 38:473-474, July, 1973.

"Vaginal administration of prostaglandins and early abortion," by R. J. Pion, et al. J REPROD MED 9:413-415, December, 1972.

"Vaginal administration of prostaglandin F2a for inducing therapeutic abortion," by W. E. Brenner, et al. PROSTAGLANDINS 1:455-467, 1972.

"Vaginal mid-trimester abortion," by D. T. Liu. LANCET 1:433, February 24, 1973.

"Value of Salbutamol in obstetrics," by P. Dellenbach, et al. THERA-PEUTIQUE 48:671-675, December, 1972.

"The velvet glove or the iron fist?" by J. Brennan. LINACRE 40:128-132, May, 1973.

"Viability, abortion, and the difference between a fetus and an infant," by H. T. Engelhardt, Jr. AM J OBSTET GYNECOL 116:429-434, June 1, 1973.

"The viability of fetal skin of abortuses induced by saline or prosta-glandin," by I. J. Park, et al. AM J OBSTET GYNECOL 115:274-275, January 15, 1973.

"Vibrio infections in goats," by A. I. Krylov, et al. VETERINARIIA 8:104-105, August, 1972.

"Vibrionic abortion in ewes in South Africa: preliminary report," by A. P. Schutte, et al. J S AFR VET MED ASSOC 42:223-226, September, 1971.

"Voluntary abortion. Its social and biological consequences," by J. Botella Llusia. AN R ACAD NACL MED 90:285-295, 1973.

"Wages of crying wolf: a comment on Roe v. Wade (93 Sup Ct 705)," by J. H. Ely. YALE L J 82:920, April, 1973.

"Wanderer Forum backs amendment," by D. Effenberger. NAT CATH REP 9:17, July 20, 1973.

"Water vacuum suction curettage (WVSC): one year's experience," by J. R. Woods, Jr., et al. OBSTET GYNECOL 41:720-725, May, 1973.

"What about me?" by P. W. Lang. J CAN BA 4:27, January, 1973.

"What the bishops say," by M. Walsh. MONTH 6:172-175, May, 1973.

"What chance do prolife amendments have," by R. Shaw. COLUMBIA 53:10, October, 1973.

"What does theology say about abortion?" by J. R. Nelson. CHR CENT 90:124-128, January 31, 1973.

"What liberal abortion has done to Hungary," by H. Szablya. OSV 61:1 plus, September 23, 1973.

"What sisters should know about euthanasia; interview by D. Durken," by P. Marx. SISTERS 45:90-101, October, 1973.

"What will abortion regulations be if law is reformed? Here are clues," by J. W. Eliot. MICH MED 71:959-962, November, 1972.

"What you should know about abortion," by S. A. Kaufman. PARENTS MAG 48:62-64, April, 1973.

"When the barbarians came," by D. Francis. J LA STATE MED SOC 125: 138-139, April, 1973.

"White: beyond the Constitution," by B. White. NAT CATH REP 9:14, February 2, 1973.

"Why I favor liberalized abortion," by A. F. Guttmacher. READ DIGEST 103:143-147, November, 1973.

"Why I reversed my stand on laissez-faire abortion," by C. E. Lincoln. CHR CENT 90:477-479, April 25, 1973.

"Why they didn't kill my son," by R. Scheiber. OSV 61:7, February 11, 1973.

"Why the topic legalized abortion?" NURSING 45:22-23, January-February 1973.

"Wife of Onan and the sons of Cain: danger inherent in social technology," by J. A. Miles, Jr. NAT R 25:891-894, August 17, 1973; Discussion 25:1024 plus, September 28, 1973.

"Women claim abortion, feminism contradictory." NAT CATH REP

9:5, March 2, 1973.

"Women who seek abortions: a study," by A. T. Young, et al. SOC WORK 18:60-65, May, 1973.

"Women's rights vs. Catholic dogma: why the church fathers oppose abortion," by C. Moriarty. INTERNAT SOCIALIST R 34:8-11 plus, March, 1973.

"The work of the women's consultation for the prevention of artificial abortions," by S. L. Polchanova. AKUSH GINEKOL 48:54-56, September, 1972.

"The wounded uterus: pregnancy after hysterotomy," by W. M. Clow, et al. BR MED J 1:321-323, February 10, 1973.

"Y to X translocation in a woman with reproductive failure. A new rearrangement," by G. Khudr, et al. JAMA 226:544-549, October 29, 1973.

PERIODICAL LITERATURE

SUBJECT INDEX

ABNORMALITIES
see: Complications

ABORTION (GENERAL)
"Abortion: patterns, technics, and results," by E. B. Connell.
FERTIL STERIL 24:78-91, January, 1973.

"Abortion; postscript." ECONOMIST 247:28, June 2, 1973.

"The abortionist dictionary: gilded words for guilty deeds," by J.
Allen. LIGUORIAN 61:36-37, May, 1973.

"Telling it like it is about abortion," by J. Breig. OSV 62:1 plus,
August 26, 1973.

"The velvet glove or the iron fist?" by J. Brennan. LINACRE 40:128-
132, May, 1973.

ABORTION ACT
see: Laws and Legislation

ABORTION: AUSTRALIA
"Abortion in Victoria after Menhennit," by J. Smibert. MED J AUST
1:1016-1017, May 19, 1973.

"Experience with the suction curette in termination of pregnancy at a
Sydney Teaching hospital," by R. H. Picker, et al. AUST NZ J
OBSTET GYNAECOL 13:49-50, February, 1973.

"Legal abortion, the South Australian experience." MED J AUST
1:821-823, April 28, 1973.

"Maternal deaths in Australia compared with England and Wales in 1964-1966," by J. R. Neil, et al. MED J AUST 59-1:682-685, 1972.

"Medical abortion in South Australia. A critical assessment of early complications," by J. M. Miller. MED J AUST 1:825-830, April 28, 1973.

"Psychiatric sequelae to legal abortion in South Australia," by F. Weston. MED J AUST 1:350-354, February 17, 1973.

"Storm rages over abortion in Australia," by R. Mathias. CHR CENT 90:810-811, August 15, 1973.

"Termination of pregnancy, Sydney, 1972," by D. Pfanner, et al. MED J AUST 1:710-711, April 7, 1973.

"Trends in legalized abortion in South Australia," by A. F. Connon. MED J AUST 1:231-234, February 3, 1973.

ABORTION: BELGIUM
"The law on abortion and the defence of life; a declaration of the Belgian bishops." OR 24,272:9, June 14, 1973.

ABORTION: CANADA
"Abortion in Canada as a public health problem and as a community health measure," by C. W. Schwenger. CAN J PUBLIC HEALTH 64:223-230, May-June, 1973.

"Abortions rise 33 per cent in nation-wide Canadian survey." HOSP ADMIN CAN 15:8, February, 1973.

"Declartions des eveques du Quebec." DOC CATH 70:382-384, April 15, 1973.

"Pregnancy loss among British Columbia mothers." CANAD J PUBLIC HEALTH 64:25-35, January-February, 1973.

"Student opinion on legalized abortion at the University of Toronto," by F. M. Barrett. CANAD J PUBLIC HEALTH 64:294-299, May-June, 1973.

"Therapeutic abortion and its complications in Halifax, N. S.," by
C. Resch, et al. NS MED BULL 52:67-70, April, 1973.

ABORTION: CHILE
"Fecundity, abortion and standard of living among Mapuche women,"
by T. Monreal. REV MED CHIL 100:1273-1286, October, 1972.

ABORTION: DENMARK
"The abortion situation in Denmark and conditions in Finland," by
M. Johansson. LAKARTIDNINGEN 70:344, January 31, 1973.

"Development concerning legal abortions under the present Danish
abortion law," by V. Skalts. UGESKR LAEGER 134:2505-2507,
November 20, 1972.

"Development in the incidence of abortions in recent years. Investigations and calculations concerning the incidence of criminal abortions
prior to and after the Danish abortion law of 1970," by V. Sele, et al.
UGESKR LAEGER 134:2493-2505, November 20, 1972.

"Free abortion in Denmark?" by M. Johansson. NORD MED 88:13,
January, 1973.

"Legal abortion. An assessment following the Danish abortion law of
1.IV.1970," by E. Gregersen. UGESKR LAEGER 135:417-420,
February 19, 1973.

ABORTION: FINLAND
"Abortion in Finland today," by K. Wichmann. DUODECIM 89:649-651,
1973.

"The abortion situation in Denmark and conditions in Finland," by
M. Johansson. LAKARTIDNINGEN 70:344, January 31, 1973.

ABORTION: FRANCE
"L'adoption, une alternative meconnue a l'avortement; France," by
F. Dardot. ETUDES 338:701-714, May, 1973.

"Les chretiens face a l'avortement," by B. Ribes. ETUDES 339:
405-423, October, 1973.

"Le Conseil permanent de l' Episcopat francais, Paris, 19-21 juin 1973, introduction," by F. Marty. DOC CATH 70:672-674, July 15, 1973.

"Data for reform of French legislation on abortion," by R. Veylon. NOUV PRESSE MED 2:475-478, February 24, 1973.

"Declaration du Conseil permanent de l' Episcopat francais sur l'avortement." DOC CATH 70:676-679, July 15, 1973.

"Dossier sur l'avortement, l'apport de nos lecteurs," by B. Ribes. ETUDES 338:511-534, April, 1973.

"France: abortion, oui!" NEWSWEEK 81:46 plus, June 11, 1973.

"France; the power to start and end a life." ECONOMIST 245:45, December 2, 1972.

"The French Episcopate, firm and clear against revision of abortion law." OR 33,281:3 plus, August 16, 1973.

"French manifesto." TIME 101:76, February 19, 1973.

"French medicine: the abortion battle." MED WORLD NEWS 14:4-5, March 2, 1973.

"Lib and let live," by N. Roberts. GUARDIAN p. 12, February 15, 1973.

"Pour une reforme de la legislation francaise relative a l'avortement," by D. Albe-Fessard. ETUDES 338:55-84, January, 1973.

ABORTION: GERMANY
"Abortion law reform controversy rages in West Germany," by F. Lupsen. CHR CENT 90:487-488, April 25, 1973.

"Appeal to all: protect human life; pastoral letter of the German Episcopate." OR 28,276:9-10, July 12, 1973.

"Development of the clinical abortion situation at the gynecologic hospital of Karl-Marx-University, Leipzig from 1.1.1960 to

30.6.1972," by S. Schulz, et al. ZENTRALBL GYNAEKOL 95:952-957, July 13, 1973.

"Reactions against the bill for the liberalization of abortion; in Germany." OR 22,270:10, May 31, 1973.

ABORTION: HUNGARY

"The demographic effects of legal abortion on the Hungarian labor force (conference paper)," by B. Kapotsy. EUROPEAN DEMOGRAPHIC INFO BUL 4:136-143, November 3, 1973.

"What liberal abortion has done to Hungary," by H. Szablya. OSV 61:1 plus, September 23, 1973.

ABORTION: INDIA

"Opinion towards induced abortion among urban women in Delhi, India," by S. B. Kar. SOC SCI MED 6:731-736, December, 1972.

ABORTION: ITALY

"Discipline or liberalization of abortion? Proposal for the Fortuna law: its function and applicability in Italy," by S. Fossati. MINERVA GINECOL 25:364-370, June, 1973.

"Italian abortion law faces opposition." NAT CATH REP 9:5, February 9, 1973.

ABORTION: JAPAN

"Abortion programme in Duchenne muscular dystrophy in Japan," by K. Kondo, et al. LANCET 1:543, March 10, 1973.

ABORTION: NEW ZEALAND

"Abortion in New Zealand," by W. A. Facer, et al. J BIOSOC SCI 5:151-158, April, 1973.

"Criminal abortion in New Zealand," by W. A. P. Facer. HEALTH PEOPLE 6:18-20 plus, October, 1972.

"Maori attitudes toward abortion," by L. Gluckman. LINACRE 40:44-48, February, 1973.

ABORTION: PUERTO RICO
"Abortion decision and Puerto Rico," by J. L. Simon. REV C ABO PR
34:505-513, August, 1973.

ABORTION: ROMANIA
"The dynamics of therapeutic abortions in the town of Bucharest
during the 1967-1969 period," by V. Coroi, et al. OBSTET GINECOL
20:267-272, 1972.

ABORTION: SWEDEN
"Report of the Swedish Abortion Committee," by C. Tietze. STUD
FAM PLANN 3:28, February, 1972.

ABORTION: UGANDA
"Prostaglandin developments in Uganda," by S. M. Karim. J REPROD
MED 9:255-257, December, 1972.

ABORTION: UNITED KINGDOM
"The Abortion Act of 1967; Society for the Protection of Unborn
Children." TABLET 227:237-239, March 10, 1973.

"Abortion and liberation," by M. Simms. NEW HUMANIST 88:479-481,
April, 1973.

"Abortion deaths: England and Wales." LANCET 1:1199, May 26, 1973.

"Abortions at charity prices." SOC JUST 66:87-88, June, 1973.

"Maternal deaths in Australia compared with England and Wales in
1964-1966," by J. R. Neil, et al. MED J AUST 59:682-685, 1972.

"The medical profession and the 1967 Abortion Act in Britain," by
S. J. Macintyre. SOC SCI MED 7:121-134, February, 1973.

"Numbers go on rising." ECONOMIST 247:30, May 26, 1973.

"On the incidence of illegal abortion (Great Britain); with a reply to
Dr. W. H. James," by C. B. Goodhart. POPULATION STUDIES
27:207-233, July, 1973.

"Salmonella dublin abortion in a New South Wales dairy herd," by

K. R. Davidson. AUST VET J 49:174, March, 1973.

"Scottish abortion statistics--1971." HEALTH BULL 31:39-50, January, 1973.

ABORTION: UNITED STATES
ARKANSAS
"Abortion applicants in Arkansas," by F. O. Henker, 3d. J ARKANSAS MED SOC 69:293-295, March, 1973.

CALIFORNIA
"California abortion law overturned." NEWSLETTER 6:6, January, 1973.

"The effects of legal abortion on legitimate and illegitimate birth rates: the California experience (figures for the period 1966-1972)," by J. Sklar, et al. STUDIES IN FAMILY PLANNING 4:281-292, November, 1973.

"Law of consent and abortion in California," by A. H. Bernstein. HOSPITALS 47:132 passim, February 1, 1973.

"Trends in therapeutic abortion in San Francisco," by P. Goldstein, et al. AM J PUBLIC HEALTH 62:695-699, 1972.

COLORADO
"Colorado Nurses' Association statement on abortion." COLO NURSE 73:10, February, 1973.

"Colorado Supreme Court applies Wade and Bolton." NEWSLETTER 6:5-6, May, 1973.

CONNECTICUT
"Connecticut asks new look at abortion." NAT CATH REP 9:2, April 13, 1973.

FLORIDA
"Father may not restrain unwed mother from obtaining an abortion: Florida." NEWSLETTER 6:3, June, 1973.

GEORGIA
"Constitutional law--the right of privacy--Georgia's abortion law declared unconstitutional." GA SB J 10:153-162, August, 1973.

"Georgia, Texas file appeals." NAT CATH REP 9:3, February 23, 1973.

"The new Georgia abortion law," by J. W. Huff. J MED ASSOC GA 62:241-242, June, 1973.

HAWAII
"Abortion in Hawaii," by M. Diamond, et al. FAMILY PLANN PERSPECT 5:54-60, Winter, 1973.

"Abortion in Hawaii: 1970-1971," by R. G. Smith, et al. HAWAII MED J 32:213-220, July-August, 1973.

"A preliminary report: Abortion in Hawaii--present and future trends," by P. I. McNamee, et al. HAWAII MED J 32:220-221, July-August, 1973.

ILLINOIS
"Illinois, Massachusetts enact conscience clause legislation." HOSPITALS 47:85, August 16, 1973.

IOWA
"Prenatal mortality in Iowa, 1963," by M. Mackeprang, et al. J IOWA MED SOC 63:16-18, January, 1973.

"Termination of pregnancy: guideline statement of the Iowa Medical Society." J IOWA MED SOC 63:248 plus, June, 1973.

LOUISIANA
"Law to protect the unborn; New Orleans, Louisiana." OR 30,278: 3, July 26, 1973.

MARYLAND
"Effect of recent Supreme Court Decision on Delaware's abortion law." DEL MED J 45:141-145, May, 1973.

"Guidelines for physician performance of induced abortions."

MARYLAND STATE MED J 22:68, September, 1973.

"Liberalized abortion and birth rates changes in Baltimore," by W. Oppel, et al. AMER J PUBLIC HEALTH 63:405-408, May, 1973.

"Maryland's 'hospital only' provision in abortion law declared unconstitutional." HOSPITALS 47:17, September 1, 1973.

"Minor cannot be compelled to have abortion: Maryland." NEWS-LETTER 6:5, January, 1973.

MASSACHUSETTS
"Abortion services in Massachusetts." N ENGL J MED 288:686-687, March 29, 1973.

"Boston prelate indicts court's abortion decision." HOSPITALS 47:170, May 16, 1973.

"Illinois, Massachusetts enact conscience clause legislation." HOSPITALS 47:85, August 16, 1973.

MISSOURI
"American Civil Liberties Union suit seeks abortions in St. Louis public hospitals." HOSPITALS 47:116, September 16, 1973.

NEW JERSEY
"Constitutional law--New Jersey abortion statute unconstitutionally vague on its face; women prior to pregnancy have no standing to attack statute, but plaintiff-physicians have standing to assert deprivation of their women patients right of privacy." J URBAN L 50:505, February, 1973.

"Says no doctor or hospital can be forced to perform abortion: New Jersey's Attorney General." HOSP PROGRESS 54:96d, March, 1973.

NEW YORK
"Abortion clinics face competition: New York City." AMER MED NEWS 16:3, April 2, 1973.

"Contraceptive practice among New York abortion patients," by M. B. Bracken, et al. AM J OBSTET GYNECOL 114:967-977, December 1, 1972.

"Defending the right to abortion in New York (based on conference paper)," by D. Welch. INTERNAT SOCIALIST R 34:10-13, January, 1973.

"Impact of the liberalized abortion law in New York City on deaths associated with pregnancy: a two-year experience," by J. Pakter, et al. BULL NY ACAD MED 49:804-818, September, 1973.

"Legal abortion 1970-1971--the New York City experience," by D. Harris, et al. AM J PUBLIC HEALTH 63:409-418, May, 1973.

"Mortality with legal abortion in New York City, 1970-1972: a preliminary report," by C. Tietze, et al. J AMER MED ASS 225:507-509, July 30, 1973.

"New York State physicians and the social context of abortion," by S. Wassertheil-Smoller, et al. AM J PUBLIC HEALTH 63:144-149, February, 1973.

"Repeat abortions in New York City: 1970-1972," by E. F. Daily, et al. FAMILY PLANNING PERSPECTIVES 5:89-93, Spring, 1973.

"Two years experience in New York City with the liberalized abortion law--progress and problems," by J. Pakter, et al. AM J PUBLIC HEALTH 63:524-535, June, 1973.

"Two years' experience with a liberal abortion law: Its impact on fertility trends in New York City," by C. Tietze. FAMILY PLANN PERSPECT 5:36-41, Winter, 1973.

NORTH CAROLINA
"Abortion. The first five years at North Carolina Memorial Hospital," by W. E. Easterling, Jr., et al. TEX MED 69:61-67, April, 1973.

OKLAHOMA
"Abortion situation in Oklahoma reviewed." J OKLA STATE MED ASS 66:409-411, September, 1973.

OREGON
"Abortion bill in Oregon would be costly to Catholic hospitals."
HOSP PROGRESS 54:20, April, 1973.

PENNSYLVANIA
"A baby girl: one good argument against abortion; testimony,
Pennsylvania Abortion Law Commission, February 24, 1972,"
by C. Martin. DIMENSION 4:144-148, Winter, 1972.

TENNESSEE
"Tennessee's new abortion law," by H. Williams. J TENN MED
ASSOC 66:651-652, June, 1973.

TEXAS
"Criminal law--Texas abortion statute--criminality exceptions
limited to life-saving procedures on mother's behalf without
regard to stage of pregnancy violates due process clause of
fourteenth amendment protecting right to privacy." AM J CRIM L
2:231-243, Summer, 1973.

"Georgia, Texas file appeals." NAT CATH REP 9:3, February 23,
1973.

"Landmark decision; three Texas women who fought the abortion
issue," by J. N. Bell. GOOD H 176:77-79 plus, June, 1973.

ABORTION: USSR
"Experiences with the vibro dilatator from the Soviet Union," by K. H.
Beckmann, et al. DTSCH GESUNDHEITSW 28:227-228, 1973.

YUGOSLAVIA
"Outcome of pregnancy in women denied legal abortion in several
subregions of the Croatian republic," by D. Stampar. NAR ZDRAV
28:205-211, June, 1972.

ADOPTION
see: Family Planning

ALUPENT
"Use of Alupent in obstetrics. Our personal experiences," by G.
Di Terlizzi. MINERVA GINECOL 25:225-245, April, 1973.

AMERICAN COLLEGE OF OBSTETRICIANS AND GYNECOLOGISTS
"The American College of Obstetricians and Gynecologists Statement on Abortion, February 10, 1973." J MED ASSOC STATE ALA 42:736, April, 1973.

"Guidelines on abortion published: American College of Obstetricians and Gynecologists." US MED 9:6, March 1, 1973.

"Statement on abortion: the American College of Obstetricians and Gynecologists." J MED ASS STATE ALA 42:736, April, 1973.

AMERICAN HOSPITAL ASSOCIATION
"Right to refuse to perform abortions remains intact: American Hospital Association." AMER MED NEWS 16:3, February 12, 1973.

AMERICAN PUBLIC HEALTH ASSOCIATION
"Recommended program guide for abortion services: American Public Health Association." AMER J PUBLIC HEALTH 63:639-644, July, 1973.

ANESTHESIA
see also: Induced Abortion
           Therapeutic Abortion

"Anesthesia in artificial abortion," by B. P. Oleinik, et al. PEDIATR AKUSH GINEKOL 1:53-55, 1973.

"Effect of anaesthetic technique on blood loss in termination of pregnancy," by S. R. Dunn, et al. BR J ANAESTH 45:633-637, June, 1973.

"Hazards in the operating theatre. Contamination of air by anaesthetics," by A. A. Spence. ANN R COLL SURG ENGL 52:360-361, June, 1973.

"Local potentiated anesthesia in artificial abortions," by E. I. Gorobets. PEDIATR AKUSH GINEKOL 1:55-56, 1973.

"Paracervical block anaesthesia for minor gynaecological operations," by I. S. Jones. NZ MED J 78:15-18, July 11, 1973.

ANTIBODIES
"Accumulation of complement-fixing antibodies in virus abortion of
sheep," by R. K. Khamadeev, et al. VETERINARIIA 49:113-115,
May, 1973.

ARTIFICIAL ABORTION
see: Induced Abortion

ASPIRIN
"Aspirin and indomethacin: effect on instillation/abortion time of
mid-trimester hypertonic saline induced abortion," by R. Waltman,
et al. PROSTAGLANDINS 3:47-58, 1973.

BEHAVIOR
see: Sociology and Behavior

BIBLIOGRAPHY
"Abortion: locating the blind spots," by J. F. Kavanaugh. AMERICA
129:149, September 8, 1973.

"Abortion: resources for reflection (bibliographical)," by D. Friesen.
MENN p. 480, August 8, 1972.

BIRTH CONTROL
see also: Family Planning

"Abortion: the agent's perspective," by S. Hauerwas. AER 167:102-
120, February, 1973.

"Abortion and the court." C TODAY p. 32, February 16, 1973.

"Abortion and the mosaic law," by J. Cottrell. C TODAY p. 6,
March 16, 1973.

"The abortion debate is revealing our values," by G. Chamberlain.
NCW p. 206, September-October, 1972.

"The Abortion Decision," by R. Drinan. COMM p. 438, February 16,
1973.

"Abortion may be a realistic alternative," by T. Koontz, et al.

MENN p. A-2, April 17, 1973.

"Abortion: resources for reflection (bibliographical)," by D. Friesen. MENN p. 480, August 8, 1972.

"Additional births averted when abortion is added to contraception," by R. G. Potter. STUD FAM PLANN 3:53-59, April, 1972.

"Death before birth." CHR TODAY 18:43, October 12, 1973.

"Death before birth (relates to U.S. Supreme Court decision)," by E. Palmer. BANNER p. 15, March 23, 1973.

"Devaluation of human life (U.S. Supreme Court decision)," by H. Berry. GNB p. 3, April, 1973.

"The growing scandal of abortion," by K. Mitzner. C ECON p. 33, October, 1972.

"A nurse's biography of an abortion," by S. Kelberg. US CATH p. 19, February, 1973.

"Of life and death," by J. Noble. PRES J p. 7, February 14, 1973.

"Protestant Theologians debate court ruling on abortion," by E. Wright. CH HER p. 12, March 22, 1973.

"Reflections on the Supreme Court's ruling on abortion," by Haines, et al. UC HER p. 59, April, 1973.

"The sanctity of human life." CH HER p. 8, October 20, 1972.

"Sexuality, birth control and abortion: a decision-making sequence," by M. Diamond, et al. J BIOSOC SCI 5:347-361, July, 1973.

"The unborn." BANNER p. 13, April 13, 1973.

BLOOD
"ABO blood groups and abortion." BR MED J 4:547, December 2, 1972.

"Alpha-fetoprotein in abortion," by M. Seppala, et al. BR MED J

BLOOD

4:769-771, December 30, 1972.

"Analysis of prostaglandin F2a and metabolites in blood during constant intravenous infusion of prostaglandin F2a in the human female," by F. Beguin, et al. ACTA PHYSIOL SCAND 86:430-432, 1972.

"Coagulation changes during termination of pregnancy by prostaglandins and by vacuum aspiration," by M. H. Badraoui, et al. BR MED J 1:19-21, January 6, 1973.

"Coagulation changes in saline-induced abortion," by R. K. Laros, Jr., et al. AM J OBSTET GYNECOL 116:271-276, May 15, 1973.

"Evaluation of the prognosis of threatened abortion from the peripheral plasma levels of progesterone, estradiol, and human chorionic gonadotropin," by K. G. Nygren, et al. AM J OBSTET GYNECOL 116: 916-922, August 1, 1973.

"Indices of the coagulant and anticoagulant systems of the blood in threatened and incipient abortion," by A. I. Zherzhov. VOPR OKHR MATERIN DET 17:85-86, August, 1972.

CANDIDIASIS
see: Complications

CARDIOVASCULAR SYSTEM
see: Complications

CEPHALOTHIN
"Use of cephalothin in septic abortion," by C. H. Dahm, Jr., et al. OBSTET GYNECOL 41:693-696, May, 1973.

CERVICAL INCOMPETENCE AND INSUFFICIENCY
"Cervical fistula as a complication of mid-trimester abortion," by J. S. Hirsch. OBSTET GYNECOL 41:478-479, March, 1973.

"Cervical migration of laminaria tents," by L. Wellman. AM J OBSTET GYNECOL 115:870-871, March 15, 1973.

"Cervical rupture following induced abortion," by S. L. Corson, et al.

AM J OBSTET GYNECOL 116:893, July 15, 1973.

"Cervical-segmental insufficiency (CSI) as a cause of abortion. Surgical treatment. Clinico-statistical considerations," by L. Volpe, et al. MINERVA GINECOL 25:123-139, March, 1973.

CHLORMADINONE
"Evaluation of the effects of chlormadinone in the treatment of threatened abortion," by J. Cardenas. GINECOL OBSTET MEX 33:121-124, January, 1973.

CLINICAL ASPECTS
"Abortion clinics and operating sessions," by A. E. Buckle. NURS MIRROR 136:36-38, March 9, 1973.

"Clinical and hysterosalpingographical findings following interruptio," by H. J. Seewald, et al. ZENTRALBL GYNAEKOL 95:710-713, May 25, 1973.

"Clinical application of prostaglandin F2a (P.G.F2a) as a drug which can produce an interruption of pregnancy during the 1st trimester," by J. H. Luigies. NED TIJDSCHR GENEESKD 116:2368-2369, December 23, 1972.

"Clinical application of prostaglandin in obstetrics," by M. I. T'ang. CHIN MED J 9:563-569, 1973.

"Clinical evaluation of Vibravenous (doxicillin) preparation in obstetrics and gynecology," by Z. Sternadel, et al. GINEKOL POL 44:189-191, February, 1973.

"Clinical experience in prophylactic treatment of spontaneous abortion," by P. F. Tropea. ACTA EUR FERTIL 2:253-274, June, 1970.

"Clinical problems of preventive medicine. The prevention and control of infectious ovine abortion," by W. A. Watson. BR VET J 129:309-314, July-August, 1973.

"Clinical significance of organic hypomenorrhea," by W. Z. Polishuk, et al. AM J OBSTET GYNECOL 116:1058-1064, August 15, 1973.

CLINICAL ASPECTS

"Experimental clinical studies on spontaneous and habitual abortion with nephrogenic pathology," by M. Georgneva. AKUSH GINEKOL 11:109-114, 1972.

"Intra-uterine administration of prostaglandin F 2 during the second trimester of pregnancy; clinical and hormonal results," by R. Shearman, et al. J REPROD FERTIL 32:321-322, February, 1973.

"Prostaglandin-oxytocin abortion: a clinical trial of intra-amniotic prostaglandin F2alpha in combination with intravenous oxytocin," by M. Seppala, et al. PROSTAGLANDINS 2:311-319, October, 1972.

"Prostaglandins and their clinical applications in human reproduction," by E. M. Southern, et al. J REPROD MED 9:472-477, December, 1972.

"Second trimester termination by intra-uterine prostaglandin F 2. Clinical and hormonal results with observations on induced lactation and chronoperiodicity," by R. Shearman, et al. J REPROD MED 9:448-452, December, 1972.

CLOMIPHENE
"Potentiation of ovarian response to H.C.G. with clomiphene. Application to the treatment of luteal deficiency," by S. Geller, et al. J GYNECOL OBSTET BIOL REPROD 1:417-434, July-August, 1972.

COLLEGE WOMEN
see: Youth

COMPLICATIONS
see also: Hemorrhage

"Abruption of the placenta. A review of 189 cases occurring between 1965 and 1969," by R. G. Blair. J OBSTET GYNAECOL BR COMMONW 80:242-245, March, 1973.

"Accidents and sequelas of medical abortions," by B. Beric, et al. AM J OBSTET GYNECOL 116:813-821, July 15, 1973.

"Acute renal failure in obstetric septic shock. Current views on pathogenesis and management," by D. S. Emmanouel, et al. AM J OBSTET GYNECOL 117:145-159, September 1, 1973.

"Air embolism in the interruption of pregnancy by vacuum extraction," by G. H. Hartung. ZENTRALBL GYNAEKOL 95:825-828, June 15, 1973.

"Analysis of products of conception," by W. Y. Burton, Jr. AM J OBSTET GYNECOL 115:1163, April 15, 1973.

"Bovine abortion associated with Candida tropicalis," by K. Wohlgemuth, et al. J AM VET MED ASSOC 162:460-461, March 15, 1973.

"Cardiovascular and respiratory responses to intravenous infusion of prostaglandin F2a in the pregnant woman," by J. I. Fishburne, Jr., et al. AM J OBSTET GYNECOL 114:765-772, 1972.

"A case of abortion consequent upon infection with Brucella abortus biotype 2," by P. M. Poole, et al. J CLIN PATHOL 25:882-884, October, 1972.

"Case of defibrination syndrome in internal abortion," by L. Tiraboschi, et al. MINERVA GINECOL 25:205-209, April, 1973.

"A case of postabortal bilateral uveitis--adaptometric fall of a paracentral acotoma," by G. E. Jayle, et al. BULL SOC OPHTALMOL FR 72:731-736, July-August, 1972.

"Cervical fistula as a complication of mid-trimester abortion," by J. S. Hirsch. OBSTET GYNECOL 41:478-479, March, 1973.

"Cervical rupture following induced abortion," by S. L. Corson, et al. AM J OBSTET GYNECOL 116:893, July 15, 1973.

"Clinical and hysterosalpingographical findings following interruptio," by H. J. Seewald, et al. ZENTRALBL GYNAEKOL 95:710-713, May 25, 1973.

"Clinical problems of preventive medicine. The prevention and control of infectious ovine abortion," by W. A. Watson. BR VET J 129:309-314, July-August, 1973.

"Clinical significance of organic hypomenorrhea," by W. Z. Polishuk, et al. AM J OBSTET GYNECOL 116:1058-1064, August 15, 1973.

"Clostridium infection after intra-amniotic hypertonic saline injection for induced abortion," by N. Sehgal, et al. J REPROD MED 8:67-69, February, 1972.

"Coagulation disorder in abruptio placentae," by N. N. Choudhury. J INDIAN MED ASSOC 58:428-429, June 1, 1972.

"Comparison of operative morbidity in abortion-sterilization procedures," by L. L. Veltman, et al. AM J OBSTET GYNECOL 117:251-254, September 15, 1973.

"Complication rates associated with abortion," by G. Joslin. MED J AUST 1:1165, June 9, 1973.

"Complications in induced abortion," by J. M. Bedoya-Gonzalez. AN R ACAD NACL MED 90:297-306, 1973.

"Complications of abortion," by J. E. Hodgson. AM J OBSTET GYNECOL 117:293-294, September 15, 1973.

"Course of pregnancy, delivery and puerperium following induced abortion of first pregnancy," by S. Lembrych. ZENTRALBL GYNAEKOL 94:164-168, February 5, 1972.

" 'Delayed menstruation' induced by prostaglandin in pregnant patients," by P. Mocsary, et al. LANCET 2:683, September 22, 1973.

"Disseminated intravascular coagulation resulting in severe hemorrhage, following the intraamniotic injection of hypertonic saline to induce abortion," by A. Sedaghat, et al. AM J OBSTET GYNECOL 114:841-843, November 15, 1972.

"Early medical complications of abortion by saline: joint program for the study of abortion (JPSA)," by C. Tietze, et al. STUD FAM PLANN 4:133-138, June, 1973.

"The effects of intravenous infusion of graded doses of prostaglandins F2a and E2 on lung resistance in patients undergoing termination of pregnancy," by A. P. Smith. CLIN SCI 44:17-25, 1973.

"Fetal implants in uterus." BR MED J 2:133-134, April 21, 1973.

" 'Glioma' of the uterus: a fetal homograft," by P. A. Niven, et al. AM J OBSTET GYNECOL 115:534-538, February 15, 1973.

"Gonorrhea in women prior to pregnancy interruption," by M. Mesko, et al. ZENTRALBL GYNAEKOL 94:169-172, February 5, 1972.

"Hormonal therapy of spontaneous abortion and premature labor in women with menstrual disorders," by P. G. Shushanila, et al. AKUSH GINEKOL 47:54-58, October, 1971.

"Hyperosmolal crisis following infusion of hypertonic sodium chloride for purposes of therapeutic abortion," by E. D. De Villota, et al. AM J MED 55:116-122, July, 1973.

"Hypertonic saline-induced abortion complicated by consumptive coagulopathy: a case report," by J. C. Morrison, et al. SOUTH MED J 66:561-562, May, 1973.

"Hypertonic saline-induced abortion. Correlation of fetal death with disseminated intravascular coagulation," by H. I. Glueck, et al. JAMA 225:28-31, July 2, 1973.

"Induced abortion and ectopic pregnancy," by P. P. Panayotou, et al. AM J OBSTET GYNECOL 114:507-510, 1972.

"The induction of abortion and menstruation by the intravaginal administration of prostaglandin F 2a," by T. Sato, et al. AM J OBSTET GYNECOL 116:287-289, May 15, 1973.

"Infection as a complication of therapeutic abortion," by A. H. De Cherney, et al. PA MED 75:49-52, December, 1972.

"Infectious complications following legal abortion," by E. Gaziano, et al. MINN MED 56:269-272, April, 1973.

"Injuries of the cervix after induced midtrimester abortion," by P. J. Bradley-Watson, et al. J OBSTET GYNAECOL BR COMMONW 80: 284-285, March, 1973.

"Latent morbidity after abortion." BRIT MED J 1:506, March 3, 1973.

"Latent morbidity after abortion." BR MED J 1:739-740, March 24, 1973.

"Latent morbidity after abortion." BR MED J 2:51, April 7, 1973.

"Latent morbidity after abortion." BR MED J 2:611, June 9, 1973.

"Latent morbidity after abortion," by C. Buck, et al. BR MED J 3:292-293, August 4, 1973.

"Latent morbidity after abortion," by A. Hordern. BR MED J 2:368, May 12, 1973.

"Latent morbidity after abortion," by A. Ogborn. BR MED J 2:114-115, April 14, 1973.

"Latent toxoplasmosis and pregnancy," by M. Sharf, et al. OBSTET GYNECOL 42:349-354, September, 1973.

"Lesions of blood vessels in the uterine cervix as a cause of bleedings following interruption of pregnancy," by M. Cislo, et al. POL TYG LEK 27:2066-2068, December 25, 1972.

"Letter: interruption of pregnancy because of embryonal damage," by H. J. Rieger. DTSCH MED WOCHENSCHR 98:1782, September 21, 1973.

"The management of abruptio placentae," by C. B. Lunan. J OBSTET GYNAECOL BR COMMONW 80:120-124, February, 1973.

"Medical abortion in South Australia. A critical assessment of early complications," by J. M. Miller. MED J AUST 1:825-830, April 28, 1973.

"Neonatal intravascular coagulation associated with abruptio placentae," by F. L. al-Salihi. J MED SOC NJ 70:381-383, May, 1973.

"Nursing care in placenta previa and abruptio placentae," by R. C. Kilker, et al. NURS CLIN NORTH AM 8:479-487, September, 1973.

"On the pathomorphism of threatened abortion (labor complications and fetal diseases)," by A. Weidenbach. MINERVA GINECOL 25: 457-461, August, 1973.

"One death and a cluster of febrile complications related to saline abortions," by G. S. Berger, et al. OBSTET GYNECOL 42:121-126, July, 1973.

"Our experience in the premature detachment of the normally inserted placenta," by R. M. Nava y Sanchez, et al. GINECOL OBSTET MEX 33:269-284, March, 1973.

"The paramedic abortionist," by R. F. Mattingly. OBSTET GYNECOL 41:929-930, June, 1973.

"Personal experience in the premature detachment of a normally implanted placenta," by R. M. Nava y Sanchez, et al. GINECOL OBSTET 33:269-284, March, 1973.

"Placenta previa: a rare complication of midtrimester abortion by amnioinfusion," by J. A. Goldman, et al. INT SURG 58:707, October, 1973.

"The postabortal pain syndrome: a new entity," by B. N. Nathanson. OBSTET GYNECOL 41:739-742, May, 1973.

"Postabortal metastatic panophthalmia," by F. Deodati, et al. BULL SOC OPHTALMOL FR 72:729-730, July-August, 1972.

"Postabortal posterior colpotomy and sterilization," by S. S. Sheth, et al. J OBSTET GYNAECOL BR COMMONW 80:274-275, March, 1973.

"The postabortive ovarian disfunction (clinical, pathological and endocrine study)," by J. Botella-Llusia. GYNECOL PRAT 23:117-123, 1972.

"Post-abortum cervical spondylodiscitis," by A. J. Chaumont, et al. MED LEG DOMM CORPOR 5:155-156, April-June, 1972.

"Posterior cervical rupture following prostaglandin-induced midtrimester abortion," by A. C. Wentz, et al. AM J OBSTET GYNECOL

115:1107-1110, April 15, 1973.

"Pregnancy after hysterotomy," by R. F. Heys. BR MED J 1:681-682, March 17, 1973.

"Pregnancy termination and infectious diseases," by J. E. Hodgson. MINN MED 56:698-699, August, 1973.

"Premature abruptio placentae in the last 12 years in patients of the Medical Center in Mostar," by V. Martinovic. MED ARH 26:247-250, July-August, 1972.

"Recurrent abortions and chromosome abnormalities," by M. Lucas, et al. J OBSTET GYNAECOL BR COMMONW 79:1119-1127, December, 1972.

"Resumption of ovulation after incomplete abortion," by G. J. Ratten. AUST NZ J OBSTET GYNAECOL 12:217-219, November, 1972.

"Retinal detachment and interruption of pregnancy," by C. Legerlotz. KLIN MONATSBL AUGENHEILKD 159:827-832, 1971.

"Role of abortion in the etiology of iso-immunization in Rh-incompatibility pregnancies," by P. F. Bolis, et al. ARCH OSTET GINECOL 77:44-49, February, 1972.

"The role of infection in spontaneous abortion," by A. P. Egorova, et al. VOPR OKHR MATERIN DET 17:65-70, September, 1972.

"Rubella vaccination and the termination of pregnancy." BR MED J 4:666, December 16, 1972.

"A ruptured dermoid cyst in labor simulating abruptio placentae. A possible complication of amniocentesis," by F. H. Boehm, et al. J REPROD MED 4:229-230, June, 1970.

"A safer cervical dilator," by C. Michael. MED J AUST 1:1254, June 23, 1973.

"Scintiphotographic diagnosis of abruptio placentae," by M. L. Moss, et al. J NUCL MED 14:297-298, May, 1973.

"Septicemia with Listeria monocytogenes following abortion induced after 2 and one-half months," by J. F. Lemeland, et al. NOUV PRESSE MED 2:1616, June 9, 1973.

"Severe postabortal Clostridium welchii infection: trends in management," by J. P. O'Neill, et al. AUST NZ J OBSTET GYNAECOL 12:157-165, August, 1972.

"Some observations on the aetiology and management of coagulation failure complicating abruptio placentae," by H. K. Basu. J INDIAN MED ASSOC 58:409-416, June 1, 1972.

"Spontaneous abortion: the most common complication in pregnancy," by D. A. Aiken. NURS TIMES 69:898-899, July 12, 1973.

"Studies of early modifications of maternal coagulation-fibrinolysis balance in intrauterine death of the fetus," by P. Capetta, et al. MINERVA GINECOL 25:492-495, August, 1973.

"Studies of serological reactions in ovine toxoplasmosis encountered in intensively-bred sheep," by G. A. Sharman, et al. VET REC 91: 670-675, December 30, 1972.

"The syndrome of chronic abruptio placentae, hydrorrhea, and circumvallate placenta," by F. Naftolin, et al. AM J OBSTET GYNECOL 116:347-350, June 1, 1973.

"Termination of pregnancy by 'super coils': morbidity associated with a new method of second-trimester abortion," by G. S. Berger, et al. AM J OBSTET GYNECOL 116:297-304, June 1, 1973.

"Therapeutic abortion and its complications in Halifax, N. S.," by C. Resch, et al. NS MED BULL 52:67-70, April, 1973.

"Therapeutic abortion on psychiatric grounds. A follow-up study," by J. A. Ewing, et al. NC MED J 34:265-270, April, 1973.

"Thrombocytopenia indicating gram-negative infection and endotoxemia," by F. K. Beller, et al. OBSTET GYNECOL 41:521-524, April, 1973.

"Traumatic rupture of the placenta," by R. Schuhmann, et al.

COMPLICATIONS

ZENTRALBL GYNAEKOL 94:1239-1243, September 23, 1972.

"Ultrasonographic examination in hemorrhages in the 3d trimester,"
by A. Zacutti, et al. MINERVA GINECOL 25:468-475, August, 1973.

"The work of the women's consultation for the prevention of artificial
abortions," by S. L. Polchanova. AKUSH GINEKOL 48:54-56,
September, 1972.

CONTRACEPTION
"Abortion, contraception and child mental health," by L. J. Redman,
et al. FAMILY PLANN PERSPECT 5:71-72, Spring, 1973.

"Additional births averted when abortion is added to contraception,"
by R. G. Potter. STUD FAM PLANN 3:53-59, April, 1972.

"Contraception, sterilization, and abortion legal interpretation of
consent," by D. F. Kaltreider. MD STATE MED J 22:67, September,
1973.

"Contraceptive advice in connection with legal abortion," by K.
Edstrom. LAKARTIDNINGEN 70:1404-1406, April 4, 1973.

"Contraceptive practice among New York abortion patients," by
M. B. Bracken, et al. AM J OBSTET GYNECOL 114:967-977,
December 1, 1972.

"DEPO-Medroxyprogesterone acetate as a contraceptive agent: its
effect on weight and blood pressure," by G. Leiman. AM J OBSTET
GYNECOL 114:97-102, 1972.

"The influence of recent use of an oral contraceptive on early intra-
uterine development," by B. J. Poland, et al. AM J OBSTET GYN-
ECOL 116:1138-1142, August 15, 1973.

"Population, rhythm, contraception and abortion policy questions,"
by A. Hellegers. LINACRE 40:91-96, May, 1973.

CRIMINAL ABORTION
see: Laws and Legislation

DEMOGRAPHY
see also: Population

"The demographic effects of legal abortion on the Hungarian labor force (conference paper)," by B. Kapotsy. EUROPEAN DEMOGRA-PHIC INFO BUL 4:136-143, November 3, 1973.

DIAGNOSIS
"A comparative study of cervical mucus examination for arborisation in pregnancy, abortion and secondary amenorrhoea," by L. Joshi. J INDIAN MED ASSOC 58:420-421 passim, June 1, 1972.

"Determination of urinary C.G.H. in spontaneous threatened abortion. Prognostic value," by R. Hechtermans, et al. J GYNECOL OBSTET BIOL REPROD 1:869-876, December, 1972.

"Diagnosis and therapy of habitual abortion related to disorders in adrenal cortex function," by I. S. Rozovskii. AKUSH GINEKOL 48:18-23, September, 1972.

"Diagnosis and therapy of spetic abortion and bacterial shock," by G. Iliew, et al. Z AERZTL FORTBILD 67:232-235, March 1, 1973.

"Diagnosis and therapy of threatened abortion--our experience," by B. Stambolovic, et al. ZENTRALBL GYNAEKOL 95:808-810, June 15, 1973.

"Diagnosis of premature separation of the normally implanted placenta with ultrasonic B-scan," by K. H. Schlensker. GEBURTSHILFE FRAUENHEILKD 32:773-780, September, 1972.

"Early termination of an encephalic pregnancy after detection by raised alpha-fetoprotein levels," by M. J. Seller, et al. LANCET 2:73, July 14, 1973.

"Evaluation of the prognosis of threatened abortion from the peripheral plasma levels of progesterone, estradiol, and human chorionic gona-dotropin," by K. G. Nygren, et al. AM J OBSTET GYNECOL 116: 916-922, August 1, 1973.

"Laparotomy during pregnancy: an assessment of diagnostic accuracy and fetal wastage," by P. Saunders, et al. BR MED J 3:165-167, July 21, 1973.

"Prenatal diagnosis and selective abortion," by K. Lebacqz. LINACRE 40:109-127, May, 1973.

"Prognostic value of immunologic determinations of chorionic gonado-tropins (C.G.H.) in threatened abortion," by D. Chouvacovic, et al. BULL FED SOC GYNECOL OBSTET LANG FR 23:629-630, November-December, 1971.

"A ruptured dermoid cyst in labor simulating abruptio placentae. A possible complication of amniocentesis," by F. H. Boehm, et al. J REPROD MED 4:229-230, June, 1970.

"Scintiphotographic diagnosis of abruptio placentae," by M. L. Moss, et al. J NUCL MED 14:297-298, May, 1973.

"Thrombotic thrombocytopenic purpura and gynaecological manifestations," by M. Yudis. LANCET 1:1445, June 23, 1973.

"Ultrasonography in abortion diagnosis," by H. Meyenberg. GEBURT-SHILFE FRAUENHEILKD 33:272-276, April, 1973.

"Use of vaginal wall cytologic smears to predict abortion in high-risk pregnancies," by M. T. McLennan, et al. AM J OBSTET GYNECOL 114:857-860, December 1, 1972.

DIETHYLSTILBESTROL
"Vaginal adenocarcinoma as a late result of treatment of threatened abortion with diethylstilbestrol," by J. Presl. CESK GYNEKOL 38:473-474, July, 1973.

DOXICILLIN
"Clinical evaluation of Vibravenous (doxicillin) preparation in obstetrics and gynecology," by Z. Sternadel, et al. GINEKOL POL 44:189-191, February, 1973.

DRUG THERAPY
  see: Induced Abortion
        Surgical Treatment and Management
        Techniques of Abortion
        Under Specific Drugs

EDUCATION
  "From abortion to sex education," by K. Whitehead. HPR 74:60-69,
    November, 1973.

  "Health education for prevention of abortion," by S. L. Polchanova.
    FELDSHER AKUSH 37:28-32, November, 1972.

  "Learning abortion care," by A. Goldmann. NURS J INDIA 63:153-
    154 plus, May, 1972.

ENDOTOXIN
  "Inhibition of abortion and fetal death produced by endotoxin or
    prostaglandin F2alpha," by M. J. Harper, et al. PROSTAGLANDINS
    2:295-309, October, 1972.

ESTRADIOL
  "Evaluation of the prognosis of threatened abortion from the peripheral
    plasma levels of progesterone, estradiol, and human chorionic
    gonadotropin," by K. G. Nygren, et al. AM J OBSTET GYNECOL
    116:916-922, August 1, 1973.

ETHYL ALCOHOL
  "Death from an attempt to procure an abortion by intra-uterine in-
    jection of ethyl alcohol," by T. Marcinkowski. FORENSIC SCI
    2:245-246, May, 1973.

FAMILY PLANNING
  see also: Sociology and Behavior

  "Abortion and family planning," by K. N. Rao. J INDIAN MED ASSOC
    59:337-341, October 16, 1972.

  "Family Plann Digest." US DEPT HEW PUBL 1:1-16, September, 1972.

  "Legal abortion as a positive mental health measure in family plann -

ing," by Z. M. Lebensohn. COMPR PSYCHIATRY 14:95-98, March-April, 1973.

"The physician and family planning," by A. Alvarez-Bravo. GAC MED MEX 105:498-507, May, 1973.

"Status of abortions, fertility and family planning in the Rostock region during 1962-1971," by K. H. Mehlan, et al. Z AERZTL FORTBILD 67:539-545, June, 1973.

FEES AND PUBLIC ASSISTANCE
see also: Sociology and Behavior

"Abortions at charity prices." SOC JUST 66:87-88, June, 1973.

"Free abortion in Denmark?" by M. Johansson. NORD MED 88:13, January, 1973.

"Free standing abortion clinics: a new phenomenon," by R. U. Hausknecht. BULL NY ACAD MED 49:985-991, November, 1973.

"Most insurers are paying for abortions: legality still the key question." AMER MED NEWS 16:7, March 26, 1973.

FERTILITY
see: Sterility

FETUS
"Body composition studies in the human fetus after intra-amniotic injection of hypertonic saline," by J. Wang, et al. AM J OBSTET GYNECOL 117:57-63, September 1, 1973.

"Detection of fetal heart activity in first trimester," by O. Piiroinen. LANCET 2:508-509, September 1, 1973.

"Fetal implants in uterus." BR MED J 2:133-134, April 21, 1973.

"Fetal rights and abortion laws," by S. F. O'Beirn. BR MED J 1:740, March 24, 1973.

"The fetus: whose property?" by A. Etzioni. COMM 98:493,

September 21, 1973.

"Figures and fetuses," by R. J. Neuhaus; Discussion COMMONWEAL 97:358-359, January 19, 1973.

"Malnutrition of the fetus as a cause of abortion," by S. J. van Rensburg. J S AFR VET MED ASSOC 42:305-308, December, 1971.

"New law gives rights to fetus." NAT CATH REP 9:1, March 23, 1973.

"Pathohistologic changes of the fetus in enzootic virus abortion of sheep," by A. Djurov. ZENTRALBL VETERINAERMED 19:578-587, August, 1972.

"Viability, abortion, and the difference between a fetus and an infant," by H. T. Engelhardt, Jr. AM J OBSTET GYNECOL 116:429-434, June 1, 1973.

FLUMETHASONE
"A note on the effects of maternal or fetal injection of flumethasone and of thyroidectomy on the termination of pregnancy," by J. M. Van Der Westhuysen. S AFR J ANIM SCI 1:67, 1971.

GENETICS
"Abortion and chromosome aberrations," by G. Neuhauser. HIPPO-KRATES 44:85-87, March, 1973.

"Banding analysis of abnormal karyotypes in spontaneous abortion," by T. Kajii, et al. AM J HUM GENET 25:539-547, September, 1973.

"Chromosomal abnormalities in 32 cases of repeated abortions," by S. Warter, et al. REV FR GYNECOL OBSTET 67:321-325, May, 1972.

"Chromosomal findings in women with repeated spontaneous abortions," by J. Malkova, et al. CESK GYNEKOL 38:193-194, April, 1973.

"Chromosome investigation in married couples with repeated spontaneous abortions," by M. E. Kaosaar, et al. HUMANGENETIK 17:277-283, 1973.

"Chromosome studies in couples with repeated abortions," by H. D.

Rott, et al. ARCH GYNAEKOL 213:110-118, 1972.

"Cytogenetic causes of abortion," by L. Peiz. ZENTRALBL GYNAE-KOL 94:145-155, February 5, 1972.

"A cytogenetic study of recurrent abortion," by M. K. Bhasin, et al. HUMANGENETIK 18:139-148, April 16, 1973.

"Double heteroploidy, 46, XY, t(13q14q), 18, in a spontaneous abortus," by S. Avirachan, et al. CLIN GENET 4:101-104, 1973.

"Frequency of chromosome abnormalities in abortions," by I. H. Pawlowitzki. HUMANGENETIK 16:131-136, 1972.

"Increased frequency of chromosomal anomalies in abortions after induced ovulation," by J. G. Boue, et al. LANCET 1:679-680, March 24, 1973.

"Giemsa banding in the t(13q13q) carrier mother of a translocation trisomy 13 abortus," by M. I. Parslow, et al. HUMANGENETIK 18: 183-184, April 16, 1973.

"Maternal x-radiation and chromosome abnormalities in subsequent conceptions," by E. D. Alberman. BR J PREV SOC MED 27:67-68, February, 1973.

"Morphological, autoradiographic, immunochemical and cytochemical investigation of a cell strain with trisomy 7 from a spontaneous abortus," by A. M. Kuliev, et al. HUMANGENETIK 17:285-296, 1973.

"The mortality of human XO embryos," by B. Santesson, et al. J REPROD FERTIL 34:51-55, July, 1973.

"Outcome of pregnancies following a spontaneous abortion with chromosomal anomalies," by J. G. Boue, et al. AM J OBSTET GYNECOL 116:806-812, July 15, 1973.

"Parental x-irradiation and chromosomes constitution in their spontaneously aborted foetuses," by E. Alberman, et al. ANN HUM GENET 36:185-194, November, 1972.

"Physiology and pathology of female reproductive functions," by M. A. Petrov-Maslakov. VESTN AKAD MED NAUK SSSR 28:53-61, 1973.

"Products of late abortion. Occurrence of chromosome aberrations," by S. Foussereau, et al. J GYNECOL OBSTET BIOL REPROD 1:651-656, October-November, 1972.

"Recurrent abortions and chromosome abnormalities," by M. Lucas, et al. J OBSTET GYNAECOL BR COMMONW 79:1119-1127, December, 1972.

"Round table discussion on abortions of chromosomal origin." CAH MED 14:191-203, March, 1973.

"The selective effect of therapeutic abortion when children thus eliminated are carriers of a recessive autosomic or x-chromosome-linked defect," by U. Pfandler, et al. J GENET HUM 20:135-150, June, 1972.

"Y to X translocation in a woman with reproductive failure. A new rearrangement," by G. Khudr, et al. JAMA 226:544-549, October 29, 1973.

GESTANON
"Human chorionic gonadotropin (HCG) excretion in the urine in habitual threatened abortion treated with gestanon," by R. Wawryk, et al. GINEKOL POL 44:665-670, June, 1973.

GONORRHEA
see: Complications

GYNAECOLOGY
"Achievements, changes and challenges in gynecology," by A. Peretz. HAREFUAH 85:1-3, July 1, 1973.

"Attitudes of obstetric and gynecologic residents toward abortion," by P. R. Mascovich, et al. CALIF MED 119:29-34, August, 1973.

"Clinical evaluation of Vibravenous (doxicillin) preparation in obstetrics and gynecology," by Z. Sternadel, et al. GINEKOL POL 44:189-191, February, 1973.

"The induced abortion and the gynecologist," by Z. Polishok. HAREFUAH 83:264-265, September 15, 1972.

"Neuroleptanalgesia using innovar in minor gynecological procedures," by L. D. McLaughlin, Jr., et al. J AM ASSOC NURSE ANESTH 41: 211-215, June, 1973.

"Prostaglandins in gynecology," by M. Breckwoldt, et al. HIPPO-KRATES 43:494-495, December, 1972.

GYNESTHESIN
"Legal interruption of pregnancy by the aspiration method and the pericervical block with Gynesthesin," by M. Beric. SCHWEIZ Z GYNAEKOL GEBURTSHILFE 3:151-159, 1972.

HABITUAL ABORTION
"Abortion and chromosome aberrations," by G. Neuhauser. HIPPO-KRATES 44:85-87, March, 1973.

"Balanced translocation t(15q-;16p) as cause of habitual abortions," by T. Hasegawa, et al. GEBURTSHILFE FRAUENHEILKD 33:541-544, July, 1973.

"Body built and endocrine changes in women with habitual abortions," by G. P. Koreneva, et al. VOPR OKHR MATERIN DET 17:48-51, November, 1972.

"Cervical-segmental insufficiency (CSI) as a cause of abortion. Surgical treatment. Clinico-statistical considerations," by L. Volpe, et al. MINERVA GINECOL 25:123-139, March, 1973.

"Chromosomal abnormalities in 32 cases of repeated abortions," by S. Warter, et al. REV FR GYNECOL OBSTET 67:321-325, May, 1972.

"Chromosome investigation in married couples with repeated spon-taneous abortions," by M. E. Kaosaar, et al. HUMANGENETIK 17:277-283, 1973.

"Chromosome studies in couples with repeated abortions," by H. D. Rott, et al. ARCH GYNAEKOL 213:110-118, 1972.

"Clinical experience in prophylactic treatment of spontaneous abortion," by P. F. Tropea. ACTA EUR FERTIL 2:253-274, June, 1970.

"Clinical significance of organic hypomenorrhea," by W. Z. Polishuk, et al. AM J OBSTET GYNECOL 116:1058-1064, August 15, 1973.

"A comparative study of cervical mucus examination for arborisation in pregnancy, abortion and secondary amenorrhoea," by L. Joshi. J INDIAN MED ASSOC 58:420-421 passim, June 1, 1972.

"A cytogenetic study of recurrent abortion," by M. K. Bhasin, et al. HUMANGENETIK 18:139-148, April 16, 1973.

"Detection of anti-immunoglobulins by the Waaler-Rose reaction in the serum of women with habitual abortion," by D. Vladimirova, et al. AKUSH GINEKOL 11:214-218, 1972.

"Diagnosis and therapy of habitual abortion related to disorders in adrenal cortex function," by I. S. Rozovskii. AKUSH GINEKOL 48:18-23, September, 1972.

"Disorders in catecholamine and serotonin excretion in premature labor," by L. P. Grokhovskii. AKUSH GINEKOL 48:30-32, September, 1972.

"Experimental clinical studies on spontaneous and habitual abortion with nephrogenic pathology," by M. Georgneva. AKUSH GINEKOL 11:109-114, 1972.

"A familial translocation t(6q ;8q-) identified by fluorescence microscopy," by E. Niebuhr. HUMANGENETIK 18:189-192, April 16, 1973.

"The functional state of the thyroid gland and iodine metabolism in habitual abortion," by E. A. Danilova. ZH EKSP KLIN MED 11:60-65, 1971.

"Giemsa banding in the t(13q13q) carrier mother of a translocation trisomy 13 abortus," by M. I. Parslow, et al. HUMANGENETIK 18: 183-184, April 16, 1973.

"Histological study of the placenta and basal decidua in habitual abortion caused by hyperandrogenism. Spontaneously interrupted pregnancies during the 1st 6 months and pregnancies treated successfully by corticotherapy," by L. Badarau, et al. REV FR GYNECOL OBSTET 67:685-697, December, 1972.

"Hormonal therapy of spontaneous abortion and premature labor in women with menstrual disorders," by P. G. Shushaniia, et al. AKUSH GINEKOL 47:54-58, October, 1971.

"Human chorionic gonadotropin (HCG) excretion in the urine in habitual threatened abortion treated with gestanon," by R. Wawryk, et al. GINEKOL POL 44:665-670, June, 1973.

"Latent toxoplasmosis and pregnancy," by M. Sharf, et al. OBSTET GYNECOL 42:349-354, September, 1973.

"Letter: Trisomy in abortion material," by H. R. McCreanor, et al. LANCET 2:972-973, October 27, 1973.

"Male factor as a possible cause of habitual abortion and infertility," by C. A. Joel. SCHWEIZ MED WOCHENSCHR 102:1377-1383, September 30, 1972.

"Organization of dispensary care women with habitual abortions," by G. P. Koreneva, et al. PEDIATR AKUSH GINEKOL 6:39-43, 1972.

"Ovarian function in women with habitual abortion," by M. A. Petrov-Maslakov, et al. AKUSH GINEKOL 48:27-30, September, 1972.

"The pathogenesis and prevention of habitual abortion," by V. I. Bodiazhina. AKUSH GINEKOL 48:12-18, September, 1972.

"Potentiation of ovarian response to H.C.G. with Clomiphene. Application to the treatment of luteal deficiency," by S. Geller, et al. J GYNECOL OBSTET BIOL REPROD 1:417-434, July-August, 1972.

"Preconception surgical treatment of uterine insufficiency in women with habitual abortions," by A. Zwinger, et al. CESK GYNEKOL 38:256-258, May, 1973.

"Prevention of abortion in the presence of developmental anomalies of the uterus," by N. L. Piganova. AKUSH GINEKOL 48:38-42, September, 1972.

"Recurrent abortions and chromosome abnormalities," by M. Lucas, et al. J OBSTET GYNAECOL BR COMMONW 79:1119-1127, December, 1972.

"Repeated abortive pregnancy," by J. O. Mastboom. NED TIJDSCHR GENEESKD 117:740-743, May 12, 1973.

"Repeated pregnancy loss," by J. Schneider. CLIN OBSTET GYNECOL 16:120-133, March, 1973.

"RNA concentration in the endometrium of women with habitual abortion," by R. K. Ryzhova. AKUSH GINEKOL 48:23-27, September, 1972.

"Spontaneous premature interruption of pregnancy and its causes," by M. A. Petrov-Maslakov. AKUSH GINEKOL 48:7-11, September, 1972.

"Transplantation in a system of complex treatment of habitually aborted pregnancy," by O. V. Nadeina, et al. AKUSH GINEKOL 48:35-38, September, 1972.

"Unfavorable outcome of pregnancy: repeated losses," by R. L. Naeye, et al. AM J OBSTET GYNECOL 116:1133-1137, August 15, 1973.

"Y to X translocation in a woman with reproductive failure. A new rearrangement," by G. Khudr, et al. JAMA 226:544-549, October 29, 1973.

HEMORRHAGE
see also: Complications

"Disseminated intravascular coagulation resulting in severe hemorrhage, following the intra-amniotic injection of hypertonic saline to induce abortion," by A. Sedaghat, et al. AM J OBSTET GYNECOL 114:841-843, 1972.

"Effect of anaesthetic technique on blood loss in termination of pregnancy," by S. R. Dunn, et al. BR J ANAESTH 45:633-637, June, 1973.

"Ultrasonographic examination in hemorrhages in the 3d trimester," by A. Zacutti, et al. MINERVA GINECOL 25:468-475, August, 1973.

HEPARIN

"Experience with the administration of heparin for the prevention of the Sanarelli-Shwartzman reaction (SSP) in cases of septic abortions," by H. H. Koch, et al. GEBURTSHILFE FRAUENHEILKD 33:460-463, June, 1973.

HISTORY

"The abortion constellation. Early history and present relationships," by V. Abernethy. ARCH GEN PSYCHIATRY 29:346-350, September, 1973.

"Abortion: history, opinions, and what's new in the United States," by E. D. Jubb, et al. CAN B J 4:8-12, July, 1973.

"Amazing historical and biological errors in abortion decision - Dr. Hellegers; reprint from Washington Star-News, excerpt from interview by T. Ascik," by A. Hellegers. HOSP PROG 54:16-17, May, 1973.

"History and evolution of abortion laws in the United States," by D. L. Brown. SOUTHERN MED 61:11-14, August, 1973.

HORMONES

"Effect of infused prostaglandin F 2 on hormonal levels during early pregnancy," by A. C. Wentz, et al. AM J OBSTET GYNECOL 114: 908-913, December 1, 1972.

"Hormonal changes during induction of midtrimester abortion by prostaglandin F 2," by B. Cantor, et al. AM J OBSTET GYNECOL 113:607-615, July 1, 1972.

"Hormonal therapy of spontaneous abortion and premature labor in women with menstrual disorders," by P. G. Shushanila, et al. AKUSH GINE-KOL 47:54-58, October, 1971.

"Hormone therapy of threatened abortion during the early stages of pregnancy," by S. Trepechov, et al. AKUSH GINEKOL 11:152-160, 1972.

"Intra-uterine administration of prostaglandin F 2 during the second trimester of pregnancy; clinical and hormonal results," by R. Shearman, et al. J REPROD FERTIL 32:321-322, February, 1973.

"Second trimester termination by intra-uterine prostaglandin F 2. Clinical and hormonal results with observations on induced lactation and chronoperiodicity," by R. Shearman, et al. J REPROD MED 9:448-452, December, 1972.

"Urinary excretion of various steroid hormones during the physiological course of pregnancy and in threatened spontaneous premature interruption," by L . V. Timoshenko, et al. PEDIATR AKUSH GINEKOL 5:38-40, October, 1972.

HOSPITALS

"Abortion bill in Oregon would be costly to Catholic hospitals." HOSP PROGRESS 54:20, April, 1973.

"Abortion clinic design emphasizes restraint to minimize patients' tension," by H. McLaughlin. MOD HOSP 121:74-75, September, 1973.

"Abortion clinics and operating sessions," by A. E. R. Buckle. NURSING MIRROR 136:36-38, March 9, 1973.

"Abortion clinics face competition: New York City." AMER MED NEWS 16:3, April 2, 1973.

"Abortion: the first five years at North Carolina Memorial Hospital," by W. E. Easterling, Jr., et al. TEX MED 69:61-67, April, 1973.

"Abortion services in Massachusetts." N ENGL J MED 288:686-687, March 29, 1973.

"Appeals court rules private hospital has right to refuse abortions," by E. W. Springer. HOSP TOP 51:24-25, August, 1973.

"Community abortion services: the role of organized medicine," by J. E. Hodgson. MINN MED 56:239-242, March, 1973.

"Digest of recommended guidelines for facilities performing pregnancy terminations: Michigan." MICH MED 72:359-360, May, 1973.

"Federal appeals court rules hospital may refuse abortions." HOS-PITALS 47:96, July 1, 1973.

"Federally funded hospitals not required to perform abortion." NEWS-LETTER 6:3-4, July, 1973.

"Hazards in the operating theatre. Contamination of air by anaesthetics ," by A. A. Spence. ANN R COLL SURG ENGL 52:360-361, June, 1973.

"Hospitals and the abortion ruling." NEWSLETTER 6:2, March, 1973.

"Infectious complications following legal abortion," by E. Gaziano, et al. MINN MED 56:269-272, April, 1973.

"Investigation of women admitted to hospital with abortion," by L. Freundt. ACTA PSYCHIATR SCAND 242:1-221, 1973.

"Legal abortion and the attitude of hospital staff," by L. Jacobsson, et al. LAKARTIDNINGEN 70:273-275, January 24, 1973.

"Letter: intrauterine prostaglandins for outpatient termination of very early pregnancy," by S. M. Karim. LANCET 2:794, October 6, 1973.

"A methodology for the planning of therapeutic abortion services," by S. J. Williams. HEALTH SERVS REPS 87:983-991, December, 1972.

"Organizing an abortion service," by A. H. Danon. NURSING OUTLOOK 21:460-464, July, 1973.

"Outpatient termination of pregnancy by vacuum aspiration," by A. Y. Ng, et al. SINGAPORE MED J 14:23-25, March, 1973.

"Says no doctor or hospital can be forced to perform abortion: New Jersey's Attorney General." HOSP PROGRESS 54:96d, March, 1973.

"Standards for outpatient facilities for abortion service." MARYLAND STATE MED J 22:69-70, September, 1973.

IMMUNITY

"Detection of anti-immunoglobulins by the Waaler-Rose reaction in the serum of women with habitual abortion," by D. Vladimirova, et al. AKUSH GINEKOL 11:214-218, 1972.

"Experimentally induced immunity to chlamydial abortion of cattle," by D. G. McKercher, et al. J INFECT DIS 128:231-234, August, 1973.

"Incidence of Rh immunization following abortion: possible detection of lymphocyte priming to Rh antigen," by J. Katz, et al. AM J OBSTET GYNECOL 117:261-267, September 15, 1973.

"Isoimmunization of women during pregnancy," by G. S. Aleskerov. AKUSH GINEKOL 48:65-67, November, 1972.

"Prevention of Rh immunization by anti-D globulin injection after birth and abortion," by J. Vardy, et al. HAREFUAH 83:115-120, August 1, 1972.

"Prevention of Rh immunization following abortion," by J. A. Goldman, et al. HAREFUAH 83:100-101, August 1, 1972.

"Rh immunization in induced abortion," by J. A. Goldman, et al. MINERVA GINECOL 25:100-102, February, 1973.

"Role of abortion in the etiology of iso-immunization in Rh-incompatibility pregnancies," by P. F. Bolis, et al. ARCH OSTET GINECOL 77:44-49, February, 1972.

INDUCED ABORTION
see also: Techniques of Abortion

"Abortion and coagulation by prostaglandin. Intra-amniotic dinoprost tromethamine effect on the coagulation and fibrinolytic systems," by W. R. Bell, et al. JAMA 225:1082-1084, August 27, 1973.

"Abortion and sexual behavior in college women," by K. J. Monsour, et al. AM J ORTHOPSYCH 43:804-814, October, 1973.

"Abortion clinics and operating sessions," by A. E. Buckle. NURS MIRROR 136:36-38, March 9, 1973.

"The abortion constellation. Early history and present relationships," by V. Abernethy. ARCH GEN PSYCHIATRY 29:346-350, September, 1973. •

"Abortion decision may set precedent to resolve 1st Amendment conflicts," by E. J. Schulte. HOSP PROG 54:85-87 passim, September, 1973.

"Abortion in Hawaii: 1970-1971," by R. G. Smith, et al. HAWAII MED J 32:213-220, July-August, 1973.

"Abortion of early pregnancy by the intravaginal administration of prostaglandin F2alpha," by R. J. Bolognese, et al. AM J OBSTET GYNECOL 117:246-250, September 15, 1973.

"The abortion ruling: analysis & prognosis." HOSP PROG 54:81-83 passim, March, 1973.

"Abortion surveillance program of the center for disease control," by J. C. Smith, et al. HEALTH SERV REP 88:255-259, March, 1973.

"Abortions: a national dilemma," by J. A. Paulsen. J AM COLL HEALTH ASSOC 21:495-497, June, 1973.

"Accidents and sequelae of medical abortions," by B. Beric, et al. AM J OBSTET GYNECOL 116:813-821, July 15, 1973.

"Achievements, changes and challenges in gynecology," by A. Peretz. HAREFUAH 85:1-3, July 1, 1973.

"Age of the woman and spontaneous and induced abortions," by Z. Gizicki. GINEKOL POL 43:443-447, April, 1972.

"Amazing historical and biological errors in abortion decision," by A. E. Hellegers. HOSP PROG 54:16-17, May, 1973.

"Analysis of induced abortions at a regional hospital," by B. Deidesheimer. ZENTRALBL GYNAEKOL 95:819-824, June 15, 1973.

"Analysis of products of conception," by W. Y. Burton, Jr. AM J OBSTET GYNECOL 115:1163, April 15, 1973.

"Anesthesia in artificial abortion," by B. P. Oleinik, et al. PEDIATR AKUSH GINEKOL 1:53-55, 1973.

"Aspirin and indomethacin: effect on instillation/abortion time of mid-trimester hypertonic saline induced abortion," by R. Waltman, et al. PROSTAGLANDINS 3:47-58, 1973.

"Attitudes of unmarried college women toward abortion," by M. Vincent, et al. J SCH HEALTH 43:55, January, 1973.

"Births averted by induced abortion: an application of renewal theory," by R. G. Potter. THEOR POPUL BIOL 3:69-86, March, 1972.

"Body composition studies in the human fetus after intra-amniotic injection of hypertonic saline," by J. Wang, et al. AM J OBSTET GYNECOL 117:57-63, September 1, 1973.

"Brook Lodge symposium on prostaglandins. Moderator's summary," by M. P. Embrey. J REPROD MED 9:464-465, December, 1972.

"Cervical fistula as a complication of mid-trimester abortion," by J. S. Hirsch. OBSTET GYNECOL 41:478-479, March, 1973.

"Cervical migration of laminaria tents," by L. Wellman. AM J OBSTET GYNECOL 115:870-871, March 15, 1973.

"Cervical rupture following induced abortion," by S. L. Corson, et al. AM J OBSTET GYNECOL 116:893, July 15, 1973.

"Chronoperiodicity in the response to the intra-amniotic injection of prostaglandin F 2 in the human," by I. D. Smith, et al. NATURE 241:279-280, January 26, 1973.

"Clinical and hysterosalpingographical findings following interruptio," by H. J. Seewald, et al. ZENTRALBL GYNAEKOL 95:710-713, May 25, 1973.

"Clinical application of prostaglandin F2a (P.G.F2a) as a drug which can produce an interruption of pregnancy during the 1st trimester," by J. H. Luigies. NED TIJDSCHR GENEESKD 116:2368-2369, December 23, 1972.

"Coagulation changes during termination of pregnancy by prostaglandins and by vacuum aspiration," by M. H. Badraoul, et al. BR MED J 1:19-21, January 6, 1973.

"Coagulation changes in saline-induced abortion," by R. K. Laros, et al. AM J OBSTET GYNECOL 116:271-276, May 15, 1973.

"Combined laparoscopic sterilization and pregnancy termination," by N. G. Courey, et al. J REPROD MED 10:291-294, June, 1973.

"Comparison of operative morbidity in abortion-sterilization procedures," by L. L. Veltman, et al. AM J OBSTET GYNECOL 117:251-254, September 15, 1973.

"Complications in induced abortion," by J. M. Bedoya-Gonzalez. AN R ACAD NACL MED 90:297-306, 1973.

"Complications of abortion," by J. E. Hodgson. AM J OBSTET GYNECOL 117:293-294, September 15, 1973.

"Contraception, sterilization, and abortion legal interpretation of consent," by D. F. Kaltreider. MD STATE MED J 22:67, September, 1973.

"Contraceptive practice among New York abortion patients," by M. B. Bracken, et al. AM J OBSTET GYNECOL 114:967-977, 1972.

"Course of pregnancy, delivery and puerperium following induced abortion of first pregnancy," by S. Lembrych. ZENTRALBL GYNAEKOL 94:164-168, February 5, 1972.

"A critical analysis of induced abortion," by H. Schulman. BULL NY ACAD MED 49:694-707, August, 1973.

"The current status of the use of prostaglandins in induced abortion," by I. M. Cushner. AM J PUBLIC HEALTH 63:189-190, March, 1973.

"Death from an attempt to procure an abortion by intra-uterine injection of ethyl alcohol," by T. Marcinkowski. FORENSIC SCI 2:245-246, May, 1973.

"Defibrinogenation after intra-amniotic injection of hypertonic saline," by J. L. Spivak, et al. N ENGL J MED 287:321-323, 1972.

" 'Delayed menstruation' induced by prostaglandin in pregnant patients," by P. Mocsary, et al. LANCET 2:683, September 22, 1973.

"Development in the incidence of abortions in recent years. Investigations and calculations concerning the incidence of criminal abortions prior to and after the Danish abortion law of 1970," by V. Sele, et al. UGESKR LAEGER 134:2493-2505, November 20, 1972.

"Disseminated intravascular coagulation resulting in severe hemorrhage, following the intraamniotic injection of hypertonic saline to induce abortion," by A. Sedaghat, et al. AM J OBSTET GYNECOL 114:841-843, November 15, 1972.

"Does anybody care?" AM J NURS 73:1562-1565, September, 1973.

"Dr. Jerome L. Reeves on the new sexuality," by H. A. Matthews. NC MED J 34:616-618, August, 1973.

"Drug abuse treatment and parental consent," by R. L. Epstein, et al. HOSPITALS 47:63-64 passim, September 1, 1973.

"Drugs in pregnancy." MED LETT DRUGS THER 14:94-96, December 8, 1972.

"Early medical complications of abortion by saline: joint program for the study of abortion (JPSA)," by C. Tietze, et al. STUD FAM PLANN 4:133-138, June, 1973.

"Effect of anaesthetic technique on blood loss in termination of pregnancy," by S. R. Dunn, et al. BR J ANAESTH 45:633-637, June, 1973.

"The effect of induced abortion on subsequent pregnancy ending with delivery," by A. Atanasov, et al. AKUSH GINEKOL 11:398-402, 1972.

"Effect of infused prostaglandin F 2 on hormonal levels during early pregnancy," by A. C. Wentz, et al. AM J OBSTET GYNECOL 114: 908-913, December 1, 1972.

"The effect of intra-amniotic oestriol sulphate on abortion induced by hypertonic saline," by K. J. Dennis, et al. J OBSTET GYNAECOL BR COMMONW 80:41-45, January, 1973.

"Effect of recent Supreme Court Decision on Delaware's abortion law." DEL MED J 45:141-145, May, 1973.

"The effect of spontaneous and induced abortion on prematurity and birthweight," by G. Papaevangelou, et al. J OBSTET GYNAECOL BR COMMONW 80:410-422, May, 1973.

"The effects of intravenous infusion of graded doses of prostaglandins F 2 and E 2 on lung resistance in patients undergoing termination of pregnancy," by A. P. Smith. CLIN SCI 44:17-25, January, 1973.

"The efficacy and acceptability of the 'prostaglandin impact' in inducing complete abortion during the second week after the missed menstrual period," by A. I. Csapo, et al. PROSTAGLANDINS 3:125-139, February, 1973.

"The evaluation of intra-amniotic prostaglandin F 2 in the management of early midtrimester pregnancy termination," by D. C. Leslie, et al. J REPROD MED 9:453-455, December, 1972.

"The evolution of an abortion counseling service in an adoption agency," by R. K. Heineman. CHILD WELFARE 52:253-260, April, 1973.

"Experience with the suction curette in termination of pregnancy at a Sydney Teaching hospital," by R. H. Picker, et al. AUST NZ J OBSTET GYNAECOL 13:49-50, February, 1973.

"Experiences with the vibro dilatator from the Soviet Union," by K. H. Beckmann, et al. DTSCH GESUNDHEITSW 28:227-228, 1973.

"Facing a current problem," by Hougardy. NURSING 45:1-12, January-February, 1973.

"Fecundity, abortion and standard of living among Mapuche women," by T. Monreal. REV MED CHIL 100:1273-1286, October, 1972.

"Fetal implants in uterus." BR MED J 2:133-134, April 21, 1973.

"First trimester abortions induced by the extraovular infusion of prostaglandin F2a," by A. I. Csapo, et al. PROSTAGLANDINS 1:295-303, 1972.

"First trimester abortions induced by a single extraovular injection of prostaglandin F2a," by A. I. Csapo, et al. PROSTAGLANDINS 1:365-371, 1972.

"Five thousand consecutive saline inductions," by T. D. Kerenyi, et al. AM J OBSTET GYNECOL 116:593-600, July 1, 1973.

"A follow-up study of women who request abortion," by E. M. Smith. AM J ORTHOPSYCHIATRY 43:574-585, July, 1973.

"Further experience with intrauterine prostaglandin administration," by M. Bygdeman, et al. J REPROD MED 9:392-396, December, 1972.

"Further experience with laparoscopic sterilization concomitant with vacuum curettage for abortion," by H. K. Amin, et al. FERTIL STERIL 24:592-594, August, 1973.

"Clinical application of prostaglandin in obstetrics," by M. I. T'ang. CHIN MED J 9:563-569, 1973.

"Clostridium infection after intra-amniotic hypertonic saline injection for induced abortion," by N. Sehgal, et al. J REPROD MED 8:67-69, February, 1972.

" 'Glioma' of the uterus: a fetal homograft," by P. A. Niven, et al. AM J OBSTET GYNECOL 115:534-538, February 15, 1973.

"Gonorrhea in women prior to pregnancy interruption," by M. Mesko, et al. ZENTRALBL GYNAEKOL 94:169-172, February 5, 1972.

"Guidelines for physician performance of induced abortions." MARY-LAND STATE MED J 22:68, September, 1973.

"Histopathologic changes associated with prostaglandin induced abortion," by P. D. Bullard, Jr., et al. CONTRACEPTION 7:133-144, 1973.

"Hormonal changes during induction of midtrimester abortion by prostaglandin F 2," by B. Cantor, et al. AM J OBSTET GYNECOL 113:607-615, July 1, 1972.

"Hypertonic saline-induced abortion. Correlation of fetal death with disseminated intravascular coagulation," by H. I. Glueck, et al. JAMA 225:28-31, July 2, 1973.

"Increased frequency of chromosomal anomalies in abortions after induced ovulation," by J. G. Boue, et al. LANCET 1:679-680, March 24, 1973.

"Induced abortion," by L. B. Davis. J AM OSTEOPATH ASSOC 73:74-76, September, 1973.

"Induced abortion and ectopic pregnancy," by P. P. Panayotou, et al. AM J OBSTET GYNECOL 114:507-510, October 15, 1972.

"The induced abortion and the gynecologist," by Z. Polishok. HARE-FUAH 83:264-265, September 15, 1972.

"Induced abortion: source of guilt or growth?" by F. Addelson. AM J ORTHOPSYCHIATRY 43:815-823, October, 1973.

"The induction of abortion and menstruation by the intravaginal administration of prostaglandin F 2a," by T. Sato, et al. AM J OBSTET GYNECOL 116:287-289, May 15, 1973.

"Induction of abortion by combined intra-amniotic urea and prostaglandin E 2 or prostaglandin E 2 alone," by I. Craft. LANCET 1:1344-1346, June 16, 1973.

"Induction of abortion by extra-amniotic administration of prostaglandin F2a: a preliminary report," by V. Hingorani, et al. CONTRACEPTION 6:353-359, 1972.

"Induction of abortion by intra- and extra-amniotic prostaglandin F2 administration," by P. A. Jarvinen, et al. PROSTAGLANDINS 3:491-504, April, 1973.

"Induction of abortion by intravenous and intra-uterine administration of prostaglandin F 2," by A. A. Haspels, et al. J REPROD MED 9:442-447, December, 1972.

"Induction of abortion by intravenous infusions of prostaglandin F 2," by E. Dreher, et al. ARCH GYNAEKOL 213:48-53, 1972.

"Induction of midtrimester abortion by increasing intra-uterine volume," by M. O. Pulkkinen, et al. ACTA OBSTET GYNECOL SCAND 52:9-12, 1973.

"Induction of mid-trimester abortion with intrauterine alcohol," by V. Gomel, et al. OBSTET GYNECOL 41:455-458, March, 1973.

"The induction of second trimester abortions using an intra-amniotic injection of urea and prostaglandin E2," by P. Bowen-Simpkins. J OBSTET GYNAECOL BR COMMONW 80:824-826, September, 1973.

"Influence of induced and spontaneous abortions on the outcome of subsequent pregnancies," by S. N. Pantelakis, et al. AM J OBSTET GYNECOL 116:799-805, July 15, 1973.

"IgG cold agglutinins and first trimester abortion," by K. Mygind, et al. VOX SANG 22:552-560, December, 1972.

"Inhibition of abortion and fetal death produced by endotoxin or prostaglandin F2alpha," by M. J. Harper, et al. PROSTAGLANDINS 2:295-309, October, 1972.

"Initial experiences with prostaglandin F2 in induced abortion," by H. Igel, et al. ZENTRALBL GYNAEKOL 95:353-357, March 16, 1973.

"Interrupting late-term pregnancy by means of an intra-amniotic introduction of hypertonic solutions," by K. I. Braginskii. AKUSH GINEKOL 48:61-62, 1972.

"Interrupting late-term pregnancy with an intra-amniotic administration of a hypertonic solution of sodium chloride," by G. A. Palladi, et al. AKUSH GINEKOL 48:58-61, 1972.

"Intra-amniotic prostaglandin E 2 and F 2 for induction of abortion: a dose response study," by I. Craft. J OBSTET GYNAECOL BR

COMMONW 80:46-47, January, 1973.

"Intra-amniotic prostaglandin E 2 and urea for abortion," by I. Craft. LANCET 1:779, April 7, 1973.

"Intraamniotic prostaglandin F2-alpha dose--twenty-four-hour abortifacient response," by W. E. Brenner, et al. J PHARM SCI 62:1278-1282, August, 1973.

"Intra-amniotic prostaglandin F2 alpha to induce midtrimester abortion," by S. L. Corson, et al. AM J OBSTET GYNECOL 117:27-34, September 1, 1973.

"Intra-amniotic prostaglandins and urea for abortion," by I. Craft. LANCET 2:207 passim, July, 1973.

"Intraamniotic urea for induction of mid-trimester abortion," by P. C. Weinberg, et al. OBSTET GYNECOL 41:451-454, March, 1973.

"Intra-uterine administration of prostaglandin F 2 during the second trimester of pregnancy; clinical and hormonal results," by R. Shearman, et al. J REPROD FERTIL 32:321-322, February, 1973.

"Intra-uterine suction for evacuation of the uterus in early pregnancy," by A. K. Ghosh. J INDIAN MED ASSOC 59:366-368, October 16, 1972.

"Investigation of women admitted to hospital with abortion," by L. Freundt. ACTA PSYCHIATR SCAND 242:1-221, 1973.

"Isoimmunization of women during pregnancy," by G. S. Aleskerov. AKUSH GINEKOL 48:65-67, November, 1972.

"The Karman catheter," by P. Fairbrother. AM J OBSTET GYNECOL 116:293, May 15, 1973.

"Karman catheter," by A. J. Margolis, et al. AM J OBSTET GYNECOL 115:589, February 15, 1973.

"Lack of coagulation defect after terminating second-trimester pregnancy by the catheter technique," by F. K. Beller, et al. AM J OBSTET GYNECOL 115:822-826, March 15, 1973.

"Laminaria augmentation of intra-amniotic prostaglandin F2 alpha for the induction of mid-trimester abortion," by W. E. Brenner, et al. PROSTAGLANDINS 3:879-894, June, 1973.

"Latent morbidity after abortion." BR MED J 1:506, March 3, 1973.

"Latent morbidity after abortion." BR MED J 1:739-740, March 24, 1973.

"Latent morbidity after abortion." BR MED J 2:51, April 7, 1973.

"Latent morbidity after abortion," by C. Buck, et al. BR MED J 3:292-293, August 4, 1973.

"Latent morbidity after abortion," by A. Ogborn. BR MED J 2:114-115, April 14, 1973.

"Lesions of blood vessels in the uterine cervix as a cause of bleedings following interruption of pregnancy," by M. Cislo, et al. POL TYG LEK 27:2066-2068, December 25, 1972.

"Letter: intrauterine prostaglandins for outpatient termination of very early pregnancy," by S. M. Karim. LANCET 2:794, October 6, 1973.

"Letter: orgasm-induced abortion," by J. P. Keeve. LANCET 2:970, October 27, 1973.

"Letter: prenatal treatment of hereditary diseases?" by C. Valenti. LANCET 2:797-798, October 6, 1973.

"Litigation: preparation and response," by S. M. Blaes. HOSP PROG 54:70-72 passim, August, 1973.

"Local potentiated anesthesia in artificial abortions," by E. I. Gorobets. PEDIATR AKUSH GINEKOL 1:55-56, 1973.

"Making abortion consultation therapeutic," by C. M. Friedman. AM J PSYCHIATRY 130:1257-1261, November, 1973.

"MED-CHI guidelines for physician performance of induced abortions." MD STATE MED J 22:68, September, 1973.

"Mid-trimester abortion," by A. A. Finks. LANCET 1:263-264, February 3, 1973.

"Mid-trimester abortion with intraamniotic saline and intravenous oxytocin," by C. A. Ballard, et al. OBSTET GYNECOL 41:447-450, March, 1973.

"Mid-trimester hypertonic saline-induced abortion: effect of indomethacin on induction/abortion time," by R. Waltman, et al. AM J OBSTET GYNECOL 114:829-831, 1972.

"A midtrimester procedure, not without its risks...Saline abortion: a review of the experience at Kapiolani hospital," by T. I. Hooper, et al. HAWAII MED J 32:222-225, July-August, 1973.

"Modified cervical block for elective abortion procedures," by W. D. Walden. OBSTET GYNECOL 41:473-474, March, 1973.

"Moral and medical problems concerning abortion," by M. Bermejillo. AN R ACAD NACL MED 90:307-326, 1973.

"Moral consideration of abortion from the viewpoint of the Christian value of human life," by J. M. Diaz Moreno. AN R ACAD NACL MED 90:235-261, 1973.

"New methods for interruption of very early pregnancy," by J. Presl. CESK GYNEKOL 38:474-475, July, 1973.

"New York State physicians and the social context of abortion," by S. Wassertheil-Smoller, et al. AM J PUBLIC HEALTH 63:144-149, February, 1973.

"On the mechanism of the abortifacient action of prostaglandin F 2," by A. I. Csapo. J REPROD MED 9:400-412, December, 1972; also in PROSTAGLANDINS 1:157-165, 1972.

"On the mechanism of midtrimester abortions induced by prostaglandin 'impact'," by L. Saldana, et al. PROSTAGLANDINS 3:847-858, June, 1973.

"On the topic of abortion: embryonal anthropology," by H. Scheck.

PRAXIS 62:1068-1071, August 28, 1973.

"One death and a cluster of febrile complications related to saline abortions," by G. S. Berger, et al. OBSTET GYNECOL 42:121-126, July, 1973.

"Operation on demand?" by C. O. Rice. MINN MED 56:412, May, 1973.

"Opinion towards induced abortion among urban women in Delhi, India," by S. B. Kar. SOC SCI MED 6:731-736, December, 1972.

"Outpatient termination of pregnancy by vacuum aspiration," by A. Y. Ng, et al. SINGAPORE MED J 14:23-25, March, 1973.

"Oxytocin administration in mid-trimester saline abortions," by N. H. Lauersen, et al. AM J OBSTET GYNECOL 115:420-430, February 1, 1973.

"Oxytocin augmentation of saline abortion," by F. W. Hanson, et al. OBSTET GYNECOL 41:608-610, April, 1973.

"The paramedic abortionist," by R. F. Mattingly. OBSTET GYNECOL 41:929-930, June, 1973.

"Placenta previa: a rare complication of midtrimester abortion by amnioinfusion," by J. A. Goldman, et al. INT SURG 58:707, October, 1973.

"Plasma progesterone and prostaglandin F2 levels during the insertion of prostaglandin F2 vaginal tablet," by T. Sato, et al. PROSTAGLANDINS 4:107-113, July, 1973.

"Plasma progesterone changes in abortion induced by hypertonic saline in the second trimester of pregnancy," by A. J. Tyack, et al. J OBSTET GYNAECOL BR COMMONW 80:548-552, June, 1973.

"Population-political aspects of induced abortion," by D. Klessen, et al. Z AERZTL FORTBILD 67:57-63, January 15, 1973.

"Posterior cervical rupture following prostaglandin-induced mid-trimester abortion," by A. C. Wentz, et al. AM J OBSTET GYNECOL 115:1107-1110, April 15, 1973.

"Pregnancy after hysterotomy," by R. F. Heys. BR MED J 1:681-682, March 17, 1973.

"Pregnancy and abortion: implications for career development of professional women," by M. T. Notman. ANN NY ACAD SCI 208:205-210, March 15, 1973.

"Pregnancy interruption with prostaglandins F2a," by T. Brat, et al. J GYNECOL OBSTET BIOL REPROD 1:385-387, 1972.

"Pregnancy termination and infectious diseases," by J. E. Hodgson. MINN MED 56:698-699, August, 1973.

"Pregnancy wastage in operating room personnel," by I. H. Kaiser. OBSTET GYNECOL 41:930-932, June, 1973.

"A preliminary report: Abortion in Hawaii--present and future trends," by P. I. McNamee, et al. HAWAII MED J 32:220-221, July-August, 1973.

"Prevention of Rh immunization following abortion," by J. A. Goldman, et al. HAREFUAH 83:100-101, August 1, 1972.

"The problem of legal pregnancy interruption," by C. Zwahr. ZENTRALBL GYNAEKOL 94:156-163, February 5, 1972.

"The prospects of PGs in postconceptional therapy," by A. I. Csapo. PROSTAGLANDINS 3:245-289, March, 1973.

"Prostaglandin developments in Uganda," by S. M. Karim. J REPROD MED 9:255-257, December, 1972.

"Prostaglandin-oxytocin abortion: a clinical trial of intra-amniotic prostaglandin F2alpha in combination with intravenous oxytocin," by M. Seppala, et al. PROSTAGLANDINS 2:311-319, October, 1972.

"Prostaglandins and their clinical applications in human reproduction," by E. M. Southern, et al. J REPROD MED 9:472-477, December, 1972.

"Prostaglandins for inducing labor and abortion." DRUG THER BULL 11:41-43, May 25, 1973.

"Prostaglandins in gynecology," by M. Breckwoldt, et al. HIPPO-KRATES 43:494-495, December, 1972.

"The psychological impact of abortion," by N. D. West. AORN J 17: 132-138, March, 1973.

"Psychological problems of abortion for the unwed teenage girl," by C. D. Martin. GENET PSYCHOL MONOGR 88:23-110, August, 1973.

"Reasons for delayed abortion: results of four hundred interviews," by T. D. Kerenyi, et al. AM J OBSTET GYNECOL 117:299-311, October 1, 1973.

"Recent aspects on systemic administration of prostaglandin," by N. Wiqvist, et al. J REPROD MED 9:378-382, December, 1972.

"Recent United States court decisions concerning abortion," by M. A. Olea. AN R ACAD NACL MED 90:327-335, 1973.

"Rh immunization in induced abortion," by J. A. Goldman, et al. MINERVA GINECOL 25:100-102, February, 1973.

"Saline instillation with oxytocin administration in midtrimester abortion," by L. I. Mann, et al. OBSTET GYNECOL 41:748-752, May, 1973.

"Second trimester termination by intra-uterine prostaglandin F2. Clinical and hormonal results with observations on induced lactation and chronoperiodicity," by R. Shearman, et al. J REPROD MED 9:448-452, December, 1972.

"Septic induced abortion," by J. F. Jewett. N ENGL J MED 289:748-749, October 4, 1973.

"Septicemia with Listeria monocytogenes following abortion induced after 2 and one-half months," by J. F. Lemeland, et al. NOUV PRESSE MED 2:1616, June 9, 1973.

"Sexuality, birth control and abortion: a decision-making sequence," by M. Diamond, et al. J BIOSOC SCI 5:347-361, July, 1973.

"Some recent world events in relation to pregnancy termination."
WORLD MED J 20:72-75, July-August, 1973.

"State legislation can lessen impact of Court's abortion decision," by
R. W. Stratton. HOSP PROG 54:8-9, October, 1973.

"Sterilization associated with induced abortion: JPSA findings (based
on a Joint program for the study of abortion examination of the abortion experience of 72,988 American women who had legal abortions,
1970-71)," by S. Lewit. FAMILY PLANNING PERSPECTIVES 5:177-
182, Summer, 1973.

"Studies on accidental intravascular injection in extra-amniotic saline
induced abortion and a method for reducing this risk," by B. Gustavii.
J REPROD MED 8:70-74, February, 1972.

"Studies on the pathogenesis of clotting defects during salt-induced
abortions," by L. M. Talbert, et al. AM J OBSTET GYNECOL 115:
656-662, March 1, 1973.

"The termination of adolescent out-of-wedlock pregnancies and the
prospects for their primary prevention," by W. G. Cobliner, et al.
AM J OBSTET GYNECOL 115:432-444, February 1, 1973.

"Termination of early gestation with vaginal prostaglandin F2 alpha
tablets," by R. C. Corlett, et al. PROSTAGLANDINS 2:453-464,
December, 1972.

"Termination of pregnancy." J IOWA MED SOC 63:248 passim, June,
1973.

"Termination of pregnancy," by D. Bluett. BR MED J 3:700, September
16, 1972.

"Termination of pregnancy by abdominal hysterotomy," by J. Higginbottom. LANCET 1:937-938, April 28, 1973.

"Termination of pregnancy by intra-uterine prostaglandin F 2," by A.
Korda, et al. AUST NZ J OBSTET GYNAECOL 12:166-169, August,
1972.

"The termination of pregnancy by intravenous infusion of a synthetic prostaglandin F 2 analogue," by D. S. Sharp, et al. J OBSTET GYN-AECOL BR COMMONW 80:138-141, February, 1973.

"Termination of pregnancy by 'super coils': morbidity associated with a new method of second-trimester abortion," by G. S. Berger, et al. AM J OBSTET GYNECOL 116:297-304, June 1, 1973.

"Termination of pregnancy: guideline statement of the Iowa Medical Society." J IOWA MED SOC 63:248 plus, June, 1973.

"Termination of pregnancy, Sydney, 1972," by D. Pfanner, et al. MED J AUST 1:710-711, April 7, 1973.

"Termination of pregnancy with intrauterine devices. A comparative study of coils, coils and balsa, and catheters," by B. Mullick, et al. AM J OBSTET GYNECOL 116:305-308, June 1, 1973.

"Use of combined premedication in induced abortion," by E. I. Gorobets. AKUSH GINEKOL 48:67-68, November, 1972.

"Use of laminaria tents with hypertonic saline amnioinfusion," by J. H. Lischke, et al. AM J OBSTET GYNECOL 116:586-587, June 15, 1973.

"Use of prostaglandin F 2 alpha for interruption of pregnancy in 1st and 2d trimester," by F. Havranek, et al. CESK GYNEKOL 38:432-435, July, 1973.

"The use of prostaglandin pessaries prior to vaginal termination," by I. Craft. PROSTAGLANDINS 3:377-381, March, 1973.

"Uterine contractility and placental histology in abortion by laminaria and metreurynter," by Y. Manabe, et al. OBSTET GYNECOL 41:753-759, May, 1973.

"Vaginal administration of prostaglandins and early abortion," by R. J. Pion, et al. J REPROD MED 9:413-415, December, 1972.

"Vaginal mid-trimester abortion," by D. T. Liu. LANCET 1:433, February 24, 1973.

INDUCED ABORTION

"Viability, abortion, and the difference between a fetus and an infant," by H. T. Engelhardt, Jr. AM J OBSTET GYNECOL 116:429-434, June 1, 1973.

"The viability of fetal skin of abortuses induced by saline or prostaglandin," by I. J. Park, et al. AM J OBSTET GYNECOL 115:274-275, January 15, 1973.

"Water vacuum suction curettage (WVSC): one year's experience," by J. R. Woods, et al. OBSTET GYNECOL 41:720-725, May, 1973.

"When the barbarians came," by D. Francis. J LA STATE MED SOC 125:138-139, April, 1973.

"The work of the women's consultation for the prevention of artificial abortions," by S. L. Polchanova. AKUSH GINEKOL 48:54-56, September, 1972.

"The wounded uterus: pregnancy after hysterotomy," by W. M. Clow, et al. BR MED J 1:321-323, February 10, 1973.

INDOMETHACIN
"Aspirin and indomethacin: effect on instillation/abortion time of mid-trimester hypertonic saline induced abortion," by R. Waltman, et al. PROSTAGLANDINS 3:47-58, 1973.

"Mid-trimester hypertonic saline--induced abortion: effect of indomethacin on induction-abortion time," by R. Waltman, et al. AM J OBSTET GYNECOL 114:829-831, November 15, 1972.

INFANTICIDE
"Abortion and infanticide," by M. Tooley. PHILOSOPHY AND PUBLIC AFFAIRS 2:37-66, Fall, 1972.

INFECTION
see: Complications

ISOXSUPRINE
"Use of isoxsuprine in the obstetrical pathology," by I. Signorelli, et al. ARCH OSTET GINECOL 77:115-128, April, 1972.

LAW ENFORCEMENT
see: Laws and Legislation

LAWS AND LEGISLATION
"Abortion." NEW REPUB 168:9, February 10, 1973; Reply by M. P. O'Boyle. 168:32, March 24, 1973.

"Abortion," by B. Littlewood. NZ MED J 77:126-127; February, 1973.

"Abortion," by H. Ratner. J SC MED ASSOC 69:69-70, February, 1973.

"Abortion," by P. B. Temm. NZ MED J 77:265-266, April, 1973.

"Abortion Act in Somerset," by A. P. Jones, et al. BR MED J 3:90-92, July 14, 1973.

"The Abortion Act of 1967; Society for the protection of unborn children." TABLET 227:237-239, March 10, 1973.

"Abortion after Roe (Roe v. Wade, 93 Sup Ct 705) and Doe (Doe v. Bolton, 93 Sup Ct 739): a proposed statute." VAND L REV 26:823-835, May, 1973.

"Abortion alert," by A. Altchek. OBSTET GYNECOL 42:452-454, September, 1973.

"Abortion and the court." CHR TODAY 17:32-33, February 16, 1973.

"Abortion and family planning," by K. N. Rao. J INDIAN MED ASSOC 59:337-341, October 16, 1972.

"Abortion and the principles of legislation," by P. J. Micallef. LAVAL THEOL PHIL 28:267-303, October, 1972.

"Abortion appeals rejected." NAT CATH REP 9:3, March 9, 1973.

"Abortion around the world." TIME 101:76, February 19, 1973.

"Abortion; blast and counter-blast." ECONOMIST 249:31, November 24, 1973.

"Abortion cases: a return to Lochner, or a new substantive due process?" ALBANY L REV 37:776, 1973.

"Abortion: the continuing controversy." POPULATION BULLETIN 28:1-29, August, 1972.

"Abortion controversy: ancient practice, current conflict," by M. F. Brewer. CURRENT 154:26-28, September, 1973.

"Abortion counseling: an experimental study of three techniques," by M. B. Bracken, et al. AM J OBSTET GYNECOL 117:10-20, September 1, 1973.

"Abortion: court decision removes legal uncertainty." SCI N 103:54, January 27, 1973.

"The abortion decision." COMM 97:435-436, February 16, 1973.

"Abortion decision." SCI AM 228:44-45, March, 1973.

"Abortion decision," by R. F. Drinan. COMMONWEAL 97:438-440, February 16, 1973; Reply with rejoinder by J. T. McHugh. 98:75 plus, March 30, 1973.

"Abortion decision and Puerto Rico," by J. L. Simon. REV C ABO PR 34:505-513, August, 1973.

"Abortion decision: a balancing of rights," by J. C. Evans. CHR CENT 90:195-197, February 14, 1973.

"The abortion decision; cond from a Washington Star Syndicate feature, 1973," by W. Buckley. C DGST 37:41-42, May, 1973.

"Abortion decision: a death blow?" CHR TODAY 17:48, February 16, 1973.

"Abortion decision: end of an inalienable right," by E. Melvin. OSV 61:1 plus, April 29, 1973.

"Abortion decision may set precedent to resolve 1st Amendment conflicts," by E. J. Schulte. HOSP PROGRESS 54:85 plus, September,

1973.

"Abortion decisions: Roe v. Wade (93 Sup Ct 705), Doe v. Bolton (93 Sup Ct 739)." J FAMILY L 12:459, 1972-1973.

"The abortion decisions: the Supreme Court as moralist, scientist, historian and legislator," by W. J. Curran. N ENGL J MED 288:950-951, May 3, 1973.

"Abortion: decisions to live with: conference at Southern Methodist university," by R. C. Wahlberg. CHR CENT 90:691-693, June 27, 1973.

"Abortion: a deeper look at the legal aspects," by R. Orloski. US CATH 38:39-40, September, 1973.

"Abortion--demanding litigation: preparation and response," by S. M. Blaes. HOSP PROGRESS 54:70 plus, August, 1973.

"Abortion: denial of freedom to care," by D. DeMarco. OSV 62:1 plus, July 1, 1973.

"Abortion: deterrence, facilitation, resistance." AMERICA 128:506-507, June 2, 1973.

"Abortion: the father's rights." U CIN L REV 42:441-467, 1973.

"Abortion for the asking," by H. Dudar. SAT R SOC 1:30-35, April, 1973.

"Abortion front: end of the phony war." NAT R 25:249-250, March 2, 1973.

"Abortion: history, opinions, and what's new in the United States," by E. D. Jubb, et al. CAN B J 4:8-12, July, 1973.

"Abortion in Finland today," by K. Wichmann. DUODECIM 89:649-651, 1973.

"Abortion in New Zealand," by W. A. Facer, et al. J BIOSOC SCI 5: 151-158, April, 1973.

"Abortion in the United States. Decisions of the Supreme Court," by R. Veylon. NOUV PRESSE MED 2:1952-1954, July 28, 1973.

"Abortion in Victoria after Menhennit," by J. Smibert. MED J AUST 1:1016-1017, May 19, 1973.

"Abortion is an expensive contraceptive," by L. O. Dandeneli. LAKARTIDNINGEN 70:343, January 31, 1973.

"Abortion is idling," by J. Willke, et al. COLUMBIA 53:10-19, April, 1973.

"Abortion issue." SAT N 88:10, September, 1973.

"Abortion law," by I. S. Edwards. MED J AUST 2:850, October 7, 1972.

"Abortion law in the USA." BR MED J 1:428-429, February 17, 1973.

"Abortion: law of nation or law of God; reprint from The Catholic Standard and Times, January 25, 1973," by J. Foley. DIMENSION 5:35, Spring, 1973.

"Abortion law reform controversy rages in West Germany," by F. Lupsen. CHR CENT 90:487-488, April 25, 1973.

"Abortion: legal but still wrong," by E. Gilbert. LIGUORIAN 61:2-4, October, 1973.

"Abortion--a matter of life and death," by J. F. Gwynne. NZ MED J 76:355-357, November, 1972.

"Abortion: next round." COMM 98:51-52, March 23, 1973.

"Abortion on demand," by C. Whelan. AMERICA 128:inside front cover, February 10, 1973.

"Abortion on demand." TIME 101:46-47, January 29, 1973.

"Abortion on demand in a post-Wade (Roe v. Wade 93 Sup Ct 705) context: must the state pay the bills?" FORDHAM L REV 41:921, May, 1973.

"Abortion on request: the physician's view," by A. F. Guttmacher. AM BIOL TEACH 34:514-517, December, 1972; Reply with rejoinder by P. R. Gastonguay. 35:353-355, September, 1973.

"Abortion picture still confused despite Supreme Court ruling." LIBR ED 36:17, April, 1973.

"Abortion positions; so who's the radical?" by C. Fager. NAT CATH REP 9:12, March 2, 1973.

"Abortion programme in Duchenne muscular dystrophy in Japan," by K. Kondo, et al. LANCET 1:543, March 10, 1973.

"Abortion - respect life - legality vs. morality," by P. O'Boyle. SOC JUST 65:372-373, February, 1973.

"Abortion revolution." NEWSWEEK 81:27-28, February 5, 1973.

"The abortion ruling: analysis & prognosis: symposium: CHA to conduct anti-abortion campaign. NCCB pastoral message. Commentaries by T. Shaffer, R. McCormick, A. Hellegers, J. McHugh, W. Regan, G. Reed, L. Hogan, E. Head, C. Bauda, E. D. Bishop." HOSP PROG 54:81-96b, March, 1973.

"Abortion ruling: Catholic facts and constitutional truths," by R. Marshall. SOC JUST 66:84, June, 1973.

"The abortion situation in Denmark and conditions in Finland," by M. Johansson. LAKARTIDNINGEN 70:344, January 31, 1973.

"Abortion situation in Oklahoma reviewed." J OKLA STATE MED ASS 66:409-411, September, 1973.

"Abortion trends in European socialist countries and in the United States," by H. P. David. AM J ORTHOPSYCHIATRY 43:376-383, April, 1973.

"Abortion: The United States Supreme Court decision." LANCET 1: 301-302, February 10, 1973.

"Abortion using a bicycle pump on the mistress and unusual suicide of a blind man," by F. J. Holzer. BEITR GERICHTL MED 30:187-196, 1973.

"Abortion: what happens now." NEWSWEEK 81:66 plus, February 5, 1973.

"Abortions: new legal guidelines," by C. Weissburg, et al. FAH REV 6:41 plus, April, 1973.

"Accidents and sequelae of medical abortions," by B. Beric, et al. AM J OBSTET GYNECOL 116:813-821, July 15, 1973.

"Action in the wake of death Monday," by J. Doyle. SOC JUST 66:133-135, July-August, 1973.

"Additional births averted when abortion is added to contraception," by R. G. Potter. STUD FAM PLANN 3:53-59, April, 1972.

"Administrative commission issues pastoral message on abortion." OR 10,258:9, March 8, 1973.

"L'adoption, une alternative meconnue a l'avortement; France," by F. Dardot. ETUDES 338:701-714, May, 1973.

"Aftermath of the abortion decisions: action in the legislatures and in the courts," by W. J. Curran. N ENGL J MED 289:955, November 1, 1973.

"Air embolism in the interruption of pregnancy by vacuum extraction," by G. H. Hartung. ZENTRALBL GYNAEKOL 95:825-828, June 15, 1973.

"Amazing historical and biological errors in abortion decision - Dr. Hellegers; reprint from Washington Star-News, excerpt from interview by T. Ascik," by A. Hellegers. HOSP PROG 54:16-17, May, 1973.

"American bishops and abortion." TABLET 227:268-269, March 17, 1973.

"American Civil Liberties Union suit seeks abortions in St. Louis public hospitals." HOSPITALS 47:116, September 16, 1973.

"America: there's a nigger in the woodpile," by W. Devlin. TRIUMPH 8:27, May, 1973.

"American tragedy: the Supreme Court on abortion," by R. M. Byrn. FORDHAM L REV 41:807, May, 1973.

"America's war on life; symposium: Where we have been, where we go from here. The abortion culture, by K. Mitzner. The movement coming together. The movement staying together. The Catholic obligation." TRIUMPH 8:17-32, March, 1973.

"Analysis of induced abortions at a regional hospital," by B. Deidesheimer. ZENTRALBL GYNAEKOL 95:819-824, June 15, 1973.

"Anatomy of social abortion," by J. Jurukovski, et al. GOD ZB MED FAK SKOPJE 18:61-69, 1972.

"Anti-abortion lobby fights on," by M. Elliott. DAILY TELEGRAPH p. 17, February 2, 1973.

"Appeal to all: protect human life; pastoral letter of the German Episcopate." OR 28:9-10, July 12, 1973.

"Appeals court rules private hospital has right to refuse abortions," by E. W. Springer. HOSP TOP 51:24-25, August, 1973.

"L'avortement," by P. Chauchard. REV THOMISTE 73:33-46, January-March, 1973.

"L'avortement: ethique et politique; compte rendue," by G. Bourgeault. RELATIONS 380:91-93, March, 1973.

"L'avortement; symposium: Une histoire d'amour et de mort, by M. Gillet. Sexualite, contraception et avortement, by M. Debout. Liberte de l'avortement et liberation des femmes, by H. Bonnet. Legalite et moralite face a l'avortement, by R. Boyer. La volonte de procreer: reflexion philosophique, by B. Quelquejeu. Reflexions theologiques sur la position de l'Eglise catholique, by J. M. Pohier." LUMIERE 21:6-107, August-October, 1972; Replies by Y. Milliasseau, et al. 22:81-87, January-March, 1973.

"Avorter, dit-elle," by M. Beaulieu. LE MACLEAN 13:14-15, 30 plus, February, 1973.

"A baby girl: one good argument against abortion; testimony, Pennsylvania Abortion Law Commission, February 24, 1972," by C. Martin. DIMENSION 4:144-148, Winter, 1972.

"The beginning of mental activity in man and its importance to law. A new theory," by Till-d'Aulnis de Bour. PSYCHIATR NEUROL NEUROCHIR 75:385-390, September-October, 1972.

"Bishops condemn abortion decision," by R. Casey. NAT CATH REP 9:1-2, February 23, 1973.

"Bishops issue rules on abortion laws." NAT CATH REP 9:19, April 27, 1973.

"Boston prelate indicts court's abortion decision." HOSPITALS 47:170, May 16, 1973.

"Buckley and Hatfield lead fight for antiabortion measure in Senate." NAT CATH REP 9:21, June 8, 1973.

"California abortion law overturned." NEWSLETTER 6:6, January, 1973.

"The Catholic burden." TRIUMPH 8:45, May, 1973.

"Catholic Hospital Association strengthens legal campaign against abortion." HOSP PROGRESS 54:18 plus, June, 1973.

"Catholic Hospital Association to conduct anti-abortion campaign." HOSP PROGRESS 54:82 plus, March, 1973.

"Catholics attack abortion decision." NAT CATH REP 9:3-4, February 2, 1973.

"Cerebral air embolism following intrauterine air insufflation," by K. Joschko. ZENTRALBL GYNAEKOL 94:1587-1592, November 18, 1972.

"CHA to conduct anti-abortion campaign." HOSP PROG 54:82, March,

1973.

"Les chretiens devant l'avortement; d'apres le temoignage des Peres de l'Eglise," by B. Sesboue. ETUDES 339:263-282, August-September, 1973.

"Les chretiens face a l'avortement," by B. Ribes. ETUDES 339:405-423, October, 1973.

"Christian responsibilities and abortion law." CHRIST NURSE :23-24, April, 1973.

"Church to make antiabortion drive." NAT CATH REP 9:1 plus, February 9, 1973.

"Coalition aims at abortion ban," by W. Mitchell. NAT CATH REP 9:1 plus, June 22, 1973.

"Colorado Supreme Court applies Wade and Bolton." NEWSLETTER 6:5-6, May, 1973.

"Community abortion services. The role of organized medicine," by J. E. Hodgson. MINN MED 56:239-242, March, 1973.

"Concern grows over abortion conscience bills," by J. Filteau. NAT CATH REP 9:3-4, April 13, 1973.

"Confusion at the highest level," by J. R. Nelson. CHR CENT 90:254-255, February 28, 1973.

"Congress and state legislatures pass 'conscience clause' legislation," by G. E. Reed. HOSP PROGRESS 54:18 plus, July, 1973.

"Congress faces abortion battle," by R. Casey. NAT CATH REP 9:1 plus, August 3, 1973.

"Connecticut asks new look at abortion." NAT CATH REP 9:2, April 13, 1973.

"Conscience bill survives attack." NAT CATH REP 9:20, June 8, 1973.

"Constitutional law--abortion--right of privacy--state statutes permitting abortion only for life saving procedure on behalf of mother without regard for other interests violate due process clause of the fourteenth amendment." MEMPHIS ST U L REV 3:359, Spring, 1973.

"Constitutional law--abortion--state statute prohibiting abortion except to save life of mother unconstitutional." TUL L REV 47:1159-1167, June, 1973.

"Constitutional law--abortion--statute defining 'justifiable abortional act' not unconstitutional--constitution does not confer or require legal personality for unborn--whether law should accord legal personality is policy question to be determined by legislature." NOTRE DAME LAW 48:715, February, 1973.

"Constitutional law--minor's right to refuse court-ordered abortion." SUFFOLK U L REV 7:1157-1173, Summer, 1973.

"Constitutional law--a new constitutional right to an abortion." NC L REV 51:1573-1584, October, 1973.

"Constitutional law--New Jersey abortion statute unconstitutionally vague on its face; women prior to pregnancy have no standing to attack statute, but plaintiff-physicians have standing to assert deprivation of their women patients right of privacy." J URBAN L 50:505, February, 1973.

"Constitutional law--the right of privacy--Georgia's abortion law declared unconstitutional." GA SB J 10:153-162, August, 1973.

"Criminal law--Texas abortion statute--criminality exceptions limited to life-saving procedures on mother's behalf without regard to stage of pregnancy violates due process clause of fourteenth amendment protecting right to privacy." AM J CRIM L 2:231-243, Summer, 1973.

"Contraception, sterilization, and abortion legal interpretation of consent," by D. F. Kaltreider. MD STATE MED J 22:67, September, 1973.

"Contraceptive advice in connection with legal abortion," by K. Edstrom. LAKARTIDNINGEN 70:1404-1406, April 4, 1973.

"Council withholds paper on abortion. avoids feud." NAT CATH REP 9:3, March 16, 1973.

"La cour supreme des Etats-Unis et l'avortement libre," by M. Marcotte. RELATIONS 382:144-148, May, 1973.

"Court rejects new abortion hearing." NAT CATH REP 9:2, April 27, 1973.

"Court rulings on abortions." SOUTHERN HOSP 41:8, April, 1973.

"Criminal abortion in New Zealand," by W. A. P. Facer. HEALTH PEOPLE 6:18-20 plus, October, 1972.

"Culmination of the abortion reform movement--Roe v. Wade (93 Sup Ct 705) and Doe v. Bolton (93 Sup Ct 739)." U RICHMOND L REV 8:75-.87, Fall, 1973.

"Curran: theologians on bishops' side," by P. Blice. NAT CATH REP 9:18, March 2, 1973.

"Data for reform of French legislation on abortion," by R. Veylon. NOUV PRESSE MED 2:475-478, February 24, 1973.

"Death before birth." CHR TODAY 18:43, October 12, 1973.

"Death before birth (relates to U.S. Supreme Court decision)," by E. Palmer. BANNER p. 15, March 23, 1973.

"Death of pluralism? right to abortion." NAT R 25:193, February 16, 1973.

"Deaths after legal abortion," by C. Tietze, et al. LANCET 1:105, January 13, 1973.

"Declaration du Conseil permanent de l'Episcopat francais sur l'avortement." DOC CATH 70:676-679, July 15, 1973.

"Declaration des eveques belges sur l'avortement." DOC CATH 70:432-438, May, 1973.

"Declarations des eveques du Quebec." DOC CATH 70:382-384, April 15, 1973.

"Declaration des eveques Suisses sur l'avortement." DOC CATH 70: 381, April 15, 1973.

"Declaration de 10 000 medecins de France sur l'avortement." DOC CATH 70:629, July 1, 1973.

"Defending the right to abortion in New York (based on conference paper)," by D. Welch. INTERNAT SOCIALIST R 34:10-13, January, 1973.

"Defusing the abortion debate," by J. C. Evans. CHR CENT 90:117-118, January 31, 1973.

"The demographic effects of legal abortion on the Hungarian labor force (conference paper)," by B. Kapotsy. EUROPEAN DEMOGRAPH-IC INFO BUL 4:136-143, November 3, 1973.

"Department of Defense abortion 'guidelines' liberalized." U S MED 9:1 plus, February 1, 1973.

"Devaluation of human life (U.S. Supreme Court decision)," by H. Berry. GNB p. 3, April, 1973.

"Development concerning legal abortions under the present Danish abortion law," by V. Skalts. UGESKR LAEGER 134:2505-2507, November 20, 1972.

"Development in the incidence of abortions in recent years. Investigations and calculations concerning the incidence of criminal abortions prior to and after the Danish abortion law of 1970," by V. Sele, et al. UGESKR LAEGER 134:2493-2505, November 20, 1972.

"Discipline or liberalization of abortion? Proposal for the Fortuna law: its function and applicability in Italy," by S. Fossati. MINERVA GINECOL 25:364-370, June, 1973.

"Doctor's bona fides and the Abortion Act," by C. Lerry. LANCET 2:242, July, 1973.

"Dossier sur l'avortement, l'apport de nos lecteurs," by B. Ribes.
ETUDES 338:511-534, April, 1973.

"Dred Scott case of the twentieth century," by C. E. Rice. HOUSTON
L REV 10:1059-1086, July, 1973.

"The due process clause and the unborn child," by M. McKernan, Jr.
DIMENSION 5:25-34, Spring, 1973.

"Editorial: our unborn children," by H. Berger. PAEDIATR PAEDOL
8:333-335, 1973.

"The effect of legal abortion on the rate of septic abortion at a large
county hospital," by P. N. Seward, et al. AM J OBSTET GYNECOL
115:335-338, February 1, 1973.

"Effect of recent Supreme Court decision on Delaware's abortion law."
DEL MED J 45:141-145, May, 1973.

"The effects of legal abortion on legitimate and illegitimate birth
rates: the California experience (figures for the period 1966-72)," by
J. Sklar, et al. STUDIES IN FAMILY PLANNING 4:281-292, November, 1973.

"Emotional patterns related to delay in decision to seek legal abortion. A pilot study," by N. B. Kaltreider. CALIF MED 118:23-27, May,
1973.

"L'episcopat des Etats-Unis et la decision de la Cour Supreme sur
l'avortement," by J. Krol. DOC CATH 70:271-273, March 18, 1973.

"Even if legalized, abortion is a crime," by S. Luoni. OR 23:4-5,
June 7, 1973.

"Expectant mothers--women seeking abortions, a sociopsychiatric comparison in Umea?" by H. Holmberg, et al. LAKARTIDNINGEN 69:
5920-5924, December 6, 1972.

"Experience acquired in some foreign countries after liberalization of
voluntary abortion," by G. Le Lorier. BULL ACAD NATL MED 156:
677-682, June-October, 1972.

"Factors affecting gestational age at termination of pregnancy," by F. D. Johnstone, et al. LANCET 2:717-719, September 29, 1973.

"Facts about abortions." BR MED J 2:438, May 26, 1973.

"Father may not restrain unwed mother from obtaining an abortion: Florida." NEWSLETTER 6:3, June, 1973.

"Federal appeals court rules hospital may refuse abortions." HOSPITALS 47:96, July 1, 1973.

"Federal judge rules juveniles may not be denied abortions." NAT CATH REP 9:5, February 23, 1973.

"Federally funded hospitals not required to perform abortion." NEWSLETTER 6:3-4, July, 1973.

"Fetal rights and abortion laws," by S. F. O'Beirn. BR MED J 1:740, March 24, 1973.

"The fetus: whose property?" by A. Etzioni. COMM 98:493, September 21, 1973.

"Figures and fetuses," by R. J. Neuhaus; discussion. COMMONWEAL 97:358-359, January 19, 1973.

"For American Catholics: end of an illusion," by T. O'Connell. AMERICA 128:514-517, June 2, 1973.

"Forensic problems in abortion caused by gunshot," by G. Lins, et al. Z RECHTSMED 71:108-113, November 28, 1972.

"Forest and the trees: Roe v. Wade (93 Sup Ct 705) and its critics," by P. B. Heymann, et al. BU L REV 53:765-784, July, 1973.

"Former NAL member hits abortion statement." NAT CATH REP 9:3, February 16, 1973.

"480,000 legal abortions in 1971." HOSP PROGRESS 54:96b, March, 1973.

"France: the power to start and end a life." ECONOMIST 215:45, December 2, 1972.

"Free abortion in Denmark?" by M. Johansson. NORD MED 88:13, January, 1973.

"Free standing abortion clinics: a new phenomenon," by R. U. Hausknecht. BULL NY ACAD MED 49:985-991, November, 1973.

"The French Episcopate, firm and clear against revision of abortion law." OR 33:3 plus, August 16, 1973.

"French manifesto." TIME 101:76, February 19, 1973.

"French medicine: the abortion battle." MED WORLD NEWS 14:4-5, March 2, 1973.

"Frequency of criminal abortion. Elucidated in interviews of women hospitalized for abortion," by J. G. Lauritsen. UGESKR LAEGER 135:770-771, April 23, 1973.

"Future of abortion; alternatives," by C. Behrens. CURRENT 154:28-31, September, 1973.

"Gangrene of the uterus and its sequelae," by R. A. Jones. S AFR MED J 47:1327-1330, July 28, 1973.

"Georgia, Texas file appeals." NAT CATH REP 9:3, February 23, 1973.

"Gonorrhea in women prior to pregnancy interruption," by M. Mesko, et al. ZENTRALBL GYNAEKOL 94:169-172, February 5, 1972.

"Goodbye to the Judeo-Christian era in law," by R. Byrn. AMERICA 128:511-514, June 3, 1973.

"Government, providers urged to develop abortion program: John H. Knowles, MD." HOSPITALS 47:19, April 16, 1973.

"The health system and the Supreme Court decision. An affirmative response," by J. H. Knowles. FAMILY PLANN PERSPECT 5:113-116, Spring, 1973.

"High court lifts restrictions on abortions: Catholic hospitals will resist, others move cautiously." MOD HOSP 120:31-32, February, 1973.

"High court rates privacy over fetus," by R. Casey. NAT CATH REP 9:1 plus, February 2, 1973.

"High court's abortion decision raises problems for Rxmen." AM DRUGGIST MERCH 167:26, May 15, 1973.

"History and evolution of abortion laws in the United States," by D. L. Brown. SOUTHERN MED 61:11-14, August, 1973.

"Hospitals and the abortion ruling." NEWSLETTER 6:2, March, 1973.

"Illinois, Massachusetts enact conscience clause legislation." HOSPITALS 47:85, August 16, 1973.

"The impact of the Abortion Act," by P. D. John. BR J PSYCHIATRY 122:115-116, January, 1973.

"Impact of the liberalized abortion law in New York City on deaths associated with pregnancy: a two-year experience," by J. Pakter, et al. BULL NY ACAD MED 49:804-818, September, 1973.

"Impact of a permissive abortion statute on community health care," by J. J. Rovinsky. OBSTET GYNECOL 41:781-788, May, 1973.

"In defense of liberty: a look at the abortion decisions." GEO L J 61:1559-1575, July, 1973.

"In defense of the unborn," by V. Gager. MARRIAGE 55:38-45, June, 1973.

"In defense of the unborn," by N. Walsh. STUDIES 61:303-314, Winter, 1972.

"The induced abortion and the gynecologist," by Z. Polishok. HAREFUAH 83:264-265, September 15, 1972.

"Induction of abortion by intravenous and intra-uterine administration of prostaglandin F2," by A. A. Haspels, et al. J REPROD MED

9:442-447, December, 1972.

"Is 'liberalized' abortion lawful?" by L. L. McNamara. SOUTHERN MED 61:27-31, August, 1973.

"Is the unborn child a person at law?" by J. P. Wadsworth. QUIS CUSTODIET 36:88-92, 1972.

"Italian abortion law faces opposition." NAT CATH REP 9:5, February 9, 1973. .

"Jane Roe and Mary Doe; abortion ruling." NATION 216:165, February 5, 1973.

"Judicial power and public conscience: symposium," by J. Kennedy, et al. SIGN 52:26-27, March, 1973.

"Judicial power and the right to life," by J. Noonan. TABLET 227: 323-326, April 7, 1973.

"Krol, Cooke, and McHugh denounce Supreme Court abortion ruling." HOSP PROGRESS 54:22a-b, February, 1973.

"Landmark abortion decisions: justifiable termination or miscarriage of justice?--proposals for legislative response." PACIFIC L J 4:821-860, July, 1973.

"Landmark decision; three Texas women who fought the abortion issue," by J. N. Bell. GOOD H 176:77-79 plus, June, 1973.

"Latent morbidity after abortion," by A. Hordern. BR MED J 2:368, May 12, 1973.

"Law of consent and abortion in California," by A. H. Bernstein. HOSPITALS 47:132 plus, February 1, 1973.

"The law on abortion and the defense of life; a declaration of the Belgian bishops." OR 24:9, June 14, 1973.

"Law on abortion and sterilization, 1973," by G. H. Roux. S AFR MED J 47:596, April 14, 1973.

"Law to protect the unborn; New Orleans, Louisiana." OR 30:3, July 26, 1973.

"Legal abortion and the attitude of hospital staff," by L. Jacobsson, et al. LAKARTIDNINGEN 70:273-275, January 24, 1973.

"Legal abortion as a positive mental health measure in family planning," by Z. M. Lebensohn. COMPR PSYCHIATRY 14:95-98, March-April, 1973.

"Legal abortion. An assessment following the Danish abortion law of 1.IV.1970," by E. Gregersen. UGESKR LAEGER 135:417-420, February 19, 1973.

"Legal abortion by extra-amniotic instillation of Rivanol in combination with rubber catheter insertion into the uterus after the twelfth week of pregnancy," by C. A. Ingemanson. AM J OBSTET GYNECOL 115: 211-215, January 15, 1973.

"Legal abortion in a day-ward," by E. Gregersen. UGESKR LAEGER 135:429-431, February 19, 1973.

"Legal abortion 1970-1971--the New York City experience," by D. Harris, et al. AMER J PUBLIC HEALTH 63:409-418, May, 1973.

"Legal abortion, the South Australian experience." MED J AUST 1:821-823, April 28, 1973.

"Legal counsel analyzes abortion ruling," by F. Speaker. PA MED 76: 21-22, April, 1973.

"Legal interruption of pregnancy by the aspiration method and the pericervical block with Gynesthesin," by M. Beric. SCHWEIZ Z GYNAE-KOL GEBURTSHILFE 3:151-159, 1972.

"Letter: interruption of pregnancy because of embryonal damage," by H. J. Rieger. DTSCH MED WOCHENSCHR 98:1782, September 21, 1973.

"Lib and let live," by N. Roberts. GUARDIAN p. 12, February 15, 1973.

"Liberal abortion laws are worldwide trend," by M. Ostro. NAT CATH REP·10:3-4, November 9, 1973.

"Liberalized abortion and birth rates changes in Baltimore," by W. Oppel, et al. AM J PUBLIC HEALTH 63:405-408, May, 1973.

"Lobbying for the unborn." CHR TODAY 17:44, July 20, 1973.

"Locus of control, latitude of acceptance and attitudes toward abortion," by B. Corenblum. PSYCHOL REP 32:753-754, June, 1973.

"Making abortion an accepted right of women," by P. C. Newman. MACLEAN'S 86:3, February, 1973.

"Marjory Mecklenburg is for life; pro-life movement," by J. Mahowald. C DGST 37:39-44, June, 1973.

"Maryland's 'hospital only' provision in abortion law declared unconstitutional." HOSPITALS 47:17, September 1, 1973.

"Medical abortion in South Australia. A critical assessment of early complications," by J. M. Miller. MED J AUST 1:825-830, April 28, 1973.

"The medical profession and the 1967 Abortion Act in Britain," by S. J. Macintyre. SOC SCI MED 7:121-134, February, 1973.

"Medical termination of pregnancy Act, 1971 (34 of 1971)." INDIAN J PUBLIC HEALTH 16:37-38, April, 1972.

"Medicolegal forum," by D. H. Mills. J AM OSTEOPATH ASSOC 72: 957-958, June, 1973.

"Minor cannot be compelled to have abortion: Maryland." NEWSLETTER 6:5, January, 1973.

"Misplaced allegiance," by E. Glynn. AMERICA 128:177, March 3, 1973.

"Model 'conscience clause' legislation proposed by Executive Committee of Catholic Hospital Association Board." HOSP PROGRESS 54:20, April, 1973.

"Most insurers are paying for abortions: legality still the key question." AMER MED NEWS 16:7, March 26, 1973.

"NAL applauds court for abortion ruling," by D. Gibeau. NAT CATH REP 9:3, February 9, 1973.

"National Conference of Catholic Bishops Administrative Committee rejects abortion ruling." HOSP PROGRESS 54:83 plus, March, 1973.

"The new abortion law--some salient features," by I. B. Rao. J INDIAN MED ASSOC 59:332-336, October 16, 1972.

"The new abortion ruling," by H. Creighton. SUPERV NURSE 4:8 plus, July, 1973.

"A new cause: many Americans join move to ban abortion; legislators take note," by J. A. Tannenbaum. WALL ST J 182:1 plus, August 2, 1973.

"The new Georgia abortion law," by J. W. Huff. J MED ASSOC GA 62: 241-242, June, 1973.

"New law gives rights to fetus." NAT CATH REP 9:1, March 23, 1973.

"Nixon signs hospital law." NAT CATH REP 9:15, July 6, 1973.

"Now that abortion is legal; unforeseen emotions that follow," by B. G. Harrison. MC CALLS 101:64 plus, November, 1973.

"Nursing home abortions may be permitted under Supreme Court rulings." MOD NURSING HOME 30:72-73, March, 1973.

"Objections aim at wrong target," by W. VanderMarck. NAT CATH REP 9:11, March 16, 1973.

"Of many things; constitutional right and abortion legislation," by C. M. Whelan. AMERICA 128:inside cover, February 10, 1973.

"Offers pro-life amendment." NAT CATH REP 9:18, February 9, 1973.

"On the incidence of illegal abortion (Great Britain); with a reply to

Dr. W. H. James," by C. B. Goodhart. POPULATION STUDIES 27: 207-233, July, 1973.

"On the moral and legal status of abortion," by M. A. Warren. THE MONIST 57:43-61, January, 1973.

"On the question of the liberalization of abortion," by M. Mall-Haefeli. SCHWEIZ Z GYNAEKOL GEBURTSHILFE 3:69-91, 1972.

"100,000 sign OSV pro-life petition." OSV 62:1 plus, May 20, 1973.

"Only a constitutional amendment can stop the flood of abortions," by J. Noonan, Jr. NAT CATH REP 9:9, February 16, 1973.

"Operation on demand?" by C. O. Rice. MINN MED 56:412, May, 1973.

"OR nurses face decision in abortion procedures," by E. S. Schrader. AORN J 17:13-14 plus, May, 1973.

"Outcome of pregnancy in women denied legal abortion in several sub-regions of the Croatian republic," by D. Stampar. NAR ZDRAV 28: 205-211, June, 1972.

"Pastoral guidelines for the Catholic hospitals and health care personnel in the United States." OR 25:11-12, June 21, 1973.

"Pastoral message on abortion." C MIND 71:7-9, September, 1973.

"A physician's right to practice." J LA STATE MED SOC 125:288-290, August, 1973.

"Pleasure without trouble," by A. Volg. THER GGW 111:1352-1354 passim, September, 1972.

"Politicians' and physicians' responsibility in abortion matters," by H. Lefevre. UGESKR LAEGER 135:723-726, March 26, 1973.

"Politics of abortion," by S. Alexander. READ DIGEST 102:69-71, March, 1973.

"Poll finds physicians endorse Supreme Court abortion rule."

PSYCHIAT NEWS 8:10 plus, June 20, 1973.

"Poor legislative response to Walsingham v. State (Fla) 250 S 2d 857 ," by J. M. Ellis. FLA B J 47:18, January, 1973.

"Population-political aspects of induced abortion," by D. Klessen, et al. Z AERZTL FORTBILD 67:57-63, January 15, 1973.

"Population, rhythm, contraception and abortion policy questions," by A. Hellegers. LINACRE 40:91-96, May, 1973.

"Post-abortum cervical spondylodiscitis," by A. J. Chaumont, et al. MED LEG DOMM CORPOR 5:155-156, April-June, 1972.

"Pour une reforme da la legislation francaise relative a l'avortement," by D. Albe-Fessard, et al. ETUDES 338:55-84, January, 1973.

"Pregnancy counseling and the request for abortion: tentative suggestions for Catholic Charities agencies," by E. Ryle. C CHAR 57:8-15, June, 1973.

"1970-1972. A preliminary report," by C. Tietze, et al. JAMA 225:507-509, July 30, 1973.

"A private matter." ECONOMIST 246:43, 45, January 27, 1973.

"The problem of legal pregnancy interruption," by C. Zwahr. ZENTRALBL GYNAEKOL 94:156-163, February 5, 1972.

"Le problem de l'avortement; lettre pastorale des eveques allemands." DOC CATH 70:626-629, July 1, 1973.

"The pro-life movement at the crossroads," by M. Lawrence. TRIUMPH 8:11-15, June, 1973.

"Protestant Theologians debate court ruling on abortion," by E. Wright. CH HER p. 12, March 22, 1973.

"Psychiatric sequelae to legal abortion in South Australia," by F. Weston. MED J AUST 1:350-354, February 17, 1973.

"Psychological factors in mid-trimester abortion," by N. B. Kaltreider. PSYCHIATRY MED 4:129-134, Spring, 1973.

"Public Policy on Abortion: John H. Knowles, M. D. urges affirmative response...to Supreme Court decision (9329/373) (News release and Speech)." PLANN PARENTHOOD FED AM :1-4, March 14, 1973.

"Quelques reflexions sur le droit a l'avortement dans le monde anglo-saxon," by M. Rivet. C DE D 13:591-597, 1972.

"A question of credibility," by L. R. McEvoy. POSTGRAD MED 54:33, October, 1973.

"RANF policy on abortion law." RANF REV 4:3, January, 1973.

"Raw judicial power," by J. T. Noonan, Jr. NAT R 25:260-264, March 2, 1973.

"Reaction to abortion ruling: physicians urged to await legal guidelines." AMER MED NEWS 16:3, February 12, 1973.

"Reactions against the bill for the liberalization of abortion; in Germany.' OR 22:10, May 31, 1973.

"Recent United States court decisions concerning abortion," by M. A. Olea. AN R ACAD NACL MED 90:327-335, 1973.

"Reflections on the Supreme Court's ruling on abortion," by Haines, et al. UC HER p. 59, April, 1973.

"Regulating abortions," by S. Shapiro. N ENGL J MED 288:1027-1028, May 10, 1973.

"Rehnquist: ruling confuses privacy," by W. Rehnquist. NAT CATH REP 9:14, February 2, 1973.

"Remarks on abortion." SEM HOP PARIS 49:123-127, April 8, 1973.

"Report of the Swedish Abortion Committee," by C. Tietze. STUD FAM PLANN 3:28, February, 1972.

"Responsible and demanding part of the work of National Committees: decisions on legal abortion," by B. Stipal. CESK ZDRAV 21:353-356, September, 1973.

"The right to life debate; excerpt from What a modern Catholic believes about the right to life," by R. Westley. CRITIC 31:50-59, July-August, 1973.

"The right to life vs the right to privacy," by C. Dozier. OSV 61:1 plus, April 8, 1973.

"The right to privacy," by J. Connery. LINACRE 40:138-143, May, 1973.

"Right to refuse to perform abortions remains intact: American Hospital Association." AMER MED NEWS 16:3, February 12, 1973.

" 'Right to' what? Editorial," by D. Anderson. CHATELAINE 46:1, June, 1973.

"Rights affecting human reproduction," by A. W. Diddle. OBSTET GYNECOL 41:789-794, May, 1973.

"Rights and deaths," by J. J. Thomson. PHILOSOPHY & PUBLIC AFFAIRS 2:146-160, Winter, 1973.

"The rights and wrongs of abortion: a reply to Judith Thomson." PHILOSOPHY & PUBLIC AFFAIRS 2:117-146, Winter, 1973.

"Rights before birth," by L. E. Rozovsky. CAN HOSP 50:17-18, March, 1973.

"The rights of the unborn," by T. Glenister. TABLET 227:557-559, June 16, 1973; Reply 227:603, June 30, 1973.

"The rights to abortion; expansion of the privacy through the fourteenth amendment," by D. Goldenberg. C LAWYER 19:36-57, Winter, 1973.

"Roe v. Wade - the abortion case," by B. White. C MIND 71:11-12, April, 1973.

"Roe vs. Wade: the new class warfare," by P. Riga. PRIEST 29:13-16 plus, September, 1973.

"Roe v. Wade (93 Sup Ct 705)--the abortion decision--an analysis and its implications." SAN DIEGO L REV 10:844-856, June, 1973.

"Roe v. Wade (93 Sup Ct 705) and Doe v. Bolton (93 Sup Ct 739): compelling state interest test in substantive due process." WASH & LEE L REV 30:628-646, Fall, 1973.

"Le Saint-Siege et l'avortement," by S. Luoni. DOC CATH 70:574-575, June 17, 1973.

"Scottish abortion statistics--1971." HEALTH BULL 31:39-50, January, 1973.

"Senate OKs fetal experiments ban." NAT CATH REP 9:20, September 28, 1973.

"Social hygiene and social politics," by D. Klessen, et al. Z AERZTL FORTBILD 66:1148-1150, November 15, 1972.

"Social indications for interruption of pregnancy," by W. Kokoszka, et al. POL TYG LEK 28:139-140, January 22, 1973.

"Sociologist calls U. S. abortion law 'worst law in world'." HOSP PROGRESS 54:21-22, April, 1973.

"Somatic complications after legal abortion by vacuum aspiration combined with oxytocin infusion," by E. D. Johansson, et al. LAKAR-TIDNINGEN 69:6045-6048, December 13, 1972.

"Some abortions may lead to murder charges." NAT CATH REP 9:3, April 3, 1973.

"Some additional arguments against abortion," by O. Bennett. HPR 73:50-53, January, 1973.

"Some aspects of implementation of legal abortion," by A. Chatterjee. J INDIAN MED ASSOC 59:342-343, October 16, 1972.

"La solution du voisin," by L. Martin. LE MACLEAN :18-19, 38 plus, February, 1973.

"State legislation can lessen impact of Court's abortion decision," by R. Stratton. HOSP PROG 54:8-9 plus, October, 1973.

"Statements of national conference of Catholic bishops; pastoral message." C LAWYER 19:29-35, Winter, 1973.

"Stunning approval for abortion; decision blow by blow." TIME 101: 50-51, February 5, 1973.

"Supreme Court abortion decisions," by W. A. Regan. HOSP PROGRESS 54:12 plus, April, 1973.

"Supreme Court abortion opinions," by J. H. Hedgepeth. HOSP MED STAFF 2:10-17, April, 1973; 33-39, May, 1973; 44-48, June, 1973.

"The Supreme Court and legitimate state interest (commenting on the U.S. Supreme Court's decision in Roe v. Wade, as it pertains to the right of a state to prohibit abortion), by Robert G. Stewart; The abortion decision, by John C. Robbins." RIPON FORUM 9:8-11, April, 1973.

"The Supreme Court decision on abortion," by R. E. Hall. AM J OBSTET GYNECOL 116:1-8, May 1, 1973.

"Supreme Court eases rules on abortion." U S NEWS 74:36, February 5, 1973.

"Supreme Court issues broad pronouncements on constitutionality of state abortion laws." HOSPITALS 47:108, February 16, 1973.

"Supreme Court on abortion." AMERICA 128:81, February 3, 1973.

"The Supreme Court on abortion: a dissenting opinion," by P. Conley, et al. C LAWYER 19:19-28, Winter, 1973; also in R REL 32:473-481, May, 1973.

"Supreme Court: right of privacy includes abortion; excerpts from abortion decision." NAT CATH REP 9:8 plus, February 2, 1973.

"Supreme Court refuses abortion review." AMER MED NEWS 16:1, March 5, 1973.

"Tennessee's new abortion law," by H. Williams. J TENN MED ASSOC 66:651-652, June, 1973.

"Termination of pregnancy, Sydney, 1972," by D. Pfanner, et al. MED J AUST 1:710-711, April 7, 1973.

"Three abortion amendments in Congress." NAT CATH REP 9:16, June 22, 1973.

"Toward a sound moral policy on abortion," by P. Coffey. NEW SCHOL 47:105-112, Winter, 1973.

"Trends in legalized abortion in South Australia," by A. F. Connon. MED J AUST 1:231-234, February 3, 1973.

"The tuskegee syphilis study," by W. J. Curran. N ENGL J MED 289: 730-731, October 4, 1973.

"The two separate issues in the abortion debate," by M. Dobbin. MED J AUST 1:1165-1166, June 9, 1973.

"Two years experience in New York City with the liberalized abortion law--progress and problems," by J. Pakter, et al. AM J PUBLIC HEALTH 63:524-535, June, 1973.

"Two years' experience with a liberal abortion law: its impact on fertility trends in New York City, 1970-1972," by C. Tietze. FAMILY PLANNING PERSPECTIVES 5:36-41, Winter, 1973.

"U. S. bishops oppose Supreme Court decision." OR 7:6-7, February 15, 1973.

"U. S. bishops' pastoral on abortion." OSV 61:4, March 11, 1973.

"U. S. Supreme Court lifts curbs on abortion." AMER MED NEWS 16:1 plus, January 29, 1973.

"U. S. Supreme Court on abortion." SOC JUST 65:359 plus, February,

1973.

"U. S. Supreme Court on abortion," by C. B. Goodhart. LANCET 1:429,
February 24, 1973; also in LANCET 1:663, March 24, 1973.

"U. S. Supreme Court on abortion," by M. Simms. LANCET 1:544, March
10, 1973; also in LANCET 1:721, March 31, 1973.

"U. S. Supreme Court on abortion. Roe v. Wade, 41 U.S.L.W. 4213(1973)."
CONN MED 37:279-289, June, 1973.

"United States' Cardinals protest court's decision; abortion." OR 5:5,
February 1, 1973.

"United States Supreme Court and abortion. 1.," by E. J. Holman. JAMA
225:215-216, July 9, 1973.

--3.," by E. J. Holman. JAMA 225:447-448, July, 1973.

"United States Supreme Court and abortion," by E. J. Holman. J AMER
MED ASS 225:215-216, July 9, 1973; 343-344, July 16, 1973; 447-448,
July 23, 1973.

"Voluntary abortion. Its social and biological consequences," by J.
Botella Llusia. AN R ACAD NACL MED 90:285-295, 1973.

"Wages of crying wolf: a comment on Roe v. Wade (93 Sup Ct 705)," by
J. H. Ely. YALE L J 82:920, April, 1973.

"Wanderer Forum backs amendment," by D. Effenberger. NAT CATH
REP 9:17, July 20, 1973.

"What about me?" by P. W. Lang. J CAN BA 4:27, January, 1973.

"What chance do prolife amendments have?" by R. Shaw. COLUMBIA
53:10, October, 1973.

"What liberal abortion has done to Hungary," by H. Szablya. OSV 61:1
plus, September 23, 1973.

"What will abortion regulations be if law is reformed? Here are clues," by J. W. Eliot. MICH MED 71:959-962, November, 1972.

"What you should know about abortion," by S. A. Kaufman. PARENTS MAG 48:62-64, April, 1973.

"White: beyond the Constitution," by B. White. NAT CATH REP 9:14, February 2, 1973.

"Why I favor liberalized abortion," by A. F. Guttmacher. READ DIGEST 103:143-147, November, 1973.

"Why I reversed my stand on laissez-faire abortion," by C. E. Lincoln. CHR CENT 90:477-479, April 25, 1973.

"Why they didn't kill my son," by R. Scheiber. OSV 61:7, February 11, 1973.

"Why the topic legalized abortion?" NURSING 45:22-23, January-February, 1973.

LISTERIOSIS
"Listeriosis. Occurrence in spontaneous interruptions of pregnancy," by J. R. Giraud, et al. NOUV PRESSE MED 2:215-218, January 27, 1973.

"Role of listeriosis in abortions, in utero fetal deaths and premature labor," by J. R. Giraud, et al. BULL FED SOC GYNECOL OBSTET LANG FR 23:593-594, November-December, 1971.

MALE ATTITUDES
see: Sociology and Behavior

MARCH OF DIMES
"The March of Dimes and abortion," by B. Williams. HPR 74:48-58, October, 1973.

MENSTRUATION
see: Complications
Induced Abortion

MENTALLY RETARDED
"Sterilization and therapeutic abortion counselling for the mentally retarded," by C. W. Smiley. CURR THER RES 15:78-81, February, 1973.

MICROBIOLOGY
see also: Research

"Multiple sclerosis and zoonoses. Importance of the role of the bovine abortion virus (pararickettsia X-14) in the etiopathogenesis of multiple sclerosis," by P. Le Gac. C R ACAD SCI 275:147-148, July 3, 1972.

"San Miguel sea lion virus isolation, preliminary characterization and relationship to vesicular exanthema of swine virus," by A. W. Smith, et al. NATURE 244:108-110, July 13, 1973.

MISCARRIAGES
"Characteristics of the functional state of the uterus in miscarriage in women with genital underdevelopment," by N. K. Moskvitina, et al. VOPR OKHR MATERIN DET 18:64-68, June, 1973.

MORBIDITY
see: Complications

MORTALITY
see also: Complications
　　　　　 Sepsis
　　　　　 Septic Abortion and Septic Shock

"Deaths after legal abortion," by C. Tietze, et al. LANCET 1:105, January 13, 1973.

"Impact of the liberalized abortion law in New York City on deaths associated with pregnancy: a two-year experience," by J. Pakter, et al. BULL N Y ACAD MED 49:804-818, September, 1973.

"Laboratory findings from ovine abortion and perinatal mortality," by J. W. Plant, et al. AUST VET J 48:558-561, October, 1972.

"Listeria as a cause of abortion and neonatal mortality in sheep," by D. W. Broadbent. AUST VET J 48:391-394, July, 1972.

"Maternal death due to DIC after saline abortion," by S. R. Lemkin, et al. OBSTET GYNECOL 42:233-235, August, 1973.

"Maternal deaths in Australia compared with England and Wales in 1964-1966," by J. R. Neil. MED J AUST 59-1:682-685, 1972.

"The mortality of human XO embryos," by B. Santesson, et al. J REPROD FERTIL 34:51-55, July, 1973.

"Mortality with legal abortion in New York City, 1970-1972: a preliminary report," by C. Tietze, et al. J AMER MED ASS 225:507-509, July 30, 1973.

"Prenatal mortality in Iowa, 1963," by M. Mackeprang, et al. J IOWA MED SOC 63:16-18, January, 1973.

"Prevention of mortality from abortions," by G. D. Safronenko, et al. PEDIATR AKUSH GINEKOL 5:57-59, October, 1972.

MYCOPLASMA
"Cases of mycoplasma abortion in swine," by V. Jelev, et al. ZENTRALBL VETERINAERMED 19:588-597, August, 1972.

NAL
see: Laws and Legislation

NCCB
"NCCB backs antiabortion step." NAT CATH REP 9:20, September 28, 1973.

NURSING HOMES
"Nursing home abortions may be permitted under Supreme Court rulings." MOD NURSING HOME 30:72-73, March, 1973.

NURSES
"Colorado Nurses' Association statement on abortion." COLO NURSE 73:10, February, 1973.

"The nurse and the abortion patient," by B. Clancy. NURS CLIN NORTH AM 8:469-478, September, 1973.

"A nurse's biography of an abortion," by S. Kilby-Kelberg, et al. U S CATH 38:19-21, February, 1973.

"Nurses' rights regarding abortion: Association of Operating Room Nurses policy statement." AORN J 17:191, April, 1973.

"Nursing care in placenta previa and abruptio placentae," by R. C. Kilker, et al. NURS CLIN NORTH AM 8:479-487, September, 1973.

"OR nurses face decision in abortion procedures," by E. S. Schrader. AORN J 17:13-16, May, 1973.

"Professional nursing and the abortion decisions." REGAN REP NURS LAW 13:1, February, 1973.

OBSTETRICS
"Attitudes of obstetric and gynecologic residents toward abortion," by P. R. Mascovich, et al. CALIF MED 119:29-34, August, 1973.

"Clinical application of prostaglandin in obstetrics," by M. I. T'ang CHIN MED J 9:563-569, 1973.

"Clinical evaluation of Vibravenous (doxicillin) preparation in obstetrics and gynecology," by Z. Sternadel, et al. GINEKOL POL 44:189-191, February, 1973.

"Use of Alupent in obstetrics. Our personal experiences," by G. Di Terlizzi. MINERVA GINECOL 25:225-245, April, 1973.

"Value of Salbutamol in obstetrics," by P. Dellenbach, et al. THERA-PEUTIQUE 48:671-675, December, 1972.

OUTPATIENT ABORTION
see: Hospitals and Abortion

OXYTOCIN
"Extra-amniotic prostaglandin-oxytocin abortion: comparison with the intra-amniotic method," by M. Seppala, et al. PROSTAGLANDINS 3:17-28, 1973.

"Midtrimester abortion produced by intra-amniotic prostaglandin F2a augmented with intravenous oxytocin," by N. Kochenour, et al. AM J OBSTET GYNECOL 114:516-519, 1972.

"Midtrimester abortion using prostaglandin F2alpha, oxytocin, and laminaria," by T. Engel, et al. FERTIL STERIL 24:565-568, August, 1973.

"Mid-trimester abortion with intraamniotic saline and intravenous oxytocin," by C. A. Ballard, et al. OBSTET GYNECOL 41:447-450, 1973.

"Oxytocin administration in mid-trimester saline abortions," by N. H. Lauersen, et al. AM J OBSTET GYNECOL 115:420-430, 1973.

"Oxytocin augmentation of saline abortion," by F. W. Hanson, et al. OBSTET GYNECOL 41:608-610, April, 1973.

"Prostaglandin-oxytocin abortion: a clinical trial on intra-amniotic prostaglandin F2a in combination with intravenous oxytocin," by M. Seppala, et al. PROSTAGLANDINS 2:311-319, 1972.

"Saline instillation with oxytocin administration in midtrimester abortion," by L. I. Mann, et al. OBSTET GYNECOL 41:748-752, May, 1973.

"Somatic complications after legal abortion by vacuum aspiration combined with oxytocin infusion," by E. D. Johansson, et al. LAKARTIDNINGEN 69:6045-6048, December 13, 1972.

"Therapeutic abortion employing the synergistic action of extra-amniotic prostaglandin E 2 and an intravenous infusion of oxytocin," by G. A. Morewood. J OBSTET GYNAECOL BR COMMONW 80:473-475, May, 1973.

PARAMEDICS
"The paramedic abortionist," by R. F. Mattingly. OBSTET GYNECOL 41:929-930, June, 1973.

PATIENT COUNSELING
see: Sociology and Behavior

PHARMACISTS
"High court's abortion decision raises problems for Rxmen." AM
DRUGGIST MERCH 167:26, May 15, 1973.

PHYSICIANS
see also: Psychology
Sociology and Behavior

"Abortion on request: the physician's view," by A. F. Guttmacher.
AM BIOL TEACH 34:514-517, December, 1972; Reply with rejoinder
by P. R. Gastonguay. 35:353-355, September, 1973.

"Doctor blames fathers for abortion," by J. McCann. NAT CATH REP
9:1-2, March, 1973.

"Doctor's bona fides and the Abortion Act," by C. Lerry. LANCET
2:212, July, 1973.

"Guidelines for physician performance of induced abortions." MARY-
LAND STATE MED J 22:68, September, 1973.

"MED-CHI standards for outpatient facilities for abortion service." MD
STATE MED J 22:69-70, September, 1973.

"The medical profession and the 1967 Abortion Act in Britain," by S. J.
Macintyre. SOC SCI MED 7:121-134, February, 1973.

"New York State physicians and the social context of abortion," by S.
Wassertheil-Smoller, et al. AM J PUBLIC HEALTH 63:144-149, 1973.

"The physician and family planning," by A. Alvarez-Bravo. GAC MED
MEX 105:498-507, May, 1973.

"A physician looks at the abortion problem," by J. Finn. DIMENSION
5:14-24, Spring, 1973.

"Physician's right to practice." LOUISIANA STATE MED SOC 125:
288-290, August, 1973.

"Politicians' and physicians' responsibility in abortion matters," by
H. Lefevre. UGESKR LAEGER 135:723-726, March 26, 1973.

"Poll finds physicians endorse Supreme Court abortion rule."
PSYCHIAT NEWS 8:10 plus, June 20, 1973.

"Problem of pregnancy interruption as a question for the physician,"
by R. Reimann-Hunziker. PRAXIS 62:397-399, March 27, 1973.

"Reaction to abortion ruling: physicians urged to await legal guidelines." AMER MED NEWS 16:3, February 12, 1973.

"Says no doctor or hospital can be forced to perform abortion: New
Jersey's Attorney General." HOSP PROGRESS 54:96d, March, 1973.

"Therapeutic termination of pregnancy in private practice," by J. M.
Miller. MED J AUST 1:831-834, April 28, 1973.

POPULATION
see *also:* Demography

"Abortion and population," by D. Munday. HEALTH SOC SERV J 83:
13-14, March 10, 1973.

"Population-political aspects of induced abortion," by D. Klessen, et
al. Z AERZTL FORTBILD 67:57-63, January 15, 1973.

"Population, rhythm, contraception and abortion policy questions," by
A. Hellegers. LINACRE 40:91-96, May, 1973.

PREGNANCY INTERRUPTION
see: Induced Abortion

PROGESTERONE
"Evaluation of the prognosis of threatened abortion from the peripheral
plasma levels of progesterone, estradiol, and human chorionic gonadotropin," by K. G. Nygren, et al. AM J OBSTET GYNECOL 116:
916-922, August 1, 1973.

"Maternal plasma oestrogen and progesterone levels during therapeutic
abortion induced by intra-amniotic injection of prostaglandin F 2,"
by E. M. Symonds, et al. J OBSTET GYNAECOL BR COMMONW 79:
976-980, November, 1972.

PROGESTERONE

"Plasma progesterone and prostaglandin F2 levels during the insertion of prostaglandin F2 vaginal tablet," by T. Sato, et al. PROSTA-GLANDINS 4:107-113, July, 1973.

"Plasma progesterone changes in abortion induced by hypertonic saline in the second trimester of pregnancy," by A. J. Tyack, et al. J OBSTET GYNAECOL BR COMMONW 80:548-552, June, 1973.

"Termination of early pregnancy in rats after ovariectomy is due to immediate collapse of the progesterone-dependent decidua," by R. Deanesly. J REPROD FERTIL 35:183-186, October, 1973.

PROSTAGLANDINS
"Abortifacient efficacy of intravaginal prostaglandin F2a," by A. C. Wentz, et al. AM J OBSTET GYNECOL 115:27-32, 1973.

"Abortion and coagulation by prostaglandin. Intra-amniotic dinoprost tromethamine effect on the coagulation and fibrinolytic systems," by W. R. Bell, et al. JAMA 225:1082-1084, August 27, 1973.

"Abortion of early pregnancy by the intravaginal administration of prostaglandin F2alpha," by R. J. Bolognese, et al. AM J OBSTET GYNECOL 117:246-250, September 15, 1973.

"Action of prostaglandin F2a on the corpus luteum of the gestating rat," by H. Tuchmann-Duplessis, et al. C R HEBD SEANCES ACAD SCI SER D SCI NAT 275:2033-2035, 1972.

"Analysis of prostaglandin F2a and metabolites in blood during constant intravenous infusion of prostaglandin F2a in the human female," by F. Beguin, et al. ACTA PHYSIOL SCAND 86:430-432, 1972.

"Brook Lodge symposium on prostaglandins. Moderator's summary," by M. P. Embrey. J REPROD MED 9:464-465, December, 1972.

"Cardiovascular and respiratory responses to intravenous infusion of prostaglandin F2a in the pregnant woman," by J. I. Fishburne, Jr., et al. AM J OBSTET GYNECOL 114:765-772, 1972.

"Chronperiodicity in the response to the intra-amniotic injection of prostaglandin F 2 in the human," by I. D. Smith, et al. NATURE

241:279-280, January 26, 1973.

"Clinical application of prostaglandin F2a (P.G.F2a) as a drug which can produce an interruption of pregnancy during the 1st trimester," by J. H. Luigies. NED TIJDSCHR GENEESKD 116:2368-2369, December 23, 1972.

"Clinical application of prostaglandin in obstetrics," by M. I. T'ang. CHIN MED J 9:563-569, 1973.

"Coagulation changes during termination of pregnancy by prostaglandins and by vacuum aspiration," by M. H. Badraoul, et al. BR MED J 1:19-21, January 6, 1973.

"Combination of prostaglandin F2 and paracervical block in the missed abortion and intrauterine fetal death," by E. J. Hickl, et al. KLIN WOCHENSCHR 51:140-141, February 1, 1973.

"Continuous extra-amniotic prostaglandin E2 for therapeutic termination and the effectiveness of various infusion rates and dosages," by A. Midwinter, et al. J OBSTET GYNAECOL BR COMMONW 80:371-373, April, 1973.

"Continuous intrauterine infusion of prostaglandin E2 for termination of pregnancy," by A. Midwinter, et al. J OBSTET GYNAECOL BR COMMONW 79:807-809, September, 1972.

"Continuous prostaglandin-F2 infusion for middle-trimester abortion," by N. H. Lauersen, et al. LANCET 1:1195, May 26, 1973.

"The current status of the use of prostaglandins in induced abortion," AM J PUBLIC HEALTH 63:189-190, 1973.

" 'Delayed menstruation' induced by prostaglandin in pregnant patients," by P. Mocsary, et al. LANCET 2:683, September 22, 1973.

"Disappearance of prostaglandin F2a from human amniotic fluid after intraamniotic injection," by C. Pace-Asciak, et al. PROSTAGLANDINS 1:469-477, 1972.

"Effect of infused prostaglandin F2 on hormonal levels during early pregnancy," by A. C. Wentz, et al. AM J OBSTET GYNECOL 114: 908-913, December 1, 1972.

"The effect of prostaglandin F2a and prostaglandin E2 upon luteal function and ovulation in the guinea-pig," by F. R. Blatchley, et al. J ENDOCRINOL 53:493-501, 1972.

"Effect of prostaglandin F2a upon the corpus luteum of pregnant rats," by H. Tuchmann-Duplessis, et al. C R ACAD SCI 275:2033-2035, October 30, 1972.

"The effects of intravenous infusion of graded doses of prostaglandins F 2 and E 2 on lung resistance in patients undergoing termination of pregnancy," by A. P. Smith. CLIN SCI 44:17-25, January, 1973.

"The efficacy and acceptability of the 'prostaglandin impact' in inducing complete abortion during the second week after the missed menstrual period," by A. I. Csapo, et al. PROSTAGLANDINS 3:125-139, 1973.

"The evaluation of intra-amniotic prostaglandin F 2 in the management of early midtrimester pregnancy termination," by D. C. Leslie, et al. J REPROD MED 9:453-455, December, 1972.

"Experience with intra-amniotic prostaglandin F2 alpha for abortion," by A. C. Wentz, et al. AM J OBSTET GYNECOL 117:513-521, October 15, 1973.

"Extra-amniotic prostaglandin-oxytocin abortion: comparison with the intra-amniotic method," by M. Seppala, et al. PROSTAGLANDINS 3:17-28, 1973.

"First trimester abortions induced by the extraovular infusion of prostaglandin F2a," by A. I. Csapo, et al. PROSTAGLANDINS 1:295-303, 1972.

"First trimester abortions induced by a single extraovular injection of prostaglandin F2a," by A. I. Csapo, et al. PROSTAGLANDINS 1:365-371, 1972.

"Further experience with intrauterine prostaglandin administration," by

M. Bygdeman, et al. J REPROD MED 9:392-396, December, 1972.

"Histopathologic changes associated with prostaglandin induced abortion," by P. D. Bullard, Jr., et al. CONTRACEPTION 7:133-144, 1973.

"Hormonal changes during induction of midtrimester abortion by prostaglandin F 2," by B. Cantor, et al. AM J OBSTET GYNECOL 113: 607-615, July 1, 1972.

"The induction of abortion and menstruation by the intravaginal administration of prostaglandin F 2a," by T. Sato, et al. AM J OBSTET GYNECOL 116:287-289, May 15, 1973.

"Induction of abortion by combined intra-amniotic urea and prostaglandin E 2 or prostaglandin E 2 alone," by I. Craft. LANCET 1:1344-1346, June 16, 1973.

"Induction of abortion by extra-amniotic administration of prostaglandin F2a: a preliminary report," by V. Hingorani, et al. CONTRACEPTION 6:353-359, 1972.

"Induction of abortion by intra- and extra-amniotic prostaglandin F2 administration," by P. A. Jarvinen, et al. PROSTAGLANDINS 3:491-504, April, 1973.

"Induction of abortion by intravenous and intra-uterine administration of prostaglandin F 2," by A. A. Haspels, et al. J REPROD MED 9:442-447, December, 1972.

"Induction of abortion by intravenous infusions of prostaglandin F2a," by E. Dreher, et al. ARCH GYNAEKOL 213:48-53, 1972.

"The induction of second trimester abortions using an intra-amniotic injection of urea and prostaglandin E2," by P. Bowen-Simpkins. J OBSTET GYNAECOL BR COMMONW 80:824-826, September, 1973.

"Induction of therapeutic abortion with intra-amniotically administered prostaglandin F 2. A comparison of three repeated-injection dose schedules," by W. E. Brenner, et al. AM J OBSTET GYNECOL 116: 923-930, August 1, 1973.

"Inhibition of abortion and fetal death produced by endotoxin or prostaglandin F2a," by M. J. K. Harper, et al. PROSTAGLANDINS 2: 295-309, 1972.

"Initial experiences with prostaglandin F2 in induced abortion," by H. Igel, et al. ZENTRALBL GYNAEKOL 95:353-357, March 16, 1973.

"Intra-amniotic administration of prostaglandin F 2 for induction of therapeutic abortion. A comparison of four dosage schedules," by W. E. Brenner, et al. J REPROD MED 9:456-463, December, 1972.

"Intra-amniotic administration of prostaglandin F 2 to induce therapeutic abortion. Efficacy and tolerance of two dosage schedules," by W. E. Brenner, et al. AM J OBSTET GYNECOL 114:781-787, November 15, 1972.

"Intra-amniotic prostaglandin E 2 and F 2 for induction of abortion: a dose response study," by I. Craft. J OBSTET GYNAECOL BR COMMONW 80:46-47, January, 1973.

"Intra-amniotic prostaglandin E 2 and urea for abortion," by I. Craft. LANCET 1:779, April 7, 1973.

"Intraamniotic prostaglandin F2-alpha dose--twenty-four-hour abortifacient response," by W. E. Brenner, et al. J PHARM SCI 62:1278-1282, August, 1973.

"Intra-amniotic prostaglandin F2 alpha to induce midtrimester abortion," by S. L. Corson, et al. AM J OBSTET GYNECOL 117:27-34, September 1, 1973.

"Intra-amniotic prostaglandins and urea for abortion," by I. Craft. LANCET 2:207 passim, July, 1973.

"Intra-uterine administration of prostaglandin F 2 during the second trimester of pregnancy; clinical and hormonal results," by R. Shearman, et al. J REPROD FERTIL 32:321-322, February, 1973.

"Intrauterine extra-amniotic administration of prostaglandin F 2 for therapeutic abortion. Early myometrial effects," by J. T. Braaksma, et al. AM J OBSTET GYNECOL 114:511-515, October 15, 1972.

"Laminaria augmentation of intra-amniotic prostaglandin F2 alpha for the induction of mid-trimester abortion," by W. E. Brenner, et al. PROSTAGLANDINS 3:879-894, June, 1973.

"Letter: intrauterine prostaglandins for outpatient termination of very early pregnancy," by S. M. Karim. LANCET 2:794, October 6, 1973.

"Maternal plasma oestrogen and progesterone levels during therapeutic abortion induced by intra-amniotic injection of prostaglandin F 2," by E. M. Symonds, et al. J OBSTET GYNAECOL BR COMMONW 79: 976-980, November, 1972.

"Midtrimester abortion produced by intra-amniotic prostaglandin F2a augmented with intravenous oxytocin," by N. Kochenour, et al. AM J OBSTET GYNECOL 114:516-519, 1972.

"Midtrimester abortion using intra-amniotic prostaglandin F2 alpha with intravenous Syntocinon," by G. G. Anderson, et al. J REPROD MED 9:434-436, December, 1972.

"Midtrimester abortion using prostaglandin F2alpha, oxytocin, and laminaria," by T. Engel, et al. FERTIL STERIL 24:565-568, August, 1973.

"On the mechanism of the abortifacient action of prostaglandin F 2," by A. I. Csapo. J REPROD MED 9:400-412, December, 1972; also in PROSTAGLANDINS 1:157-165, 1972.

"On the mechanism of midtrimester abortions induced by prostaglandin 'impact'," by L. Saldana, et al. PROSTAGLANDINS 3:847-858, June, 1973.

"Plasma progesterone and prostaglandin F2 levels during the insertion of prostaglandin F2 vaginal tablet," by T. Sato, et al. PROSTAGLAN-DINS 4:107-113, July, 1973.

"Possible mode of action of prostaglandins: V. Differential effects of prostaglandin F2a before and after the establishment of placental physiology in pregnant rats," by A. Chatterjee. PROSTAGLANDINS 3:189-199, 1973.

"Posterior cervical rupture following prostaglandin-induced mid-trimester abortion," by A. C. Wentz, et al. AM J OBSTET GYNECOL 115: 1107-1110, April 15, 1973.

"Pregnancy interruption with prostaglandins F2a," by T. Brat, et al. J GYNECOL OBSTET BIOL REPROD 1:385-387, 1972.

"Prostaglandin administration for induction of mid-trimester abortion in complicated pregnancies," by M. Toppozada, et al. LANCET 2:1420-1421, December 30, 1972.

"Prostaglandin developments in Uganda," by S. M. Karim. J REPROD MED 9:255-257, December, 1972.

"Prostaglandin effects on rat pregnancy. II. Interruption of pregnancy," by A. R. Fuchs, et al. FERTIL STERIL 24:275-283, April, 1973.

"Prostaglandin-oxytocin abortion: a clinical trial of intra-amniotic prostaglandin F2alpha in combination with intravenous oxytocin," by M. Seppala, et al. PROSTAGLANDINS 2:311-319, October, 1972.

"Prostaglandins," by R. K. Laros, Jr., et al. AM J NURS 73:1001-1003, June, 1973.

"Prostaglandins and their clinical applications in human reproduction," by E. M. Southern, et al. J REPROD MED 9:472-477, December, 1972.

"Prostaglandins and therapeutic abortion: summary of present status," by C. H. Hendricks. J REPROD MED 9:466-468, December, 1972.

"Prostaglandins as therapeutic agents," by J. Lee, et al. ARCH INTERN MED 131:294-300, 1973.

"Prostaglandins for inducing labor and abortion." DRUG THER BULL 11:41-43, May 25, 1973.

"Prostaglandins in gynecology," by M. Breckwoldt, et al. HIPPO-KRATES 43:494-495, December, 1972.

"Prostaglandins: a panacea in reproduction physiology?" by C. Revaz. SCHWEIZ Z GYNAEKOL GEBURTSHILFE 3:95-102, 1972.

"Prostaglandins: a synoptic study," by H. J. S. Rall. S AFR MED J 46:468-471, 1972.

"Recent aspects on systemic administration of prostaglandin," by N. Wiqvist, et al. J REPROD MED 9:378-382, December, 1972.

"Response of the midpregnant human uterus to systemic administration of 15(S)-15-methyl-prostaglandin F2a," by M. Toppozada, et al. PROSTAGLANDINS 2:239-249, 1972.

"Second trimester termination by intra-uterine prostaglandin F 2. Clinical and hormonal results with observations on induced lactation and chronoperiodicity," by R. Shearman, et al. J REPROD MED 9:448-452, December, 1972.

"Studies of prostaglandin F2 in the cow," by D. R. Lamond, et al. PROSTAGLANDINS 4:269-284, August, 1973.

"Termination of early gestation with vaginal prostaglandin F2a tablets," by R. C. Corlett, et al. PROSTAGLANDINS 2:453-464, 1972.

"Termination of pregnancy by intra-uterine prostaglandin F 2," by A. Korda, et al. AUST NZ J OBSTET GYNAECOL 12:166-169, August, 1972.

"The termination of pregnancy by intravenous infusion of a synthetic prostaglandin F2 analogue," by D. S. Sharp, et al. J OBSTET GYNAE-COL BR COMMONW 80:138-141, February, 1973.

"Termination of pregnancy with 15 methyl analogues of prostaglandins E 2 and F 2," by S. M. Karim, et al. J REPROD MED 9:383-391, December, 1972.

"Termination of second trimester pregnancy with intra-amniotic administration of prostaglandins E 2 and F 2," by S. M. Karim, et al. J REPROD MED 9:427-433, December, 1972.

"Therapeutic abortion by extra-amniotic administration of prostaglandins," by M. P. Embrey, et al. J REPROD MED 9:420-424, December, 1972.

"Therapeutic abortion by intrauterine infusion of prostaglandin F 2," by T. H. Lippert, et al. ARCH GYNAEKOL 213:197-201, 1973.

"Therapeutic abortion employing the synergistic action of extra-amniotic prostaglandin E 2 and an intravenous infusion of oxytocin," by G. A. Morewood. J OBSTET GYNAECOL BR COMMONW 80:473-475, May, 1973.

"Therapeutic abortion in the second trimester by intra-amniotic prostaglandin F 2," by C. A. Ballard, et al. J REPROD MED 9:397-399, December, 1972.

"Therapeutic abortion of early human gestation with vaginal suppositories of prostaglandin (F 2)," by D. R. Tredway, et al. AM J OBSTET GYNECOL 116:795-798, July 15, 1973.

"Therapeutic abortion utilizing local application of prostaglandin F2alpha," by F. Naftolin, et al. J REPROD MED 9:437-441, December, 1972.

"Use of prostaglandin F 2 alpha for interruption of pregnancy in 1st and 2d trimester," by F. Havranek, et al. CESK GYNEKOL 38:432-435, July, 1973.

"The use of prostaglandin pessaries prior to vaginal termination," by I. Craft. PROSTAGLANDINS 3:377-381, 1973.

" 'Uterine' and 'luteal' effects of prostaglandins (PG) in rats and guinea pigs as potential abortifacient mechanisms," by W. Elger, et al. ACTA ENDOCRINOL 173:46, 1973.

"Vaginal administration of prostaglandin F2a for inducing therapeutic abortion," by W. E. Brenner, et al. PROSTAGLANDINS 1:455-467, 1972.

"Vaginal administration of prostaglandins and early abortion," by R. J. Pion, et al. J REPROD MED 9:413-415, December, 1972.

"The viability of fetal skin of abortuses induced by saline or prostaglandin," by I. J. Park, et al. AM J OBSTET GYNECOL 115:274-275, January 15, 1973.

PSYCHOLOGY
see also: Sociology and Behavior

"Abortion constellation: early history and present relationships," by V. Abernethy. ARCH GEN PSYCHIAT 29:346-350, September, 1973.

"Abortion, contraception and child mental health," by L. J. Redman, et al. FAMILY PLANN PERSPECT 5:71-72, Spring, 1973.

"Abortion for the asking," by H. Dudar. SAT R SOC 1:30-35, April, 1973.

"Does anybody care?" AMER J NURSING 73:1562-1565, September, 1973.

"Emotional patterns related to delay in decision to seek legal abortion," by N. B. Kaltreider. CALIF MED 118:23-27, May, 1973.

"Emotional reactions in abortion services personnel," by F. J. Kane, Jr., et al. ARCH GEN PSYCHIATRY 28:409-411, March, 1973.

"Expectant mothers--women seeking abortions, a sociopsychiatric comparison in Umea?" by H. Holmberg, et al. LAKARTIDNINGEN 69: 5920-5924, December 6, 1972.

"Follow-up study of women who request abortion," by E. M. Smith. AMER J ORTHOPSYCHIAT 43:574-585, July, 1973.

"Legal abortion as a positive mental health measure in family planning, " by Z. M. Lebensohn. COMPR PSYCHIATRY 14:95-98, March-April, 1973.

"The mental health of the prospective father: a new indication for therapeutic abortion?" by R. Lacoursiere. BULL MENNINGER CLIN 36:645-650, November, 1972.

"Motivational factors in abortion patients," by F. J. Kane, Jr. AMER J PSYCHIAT 130:290-293, March, 1973.

"Now that abortion is legal; unforeseen emotions that follow," by B. G. Harrison. MC CALLS 101:64 plus, November, 1973.

"Problems of reproduction in adolescence," by J. A. Grant, et al.

WORLD MED J 20:57, May-June, 1973.

"Psychiatric sequelae to legal abortion in South Australia," by F. Weston. MED J AUST 1:350-354, February 17, 1973.

"Psychological factors in mid-trimester abortion," by N. B. Kaltreider. PSYCHIATRY MED 4:129-134, Spring, 1973.

"The psychological impact of abortion," by N. D. West. AORN J 17:132 plus, March, 1973.

"Psychological problems of abortion for the unwed teenage girl," by C. D. Martin. GENET PSYCHOL MONOGR 88:23-110, August, 1973.

"Psychological sequelae of abortion: anxiety and depression," by M. E. Fingerer. J COMMUNITY PSYCHOL 1:221-225, April, 1973.

"Some psychiatric problems related to therapeutic abortion," by D. S. Werman, et al. NC MED J 34:274-275, April, 1973.

"Therapeutic abortion and a prior psychiatric history," by J. A. Ewing, et al. AM J PSYCHIATRY 130:37-40, January, 1973.

"Therapeutic abortion on psychiatric grounds: a follow-up study," by J. A. Ewing, et al. N C MED J 34:265-270, April, 1973.

"Women who seek abortions: a study," by A. T. Young, et al. SOC WORK 18:60-65, May, 1973.

RADIOLOGISTS
"Cancer as a cause of abortions and stillbirths: the effect of these early deaths on the recognition of radiogenic leukaemias," by A. M. Stewart. BR J CANCER 27:465-472, June, 1973.

"Pelvic venography," by P. W. Silverberg, et al. RADIOLOGY 107:523-526, June, 1973.

REFERRAL AGENCIES SERVICES
see: Sociology and Behavior

RELIGION AND ETHICS
see also: Sociology and Behavior

"The Abortion Act of 1967; Society for the Protection of unborn children." TABLET 227:237-239, March 10, 1973.

"Abortion and the Church." AMERICA 128:110-111, February 10, 1973.

"Abortion and the Mosaic law," by J. W. Cottrell. CHR TODAY 17:6-9, March 16, 1973.

"Abortion and population," by D. Munday. HEALTH SOC SERV J 83: 13-14, March 10, 1973.

"Abortion and the sanctity of human life," by B. A. Brody. AM PHIL QUART 10:133-140, April, 1973.

"Abortion and U. S. Protestants." AMERICA 128:156-157, February 24, 1973.

"Abortion bill in Oregon would be costly to Catholic hospitals." HOSP PROGRESS 54:20, April, 1973.

"Abortion culture," by N. Thimmesch. NEWSWEEK 82:7, July 9, 1973.

"Abortion debate is revealing our values," by G. L. Chamberlain. NEW CATH WORLD 215:206-208, September, 1972.

"Abortion decision: a death blow?" CHR TODAY 17:48, February 16, 1973.

"Abortion: deterrence, facilitation, resistance." AMERICA 128:506-507, June 2, 1973.

"Abortion: an ecumenical dilemma," by G. Baum. COMM 99:231-235, November 30, 1973.

"Abortion: the fight goes on." HOSP WORLD 2:7, May, 1973.

"Abortion information can be mailed." NEWSLETTER 6:5, January, 1973.

"Abortion: the inhumanity of it all," by J. McHugh. ST ANTH 80:12-22, February, 1973.

"Abortion is morally wrong says Italian Bishops' Council." OR 9:5, March 1, 1973.

"Abortion: law of nation or law of God; reprint from The Catholic Standard and Times, January 25, 1973," by J. Foley. DIMENSION 5:35, Spring, 1973.

"Abortion: legal but still wrong," by E. Gilbert. LIGUORIAN 61:2-4, October, 1973.

"Abortion: mixed feelings." MED WORLD NEWS 14:4-6, February 9, 1973.

"Abortion: the moment of truth," by V. Dillon. US CATH 38:37-38, September, 1973.

"Abortion: next round." COMMONWEAL 98:51-52, March 23, 1973.

"Abortion: no present changes." MED WORLD NEWS 14:4-5, March 23, 1973.

"The abortion question and the evangelical tradition," by R. Wolfe. DIMENSION 5:84-89, Summer, 1973.

"Abortion--respect life--legality vs. morality," by P. O'Boyle. SOC JUST 65:372-373, February, 1973.

"Abortion: a review article," by P. Ramsey. THOMIST 37:174-226, January, 1973.

"Abortion revolution." NEWSWEEK 81:27-28, February 5, 1973.

"Abortion revolution: don't rush it," by C. L. Rosenberg. MED ECON 50:31 plus, March 5, 1973.

"Abortion ruling: Catholic facts and constitutional truths," by R. Marshall. SOC JUST 66:84, June, 1973.

"Abortion--the theological argument," by M. Alsopp. FURROW 24:202-206, April, 1973.

"Abortion: two views: keep abortion under the criminal code," by V. Macdonald. CHATELAINE 46:38, 106-107, November, 1973.

"Abortion: two views: let the individual conscience decide," by I. LeBourdais. CHATELAINE 46:38, 105-106, November, 1973.

"Abortions," by C. D. Davis. TEX HOSP 28:28-29, March, 1973.

"Abortions: fallacies and pitfalls," by W. I. Weyl. VIRGINIA MED MON 100:172, February, 1973.

"American bishops and abortion." TABLET 227:268-269, March 17, 1973.

"Because the Lord loved you," by K. O'Rourke. HOSP PROG 54:73-77, August, 1973.

"Bishop offers diocesan aid to prevent abortions." NAT CATH REP 9:5, February 23, 1973.

"Bishops condemn abortion decision," by R. Casey. NAT CATH REP 9:1-2, February 23, 1973.

"Bishops issue rules on abortion laws." NAT CATH REP 9:19, April 27, 1973.

"Boston prelate indicts court's abortion decision." HOSPITALS 47:170, May 16, 1973.

"Callahan on abortion: statements," by D. Callahan. COMMONWEAL 97:410, February 9, 1973.

"The Catholic burden." TRIUMPH 8:45, May, 1973.

"Catholic hospitals won't allow abortions." NAT CATH REP 9:4, February 2, 1973.

"Catholic Hospital Association acts on abortion campaign; statement of philosophy; medico-moral center." HOSP PROGRESS 54:22-23,

March, 1973.

"Catholic Hospital Association strengthens legal campaign against abortion." HOSP PROGRESS 54:18 plus, June, 1973.

"Catholic Hospital Association to conduct anti-abortion campaign." HOSP PROGRESS 54:82 plus, March, 1973.

"The Catholic interest." TRIUMPH 8:15, November, 1973.

"Catholics attack abortion decision." NAT CATH REP 9:3-4, February 2, 1973.

"Christian responsibilities and abortion law." CHRIST NURSE :23-24, April, 1973.

"Church abortion stand called sexist," by R. Parenteau. NAT CATH REP 10:3 plus, November 2, 1973.

"Church authorities must do much more," by G. Devine. NAT CATH REP 9:13, April 20, 1973.

"Church to make antiabortion drive." NAT CATH REP 9:1 plus, February 9, 1973.

"Compassion is needed," by E. Bianchi. NAT CATH REP 9:14, June 8, 1973.

"Confusion at the highest level," by J. R. Nelson. CHR CENT 90:254-255, February 28, 1973.

"The courage to speak; cond from a speech to the John Carroll Society," by E. Hanify. C DGST 37:22-24, April, 1973.

"Early discovery of birth defects; abortion as a consequence of discovering defects by amniocentesis," by P. R. Gastonguay. AMERICA 129:218, September 29, 1973.

"Ethical considerations of some biologic dilemmas," by J. A. Noonan. SOUTHERN MED J 66:937-939, August, 1973.

"Five popular myths about abortion," by T. Jermann. OSV 62:1 plus, May 27, 1973.

"Foes of abortion vow to continue efforts." AMER MED NEWS 16:7, January 29, 1973.

"For American Catholics: end of an illusion," by T. O'Connell. AMERICA 128:514-517, June 2, 1973.

"France: abortion, oui!" NEWSWEEK 81:46 plus, June 11, 1973.

"Georgetown University statement on abortion," by R. Henle. C MIND 71:9-10, September, 1973.

"The growing scandal of abortion," by K. Mitzner. C ECON p. 33, October, 1972.

"Hot rhetoric; abortion issue in Catholic diocesan press," by S. J. Adamo. AMERICA 128:375-376 plus, April 21, 1973.

"Induced Maude abortion charged." NAT CATH REP 10:12, November 9, 1973.

"Is abortion advertising ethical?" MED WORLD NEWS 14:53-54, September 7, 1973.

"It's time to speak out for all life," by K. Katafiasz. ST ANTH 81:26-27, October, 1973.

"Jewish religious tradition and the issue of abortion," by S. Freedman. DIMENSION 5:90-93, Summer, 1973.

"Litigation: preparation and response," by S. Blaes. HOSP PROG 54:70-72 plus, August, 1973.

"Maude dropouts threatened by boycott." BROADCASTING 85:74, August 20, 1973.

"Measure of attitudes toward abortion," by H. S. Lackey, Jr., et al. J COMMUNITY PSYCHOL 1:31-33, January, 1973.

"Medicine and abortion; interview by Vatican Radio," by A. Bompiani. OR 13:4, March 29, 1973.

"Moccasins and abortion; reprint from The Camillan," by M. Flynn. C CHAR 57:16-23, June, 1973.

"Moral and medical problems concerning abortion," by M. Bermejillo. AN R ACAD NACL MED 90:307-326, 1973.

"Moral consideration of abortion from the viewpoint of the Christian value of human life," by J. M. Diaz Moreno. AN R ACAD NACL MED 90:235-261, 1973.

"The morality of abortion," by R. B. Brandt. MONIST 56:503-526, October, 1972.

"Must the Church eliminate morality?" by D. Barsotti. OR 14:8, April 5, 1973.

"National Conference of Catholic Bishops Administrative Committee rejects abortion ruling." HOSP PROGRESS 54:83 plus, March, 1973.

"A new approach to the abortion problem," by L. Durpe. THEOL STDS 34:481-488, September, 1973.

"A new Catholic strategy on abortion." MONTH 6:163-171, May, 1973.

"Objectifs de morale chretienne," by H. de Lavalette. ETUDES 338: 499-509, April, 1973.

"On killing inconvenient people," by A. Roche. SAT N 88:29-31, September, 1973.

"On the moral and legal status of abortion," by M. A. Warren. MONIST 57:43-61, January, 1973.

"One man's love for life," by L. Lueras. COLUMBIA 53:20-27, April, 1973.

"100,000 sign OSV pro-life petition." OSV 62:1 plus, May 20, 1973.

"Parallels in treachery," by D. DeMarco. SISTERS 45:82-89, October, 1973.

"A pastoral approach to the abortion dilemma," by F. Meehan, et al. DIMENSION 4:131-143, Winter, 1972.

"Pastoral guidelines for the Catholic hospitals and health care personnel in the United States." OR 25:11-12, June 21, 1973.

"Pastoral message on abortion." C MIND 71:7-9, September, 1973.

"Prenatal diagnosis and selective abortion," by K. Lebacqz. LINACRE 40:109-127, May, 1973.

"Present concepts of abortion," by E. C. Smith. SOUTHERN MED 61: 15-19, August, 1973.

"Protestant Theologians debate court ruling on abortion," by E. Wright. CH HER p. 12, March 22, 1973.

"The right to be born," by D. DeMarco. SISTERS 44:490-495, April, 1973.

"The right to life debate; excerpt from What a modern Catholic believes about the right to life," by R. Westley. CRITIC 31:50-59, July-August, 1973.

"The right to life; pastoral letter," by J. Camey. OR 32:4 plus, August 9, 1973.

"The right to life vs the right to privacy," by C. Dozier. OSV 61:1 plus, April 8, 1973.

"The rights of the unborn," by T. Glenister. TABLET 227:557-559, June 16, 1973; Reply 227:603, June 30, 1973.

"The sanctity of human life." CH HER p. 8, October 20, 1972.

"A second look at 'Humanae Vitae'," by H. Klaus. HPR 74:59-67, October, 1973.

"Some additional arguments against abortion," by O. Bennett. HPR

73:50-53, January, 1973.

"Statement by Sisters of Charity of the Incarnate Word." HOSP PRO-
GRESS 54:96b, March, 1973.

"Statements of national conference of Catholic bishops; pastoral message." C LAWYER 19:29-35, Winter, 1973.

"Stunning approval for abortion by the Supreme Court." TIME 101:50-
51, February 5, 1973.

"Suffer, little children," by E. Figes. NEW HUMANIST 89:521, May,
1973.

"Theological reasons for the sanctity of life," by Rev. K. D. O'Rourke.
HOSP PROGRESS 54:73-77, August, 1973.

"To respect human life," by N. Pole. PHIL CONTEXT 2:16-22, 1973.

"Two essays on abortion," by D. DeMarco. R REL 32:1064-1069,
September, 1973.

"U. S. bishops oppose Supreme Court decision." OR 7:6-7, February 15,
1973.

"U. S. bishops' pastoral on abortion." OSV 61:4, March 11, 1973.

"United States' Cardinals protest court's decision: abortion." OR 5:5,
February 1, 1973.

"The unwilling dead," by S. M. Harrison. PROC CATH PHIL ASS
46:199-208, 1972.

"What the bishops say," by M. Walsh. MONTH 6:172-175, May, 1973.

"What does theology say about abortion?" by J. R. Nelson. CHR CENT
90:124-128, January 31, 1973.

"What sisters should know about euthanasia; interview by D. Durken,"
by P. Marx. SISTERS 45:90-101, October, 1973.

"Why I reversed my stand on laissez-faire abortion," by C. E. Lincoln. CHR CENT 90:477-479, April 25, 1973.

"Women's rights vs. Catholic dogma: why the church fathers oppose abortion," by C. Moriarty. INTERNAT SOCIALIST R 34:8-11 plus, March, 1973.

RESEARCH

"Abortion associated with Brucella abortus (Biotype 1) in the T.B. mare," by F. J. Robertson, et al. VET REC 92:480-481, May 5, 1973.

"Abortion in cattle associated with Bacillus cereus," by K. Wohlgemuth, et al. J AM VET MED ASSOC 161:1688-1690, December 15, 1972.

"Abortus provocatus in cattle," by L. Schjerven. NORD VET MED 24:537-543, November, 1972.

"Accumulation of complement-fixing antibodies in virus abortion of sheep," by R. K. Khamadeev, et al. VETERINARIIA 49:113-115, May, 1973.

"Action of prostaglandin F2a on the corpus luteum of the gestating rat," by H. Tuchmann-Duplessis, et al. C R HEBD SEANCES ACAD SCI SER D SCI NAT 275:2033-2035, 1972.

"Analysis of the etiology of abortions in cattle," by B. A. Timofeev, et al. VETERINARIIA 7:104-106, July, 1972.

"Arizona infections in sheep associated with gastroenteritis and abortion," by J. Greenfield, et al. VET REC 92:400-401, April 14, 1973.

"Association of Salmonella dublin with abortion in cattle," by A. P. MacLaren. VET REC 91:687-688, December 30, 1972.

"The association of Salmonella dublin with bovine abortion in Victoria," by R. G. Russell, et al. AUST VET J 49:173-174, March, 1973.

"Bovine abortion associated with Candida tropicalis," by K. Wohlgemuth, et al. J AM VET MED ASSOC 162:460-461, March 15, 1973.

"Bovine abortions in five Northeastern states, 1960-1970: evaluation of diagnostic laboratory data," by W. T. Hubbert, et al. CORNELL VET 63:291-316, April, 1973.

"Cases of mycoplasma abortion in swine," by V. Jelev, et al. ZENTRALBL VETERINAERMED 19:588-597, August, 1972.

"Changes in the rat placenta following inoculation with Salmonella dublin," by G. A. Hall. AM J PATHOL 72:103-118, July, 1973.

"Characteristics of a paramyxovirus isolated from an aborted bovine fetus," by J. F. Evermann, et al. CORNELL VET 63:17-28, January, 1973.

"Diagnosis of ovine vibriosis and enzootic abortion of ewes by immunofluorescence technique," by W. B. Ardrey, et al. AM J VET RES 33:2535-2538, December, 1972.

"A diagnostic survey of bovine abortion and stillbirth in the Northern Plains States," by C. A. Kirkbride, et al. J AM VET MED ASSOC 162:556-560, April 1, 1973.

"Diethylcarbamazine: lack of teratogenic and abortifacient action in rats and rabbits," by P. J. Fraser. INDIAN J MED RES 60:1529-1532, October, 1972.

"The direct fluorescent antibody test for detection of Brucella abortus in bovine abortion material," by M. J. Corbel. J HYG 71:123-129, March, 1973.

"Effect of biovariectomy on the embryo-maternal junction in pregnant rats before the placental relay," by M. Clabaut. ANN ENDOCRINOL 33:221-230, May-June, 1972.

"Effect of intramammary corticosteroid administration during late gestation in cattle," by D. D. Hagg, et al. MOD VET PRACT 54:29 passim, May, 1973.

"The effect of prostaglandin F2a and prostaglandin E2 upon luteal function and ovulation in the guinea-pig," by F. R. Blatchley, et al. J ENDOCRINOL 53:493-501, 1972.

"Effect of prostaglandin F2a upon the corpus luteum of pregnant rats," by H. Tuchmann-Duplessis, et al. C R ACAD SCI 275:2033-2035, October 30, 1972.

"Efficacy of an intramuscular infectious bovine rhinotraceitis vaccine against abortion due to the virus," by J. R. Saunders, et al. CAN VET J 13:273-278, December, 1972.

"Equine abortion (herpes) virus: properties of the hemagglutinin in virus suspensions," by B. Klingeborn, et al. VIROLOGY 56:164-171, November, 1973.

"Experiences in the control of enzootic abortion of sheep using a viable vaccine from a weakened strain of Chlamydia ovis 'P'," by S. Yilmaz, et al. BERL MUNCH TIERAERZTL WOCHENSCHR 86:361-366, October, 1973.

"Experimental study of abortifacient characteristics of vaccine strain Brucella bovis No. 21 in sheep," by G. E. Irskaya, et al. DONSKOGO S-KH INST 4:12-13, 1970.

"Experimentally induced immunity to chlamydial abortion of cattle," by D. G. McKercher, et al. J INFECT DIS 128:231-234, August, 1973.

"IBR abortion and its control," by F. E. Steves, et al. VET MED SMALL ANIM CLIN 68:164-166, February, 1973.

"The identification of Mortierella wolfii isolated from cases of abortion and pneumonia in cattle and a search for its infection source," by M. E. Di Menna, et al. RES VET SCI 13:439-442, September, 1972.

"Induction of embryonic death in sheep by intrauterine injection of a small volume of normal saline," by M. M. Bryden, et al. J REPROD FERTIL 32:133-135, January, 1973.

"Listeria as a cause of abortion and neonatal mortality in sheep," by D. W. Broadbent. AUST VET J 48:391-394, July, 1972.

"Listeric abortion in sheep. II. Feto-placental changes," by C. O. Njoku, et al. CORNELL VET 63:171-192, April, 1973.

--III. Feto-placental-myometrial interaction," by C. O. Njoku, et al. CORNELL VET 63:193-210, April, 1973.

--IV. Histopathologic comparison of natural and experimental infection," by C. O. Njoku, et al. CORNELL VET 63:211-219, April, 1973.

"Measles virus-associated endometritis, cervicitis, and abortion in a rhesus monkey," by R. A. Renne, et al. J AM VET MED ASSOC 163:639-641, September 15, 1973.

"Mid-term abortion induced in sheep by synthetic corticoids," by P. Fylling, et al. J REPROD FERTIL 32:305-306, February, 1973.

"Monkey anti-placental serum as an abortifacient," by S. J. Behrman, et al. CONTRACEPTION 5:357-368, 1972.

"Multiple sclerosis and zoonoses. Importance of the role of the bovine abortion virus (pararickettsia X-14) in the etiopathogenesis of multiple sclerosis," by P. Le Gac. C R ACAD SCI 275:147-148, July 3, 1972.

"Parainfluenza-3 and bovine enteroviruses as possible important causative factors in bovine abortion," by H. W. Dunne, et al. AM J VET RES 34:1121-1126, September, 1973.

"Passive hemagglutination test for bovine chlamydial abortion," by E. L. Belden, et al. INFECT IMMUN 7:141-146, February, 1973.

"Pathohistologic changes of the fetus in enzootic virus abortion of sheep," by A. Djurov. ZENTRALBL VETERINAERMED 19:578-587, August, 1972.

"Possible mode of action of prostaglandins: V. Differential effects of prostaglandin F2a before and after the establishment of placental physiology in pregnant rats," by A. Chatterjee. PROSTAGLANDINS 3:189-199, 1973.

"Prolonged gestation in the blue fox after treatment with choriongonadotropins," by O. M. Moller. NORD VET MED 24:492-500, October, 1972.

"Prostaglandin effects on rat pregnancy. II. Interruption of pregnancy," by A. R. Fuchs, et al. FERTIL STERIL 24:275-283, April, 1973.

"Regulation of menstrual cycle and termination of pregnancy in the monkey by estradiol and PGF2a," by A. A. Shaikh. PROSTAGLANDINS 2:227-233, 1972.

"Salmonella anatum from an aborted foal," by S. Kumar, et al. BR VET J 128:ixiv, November, 1972.

"Salmonella dublin abortion in a New South Wales dairy herd," by K. R. Davidson. AUST VET J 49:174, March, 1973.

"San Miguel sea lion virus isolation, preliminary characterization and relationship to vesicular exanthema of swine virus," by A. W. Smith, et al. NATURE 244:108-110, July 13, 1973.

"The serological response to Aspergillus fumigatus antigens in bovine mycotic abortion," by M. J. Corbel. BR VET J 128:73-75, December, 1972.

"The significance of urogenital trichomoniasis in the etiology of abortion," by S. S. Zakharchuk, et al. AKUSH GINEKOL 48:44-45, September, 1972.

"Studies of prostaglandin F2 in the cow," by D. R. Lamond, et al. PROSTAGLANDINS 4:269-284, August, 1973.

"Studies of the role of Dermacentor occidentalis in the transmission of bovine chlamydial abortion," by H. D. Caldwell, et al. INFECT IMMUN 7:147-151, February, 1973.

"Studies of serological reactions in ovine toxoplasmosis encountered in intensively-bred sheep," by G. A. Sharman, et al. VET REC 91: 670-675, December 30, 1972.

"Termination of early pregnancy in rats after ovariectomy is due to immediate collapse of the progesterone-dependent decidua," by R. Deanesly. J REPROD FERTIL 35:183-186, October, 1973.

"Use of vitamin preparations of reduce calf loss as well as to stabilise and normalise puerperium of cattle," by R. Liebetrau, et al. MONATSH VET MED 27:695-697, September 15, 1972.

" 'Uterine' and 'luteal' effects of prostaglandins (PG) in rats and guinea pigs as potential abortifacient mechanisms," by W. Elger, et al. ACTA ENDOCRINOL 173:46, 1973.

"Vaccination against vibrionic abortion in sheep with a cell-disrupted adjuvant vaccine," by N. J. Gilmour, et al. RES VET SCI 13:601-602, November, 1972.

"Vaccination of a large cattle herd against infectious pustular vulvo-vaginitis and rhinotracheitis," by O. C. Straub, et al. DTSCH TIERAERZTL WOCHENSCHR 80:73-77, February 15, 1973.

"Vibrio infections in goats," by A. I. Krylov, et al. VETERINARIIA 8:104-105, August, 1972.

"Vibrionic abortion in ewes in South Africa: preliminary report," by A. P. Schutte, et al. J S AFR VET MED ASSOC 42:223-226, September, 1971.

RESPIRATORY SYSTEM
see: Complications

RIVANOL
"Legal abortion by extra-amniotic instillation of Rivanol in combination with rubber catheter insertion into the uterus after the twelfth week of pregnancy," by C. Ingemanson. AM J OBSTET GYNECOL 115:211-215, 1973.

RIFAMPICIN
"Evaluation of rifampicin in septic abortion," by J. M. Ezeta, et al. GINECOL OBSTET MEX 32:561-566, December, 1972.

RUBELLA
see: Complications

SEPSIS
"Corticosteroid metabolism disorder in obstetrical sepsis," by M. G. Simakova. AKUSH GINEKOL 49:70-72, February, 1973.

SEPTIC ABORTION AND SEPTIC SHOCK
see also: Complications
      Sepsis

"Acute renal failure in obstetric septic shock. Current views on pathogenesis and management," by D. S. Emmanouel, et al. AM J OBSTET GYNECOL 117:145-159, September 1, 1973.

"Aggressive management of septic abortion: report of 262 cases," by W. J. Connolly, et al. SOUTH MED J 65:1480-1484, December, 1972.

"A case of postabortal bilateral uveitis--adaptometric fall of a paracentral scotoma," by G. E. Jayle, et al. BULL SOC OPHTALMOL FR 72:731-736, July-August, 1972.

"Clinical evaluation of Vibravenous (doxicillin) preparation in obstetrics and gynecology," by Z. Sternadel, et al. GINEKOL POL 44:189-191, February, 1973.

"Diagnosis and therapy of spetic abortion and bacterial shock," by G. Iliew, et al. Z AERZTL FORTBILD 67:232-235, March 1, 1973.

"The effect of legal abortion on the rate of septic abortion at a large county hospital," by P. N. Seward, et al. AM J OBSTET GYNECOL 115:335-338, February 1, 1973.

"Evaluation of rifampicin in septic abortion," by J. M. Ezeta, et al. GINECOL OBSTET MEX 32:561-566, December, 1972.

"Experience with the administration of heparin for the prevention of the Sanarelli-Shwartzman reaction (SSP) in cases of septic abortions," by H. H. Koch, et al. GEBURTSHILFE FRAUENHEILKD 33:460-463, June, 1973.

"Gram negative bacterial septicemia after abortion," by M. Vitse, et al. BULL FED SOC GYNECOL OBSTET LANG FR 23:603, November-December, 1971.

"Haemophilus influenzae in septic abortion," by J. Berczy, et al. LANCET 1:1197, May 26, 1973.

"Hysterectomy by septic processes during pregnancy," by J. Rosas Arceo, et al. GINECOL OBSTET MEX 33:559-568, June, 1973.

"Listeriosis. Occurrence in spontaneous interruptions of pregnancy," by J. R. Giraud, et al. NOUV PRESSE MED 2:215-218, January 27, 1973.

"Postabortal metastatic panophthalmia," by F. Deodati, et al. BULL SOC OPHTALMOL FR 72:729-730, July-August, 1972.

"Post-abortion and post-partum septico-pyemia. Apropos of 27 cases," by V. Vic-Dupont, et al. ANN MED INTERNE 124:291-302, April, 1973.

"Prevention of mortality from abortions," by G. D. Safronenko, et al. PEDIATR AKUSH GINEKOL 5:57-59, October, 1972.

"Septic abortion," by F. Kubli. MED KLIN 68:500-504, April 20, 1973.

"Septic abortion and septic shock," by M. Botes. S AFR MED J 47:432-435, March 10, 1973.

"Septic abortion and septic shock," by W. H. Utian. S AFR MED J 47:639, April 21, 1973.

"Septic induced abortion," by J. F. Jewett. N ENGL J MED 289:748-749, October 4, 1973.

"Severe postabortal Clostridium welchii infection: trends in management," by J. P. O'Neill, et al. AUST NZ J OBSTET GYNAECOL 12:157-165, August, 1972.

"Staphylococcal lung abscesses following septic abortion," by A. Singh, et al. INDIAN J CHEST DIS 14:274-276, October, 1972.

"Thrombocytopenia indicating gram-negative infection and endotoxemia, " by F. K. Beller, et al. OBSTET GYNECOL 41:521-524, April, 1973.

"Thrombotic thrombocytopenic purpura and gynaecological manifestations," by M. Yudis. LANCET 1:1445, June 23, 1973.

"Use of cephalothin in septic abortion," by C. H. Dahm, Jr., et al. OBSTET GYNECOL 41:693-696, May, 1973.

SOCIOLOGY AND BEHAVIOR
see *also:* Family Planning
Religion and Ethics

"Abortion and sexual behavior in college women," by K. J. Monsour, et al. AM J ORTHOPSYCHIATRY 43:804-814, October, 1973.

"Abortion, an Aquarian perspective," by D. Nugent. CRITIC 31:32-36, January-February, 1973.

"Abortion at MSU," by R. Kirk. NAT R 25:527, May 11, 1973.

"Abortion counseling: an experimental study of three techniques," by M. B. Bracken, et al. AM J OBSTET GYNECOL 117:10-20, September 1, 1973.

"Abortion cuts numbers of abandoned infants, immature births." J AMER MED ASS 224:1697-1698, June 25, 1973.

"Abortion services in Massachusetts." NEW ENGL J MED 288:686-687, March 29, 1973.

"Adolescent sexuality," by M. G. Wolfish. PRACTITIONER 210:226-231, February, 1973.

"Attitudes of Indian women towards abortion," by K. S. Bhardwaj, et al. INDIAN J SOCIAL WORK 33:317-322, January, 1973.

"The beginning of mental activity in man and its importance to law. A new theory," by T. de Bour. PSYCHIATR NEUROL NEUROCHIR 75: 385-390, September-October, 1972.

"Can't laugh at abortion," by A. Nowlan. ATLAN ADV 63:46-47, January, 1973.

"C'est pas mon probleme," by J. Pare. LE MACLEAN :16-17, 34-37, February, 1973.

"Community abortion services. The role of organized medicine," by J. E. Hodgson. MINN MED 56:239-242, March, 1973.

"Consultation for therapeutic abortion," by L. Daligand, et al. MED LEG DOMM CORPOR 5:372-378, October-December, 1972.

"Correlations between some economic, social and infectious factors and the pathology of pregnancy and of the neonate," by Y. Copelovici, et al. REV ROUM VIROL 10:23-32, 1973.

"Counseling abortion patients," by E. Naugle. NURSING 3:37-38, February, 1973.

"Counseling for elective abortion," by R. S. Sanders, et al. J AM COLL HEALTH ASSOC 21:446-450, June, 1973.

"Dr. Jerome L. Reeves on the new sexuality," by H. A. Matthews. NC MED J 34:616-618, August, 1973.

"Doctor blames fathers for abortion," by J. McCann. NAT CATH REP 9:1-2, March, 1973.

"Emotional reactions in abortion services personnel," by F. J. Kane, Jr., et al. ARCH GEN PSYCHIAT 28:409-411, March, 1973.

"Evolution of an abortion counseling service in an adoption agency; Spence-Chapin adoption service, New York city," by R. K. Heineman. CHILD WEL 52:253-260, April, 1973.

"Follow-up study of women who request abortion," by E. M. Smith. AM J ORTHOPSYCH 43:574-585, July, 1973.

"Frequency of criminal abortion. Elucidated in interviews of women hospitalized for abortion," by J. G. Lauritsen. UGESKR LAEGER 135:770-771, April 23, 1973.

"Generative activity in some groups of women and its reflection on the state of the uterine cervix," by T. Pipetkov. AKUSH GINEKOL 11: 251-258, 1972.

"Liberal thinking on abortion: not a solution in itself," by D. Laulicht. TIMES p. 13, May 2, 1973.

"Making abortion consultation therapeutic," by C. M. Friedman. AM J

PSYCHIATRY 130:1257-1261, November, 1973.

"Male factor as a possible cause of habitual abortion and infertility," by C. A. Joel. SCHWEIZ MED WOCHENSCHR 102:1377-1383, September 30, 1972.

"The mental health of the prospective father: a new indication for therapeutic abortion?" by R. Lacoursiere. BULL MENNINGER CLIN 36:645-650, November, 1972.

"More on abortion." CALIF MED 118:52-54, March, 1973.

"Motivational factors in abortion patients," by R. J. Kane, Jr., et al. AM J PSYCHIATRY 130:290-293, March, 1973.

"Need for an expanded abortion service: problems encountered, solutions," by M. B. Sell. SOUTHERN MED 61:22-26, August, 1973.

"A new cause: many Americans join move to ban abortion; legislators take note," by J. A. Tannenbaum. WALL ST J 182:1 plus, August 2, 1973.

"Organizing an abortion service," by A. H. Danon. NURS OUTLOOK 21:460-464, July, 1973.

"Postabortion attitudes," by D. A. Evans, et al. NC MED J 34:271-273, April, 1973.

"Pregnancy counseling and the request for abortion: tentative suggestions for Catholic Charities agencies," by E. Ryle. C CHAR 57:8-15, June, 1973.

"Prevention and abortion," by B. Grunfeld. TIDSSKR NOR LAEGE-FOREN 93:324-325, February 20, 1973.

"Recommended program guide for abortion services: American Public Health Association." AMER J PUBLIC HEALTH 63:639-644, July, 1973.

"Reducing the need for abortions," by M. Mead. REDBOOK 141:62 plus, September, 1973.

"Role of histoclinical studies in the prophylaxis of spontaneous abortions," by W. Waronski, et al. GINEKOL POL 44:425-429, April, 1973.

"The role of the placenta in fetal and perinatal pathology. Highlights of an eight months' study," by G. Altshuler, et al. AM J OBSTET GYNECOL 113:616-626, July 1, 1972.

"Science and the citizen." SCI AM 228:44-46 plus, March, 1973.

"Social indications for interruption of pregnancy," by W. Kokoszka, et al. POL TYG LEK 28:139-140, January 22, 1973.

"The social indications for abortion," by W. Becker. THER GGW 111: 587-604, 1972.

"Some implications of self-selection for pregnancy," by W. Z. Billewicz. BR J PREV SOC MED 27:49-52, February, 1973.

"Studies on accidental intravascular injection in extra-amniotic saline induced abortion and a method for reducing this risk," by B. Gustavii. J REPROD MED 8:70-74, February, 1972.

"Studies on the pathogeneis of clotting defects during salt-induced abortions," by L. M. Talbert, et al. AM J OBSTET GYNECOL 115:656-662, 1973.

"Voluntary abortion. Its social and biological consequences," by J. Botella Llusia. AN R ACAD NACL MED 90:285-295, 1973.

"Wife of Onan and the sons of Cain; danger inherent in social technology," by J. A. Miles, Jr. NAT R 25:891-894, August 17, 1973; Discussion. 25:1024 plus, September 28, 1973.

"Women claim abortion, feminism contradictory." NAT CATH REP 9:5, March 2, 1973.

"Women who seek abortions: a study," by A. T. Young, et al. SOCIAL WORK 18,3:60-65, May, 1973.

SODIUM CHLORIDE
"Hyperosmolal crisis following infusion of hypertonic sodium chloride

for purposes of therapeutic abortion," by E. D. De Villota, et al. AM J MED 55:116-122, July, 1973.

"Interrupting late-term pregnancy with an intra-amniotic administration of a hypertonic solution of sodium chloride," by G. A. Palladi, et al. AKUSH GINEKOL 48:58-61, 1972.

S.P.U.C.
see: Religion and Ethics

SPONTANEOUS ABORTION
see also: Threatened Abortion

"Age of the woman and spontaneous and induced abortions," by Z. Gizicki. GINEKOL POL 43:443-447, April, 1972.

"Banding analysis of abnormal karyotypes in spontaneous abortion," by T. Kajii, et al. AM J HUM GENET 25:539-547, September, 1973.

"Causes for spontaneous abortion," by M. A. Petrov-Maslakov, et al. VOPR OKHR MATERIN DET 17:58-63, July, 1972.

"Chromosomal findings in women with repeated spontaneous abortions," by J. Malkova, et al. CESK GYNEKOL 38:193-194, April, 1973.

"Chromosome investigation in married couples with repeated spontaneous abortions," by M. E. Kaosaar, et al. HUMANGENETIK 17:277-283, 1973.

"Chromosome studies in couples with repeated abortions," by H. D. Rott, et al. ARCH GYNAEKOL 213:110-118, 1972.

"Clinical experience in prophylactic treatment of spontaneous abortion," by P. F. Tropea. ACTA EUR FERTIL 2:253-274, June, 1970.

"Determination of urinary C. G. H. in spontaneous threatened abortion. Prognostic value," by R. Hechtermans, et al. J GYNECOL OBSTET BIOL REPROD 1:869-876, December, 1972.

"Double heteroploidy, 46, XY, t(13q14q), 18, in a spontaneous abortus," by S. Avirachan, et al. CLIN GENET 4:101-104, 1973.

"The effect of spontaneous and induced abortion on prematurity and birthweight," by G. Papaevangelou, et al. J OBSTET GYNAECOL BR COMMONW 80:410-422, May, 1973.

"Experimental clinical studies on spontaneous and habitual abortion with nephrogenic pathology," by M. Georgneva. AKUSH GINEKOL 11:109-114, 1972.

"Histological analysis of spontaneous abortions with triploidy," by M. Geisler, et al. HUMANGENETIK 16:283-294, 1972.

"Hormonal therapy of spontaneous abortion and premature labor in women with menstrual disorders," by P. G. Shushaniia, et al. AKUSH GINE-KOL 47:54-58, October, 1971.

"Influence of induced and spontaneous abortions on the outcome of subsequent pregnancies," by S. N. Pantelakis, et al. AM J OBSTET GYNECOL 116:799-805, July 15, 1973.

"Listeriosis. Occurrence in spontaneous interruptions of pregnancy," by J. R. Giraud, et al. NOUV PRESSE MED 2:215-218, January 27, 1973.

"Morphological, autoradiographic, immunochemical and cytochemical investigation of a cell strain with trisomy 7 from a spontaneous abortus," by A. M. Kuliev, et al. HUMANGENETIK 17:285-296, 1973.

"Outcome of pregnancies following a spontaneous abortion with chromosomal anomalies," by J. G. Boue, et al. AM J OBSTET GYNECOL 116:806-812, July 15, 1973.

"Parental X-irradiation and chromosome constitution in their spontaneously aborted foetuses," by E. Alberman, et al. ANN HUM GENET 36:185-194, 1972.

"Role of histoclinical studies in the prophylaxis of spontaneous abortions," by W. Waronski, et al. GINEKOL POL 44:425-429, April, 1973.

"The role of infection in spontaneous abortion," by A. P. Egorova, et al. VOPR OKHR MATERIN DET 17:65-70, September, 1972.

"Spontaneous abortion: the most common complication in pregnancy," by D. A. Aiken. NURS TIMES 69:898-899, July 12, 1973.

"Spontaneous abortions and triploidy," by J. Levy, et al. REV FR GYN- ECOL OBSTET 67:327-342, May, 1972.

"The triad of polyptychencephaly, embryonal resorption and spontaneous abortion," by J. Dankmeijer. NED TIJDSCHR GENEESKD 117:519- 524, March 31, 1973.

STATISTICS
"Abortions rise 33 per cent in nation-wide Canadian survey." HOSP ADMIN CAN 15:8, February, 1973.

"Abruption of the placenta. A review of 189 cases occurring between 1965 and 1969," by R. G. Blair. J OBSTET GYNAECOL BR COMMONW 80:242-245, March, 1973.

"Aggressive management of septic abortion: report of 262 cases," by W. J. Connolly, et al. SOUTH MED J 65:1480-1484, December, 1972.

"Chromosomal abnormalities in 32 cases of repeated abortions," by S. Warter, et al. REV FR GYNECOL OBSTET 67:321-325, May, 1972.

"The effects of legal abortion on legitimate and illegitimate birth rates: the California experience (figures for the period 1966-1972)," by J. Sklar, et al. STUDIES IN FAMILY PLANNING 4:281-292, November, 1973.

"Five thousand consecutive saline inductions," by T. D. Kerenyi, et al. AM J OBSTET GYNECOL 116:593-600, July 1, 1973.

"480,000 legal abortions in 1971." HOSP PROGRESS 54:96b, March, 1973.

"Hospital statistics of births, abortions, still births, premature births and neonatal deaths from Army hospitals in Western Command 1967- 70," by M. C. Sanyal. AR MED FORCES MED J INDIA 28:226-230, 1972.

"101 femmes," by J. Pare. LE MACLEAN :15, 32 plus, February, 1973.

"Post-abortion and post-partum septico-pyemia. Apropos of 27 cases," by V. Vic-Dupont, et al. ANN MED INTERNE 124:291-302, April, 1973.

"Reasons for delayed abortion: results of four hundred interviews," by T. D. Kerenyi, et al. AM J OBSTET GYNECOL 117:299-311, October 1, 1973.

"Repeat abortions in New York city: 1970-1972," by E. F. Daily, et al. FAMILY PLANNING PERSPECTIVES 5:89-93, Spring, 1973.

"A review of one thousand uncomplicated vaginal operations for abortion," by D. G. Bluett. CONTRACEPTION 7:11-25, 1973.

"Scottish abortion statistics--1971." HEALTH BULL 31:39-50, January, 1973.

"Statistical analysis of 1021 abortions. Treatment of abortus imminens," by T. J. Horvath. MED WELT 23:1929-1930, December 16, 1972.

"Sterilization associated with induced abortion: JPSA findings (based on a joint program for the study of abortion examination of the abortion experience of 72,988 American women who had legal abortions, 1970-71)," by S. Lewitt. FAMILY PLANNING PERSPECTIVES 5:177-182, Summer, 1973.

STERILITY
"Fertility control and the quality of human life," by C. Muller. AM J PUBLIC HEALTH 63:519-523, June, 1973.

"Fertility of women over the age of 40," by S. Sehovic, et al. JUGOSL GINEKOL OPSTET 11:191-196, 1971.

"Male factor as a possible cause of habitual abortion and infertility," by C. A. Joel. SCHWEIZ MED WOCHENSCHR 102:1377-1383, September 30, 1972.

"Status of abortions, fertility and family planning in the Rostock region during 1962-1971," by K. H. Mehlan, et al. Z AERZTL FORTBILD 67:539-545, June, 1973.

"Two years' experience with a liberal abortion law: its impact on

fertility trends in New York city (1970-72)," by C. Tietze. FAMILY
PLANNING PERSPECTIVES 5:36-41, Winter, 1973.

STERILIZATION

"Combined laparoscopic sterilization and pregnancy termination," by
N. G. Courey, et al. J REPROD MED 10:291-294, June, 1973.

"Comparison of operative morbidity in abortion-sterilization procedures," by L. L. Veltman, et al. AM J OBSTET GYNECOL 117:251-
254, September 15, 1973.

"Contraception, sterilization, and abortion legal interpretation of consent," by D. F. Kaltreider. MD STATE MED J 22:67, September, 1973.

"Further experience with laparoscopic sterilization concomitant with
vacuum curettage for abortion," by H. K. Amin, et al. FERTIL STERIL
24:592-594, August, 1973.

"Laparoscopic tubal sterilization coincident with therapeutic abortion by
suction curettage," by L. G. Whitson, et al. OBSTET GYNECOL 41:
677-680, May, 1973.

"Law on abortion and sterilization, 1973," by G. H. Roux. S AFR MED J
47:596, April 14, 1973.

"Postabortal posterior colpotomy and sterilization," by S. S. Sheth, et
al. J OBSTET GYNAECOL BR COMMONW 80:274-275, March, 1973.

"Sterilization and therapeutic abortion counselling for the mentally retarded," by C. W. Smiley. INT J NURS STUD 10:137-141, May, 1973.

"Sterilization associated with induced abortion: JPSA findings (based
on a joint program for the study of abortion examination of the abortion
experience of 72,988 American women who had legal abortions, 1970-
71)," by S. Lewitt. FAMILY PLANNING PERSPECTIVES 5:177-182,
Summer, 1973.

STUDENTS
see: Youth

SURGICAL TREATMENT AND MANAGEMENT
see also: Techniques of Abortion

"Cervical-segmental insufficiency (CSI) as a cause of abortion. Surgical treatment. Clinico-statistical considerations," by L. Volpe, et al. MINERVA GINECOL 25:123-139, March, 1973.

"Experience with Shirodkar's operation and postoperative alcohol treatment," by N. H. Lauersen, et al. ACTA OBSTET GYNECOL SCAND 52:77-81, 1973.

"Extended indications for cervix cerclage uteri in pregnancy," by G. Widmaier, et al. ZENTRALBL GYNAEKOL 95:16-21, January 5, 1973.

"Hysterectomy by septic processes during pregnancy," by J. Rosas Arceo, et al. GINECOL OBSTET MEX 33:559-568, June, 1973.

"The management of abruptio placentae," by C. B. Lunan. J OBSTET GYNAECOL BR COMMONW 80:120-124, February, 1973.

"Management of premature detachment of the normally implanted placenta," by R. Ortiz Arroyo, et al. GINECOL OBSTET MEX 33:209-215, February, 1973.

"Paracervical block anaesthesia for minor gynaecological operations," by I. S. Jones. NZ MED J 78:15-18, July 11, 1973.

"Preconception surgical treatment of uterine insufficiency in women with habitual abortions," by A. Zwinger, et al. CESK GYNEKOL 38: 256-258, May, 1973.

SURVEYS
see: Sociology and Behavior

SYMPOSIA
"The abortion ruling: analysis & prognosis: symposium: CHA to conduct anti-abortion campaign. NCCB pastoral message. Commentaries by T. Shaffer, R. McCormick, A. Hellegers, J. McHugh, W. Regan, G. Reed, L. Hogan, E. Head, C. Bauda, E. D. Bishop." HOSP PROG 54:81-96b, March, 1973.

"America's war on life; symposium: Where we have been, where we go from here. The abortion culture, by K. Mitzner. The movement coming together. The movement staying together. The Catholic obligation." TRIUMPH 8:17-32, March, 1973.

"L'avortement; symposium: Une histoire d'amour et de mort, by M. Gillet. Sexualite, contraception et avortement, by M. Debout. Liberte de l'avortement et liberation des femmes, by H. Bonnet. Legalite et moralite face a l'avortement, by R. Boyer. La volunte de procreer: reflexion philosophique, by B. Quelquejeu. Reflexions theologiques sur la position de l'Eglise catholique, by J. M. Pohier." LUMIERE 21:6-107, August-October, 1972; Replies by Y. Milliasseau, A. Dumas, R. Bel, J. J. Weber, D. Stein. 22:81-87, January-March, 1973.

"Brook Lodge symposium on prostaglandins. Moderator's summary," by C. H. Hendricks. J REPROD MED 9:425-426, December, 1972.

"Judicial power and public conscience: symposium, by J. Kennedy, A. McNally, M. Brennan." SIGN 52:26-27, March, 1973.

SYNTOCINON

"Midtrimester abortion using intra-amniotic prostaglandin F2 alpha with intravenous Syntocinon," by G. G. Anderson, et al. J REPROD MED 9:434-436, December, 1972.

TECHNIQUES OF ABORTION
see also: Induced Abortion
Surgical Treatment and Management

"Abortion by vacuum method." NURS J INDIA 64:205-207, June, 1973.

"Air embolism in the interruption of pregnancy by vacuum extraction," by G. H. Hartung. ZENTRALBL GYNAEKOL 95:825-828, June 15, 1973.

"The Anker dilator in therapeutic abortion," by B. von Friesen. ACTA OBSTET GYNECOL SCAND 52:191-192, 1973.

"Cervical migration of laminaria tents," by L. Wellman. AM J OBSTET GYNECOL 115:870-871, March 15, 1973.

"Coagulation changes during termination of pregnancy by prostaglandins and by vacuum aspiration," by M. H. Badraoui, et al. BR MED J 1:19-21, January 6, 1973.

"Experience with the suction curette in termination of pregnancy at a Sydney Teaching hospital," by R. H. Picker, et al. AUST NZ J OBSTET GYNAECOL 13:49-50, February, 1973.

"Experiences with the vibro dilatator from the Soviet Union," by K. H. Beckmann, et al. DTSCH GESUNDHEITSW 28:227-228, 1973.

"Further experience with laparoscopic sterilization concomitant with vacuum curettage for abortion," by H. K. Amin, et al. FERTIL STERIL 24:592-594, August, 1973.

"Intra-uterine suction for evacuation of the uterus in early pregnancy," by A. K. Ghosh. J INDIAN MED ASSOC 59:366-368, October 16, 1972.

"Lack of coagulation defect after terminating second-trimester pregnancy by the catheter technique," by F. K. Beller, et al. AM J OBSTET GYNECOL 115:822-826, March 15, 1973.

"Laminaria augmentation of intra-amniotic prostaglandin F2 alpha for the induction of mid-trimester abortion," by W. E. Brenner, et al. PROSTAGLANDINS 3:879-894, June, 1973.

"Laminaria: an underutilized clinical adjunct," by R. W. Hale, et al. CLIN OBSTET GYNECOL 15:829-850, September, 1972.

"Laparoscopic tubal sterilization coincident with therapeutic abortion by suction curettage," by L. G. Whitson, et al. OBSTET GYNECOL 41:677-680, May, 1973.

"Legal abortion by extra-amniotic instillation of Rivanol in combination with rubber catheter insertion into the uterus after the twelfth week of pregnancy," by C. A. Ingemanson. AM J OBSTET GYNECOL 115:211-215, January 15, 1973.

"Legal interruption of pregnancy by the aspiration method and the pericervical block with Gynesthesin," by M. Beric. SCHWEIZ Z GYNAEKOL GEBURTSHILFE 3:151-159, 1972.

"The Karman catheter," by P. Fairbrother. AM J OBSTET GYNECOL 116:293, May 15, 1973.

"Karman catheter," by A. J. Margolis, et al. AM J OBSTET GYNECOL 115:589, February 15, 1973.

"Midtrimester abortion using prostaglandin F2alpha, oxytocin, and laminaria," by T. Engel, et al. FERTIL STERIL 24:565-568, August, 1973.

"Modified cervical block for elective abortion procedures," by W. D. Walden. OBSTET GYNECOL 41:473-474, March, 1973.

"Outpatient termination of pregnancy by vacuum aspiration," by A. Y. Ng, et al. SINGAPORE MED J 14:23-25, March, 1973.

"A safer cervical dilator," by C. Michael. MED J AUST 1:1254, June 23, 1973.

"Somatic complications after legal abortion by vacuum aspiration combined with oxytocin infusion," by E. D. Johansson, et al. LAKARTIDNINGEN 69:6045-6048. December 13, 1972.

"Studies on accidental intravascular injection in extra-amniotic saline induced abortion and a method for reducing this risk," by B. Gustavii. J REPROD MED 8:70-74, February, 1972.

"Termination of pregnancy by abdominal hysterotomy," by J. Higginbottom. LANCET 809:937-938, April 28, 1973.

"Termination of pregnancy by 'super coils': morbidity associated with a new method of second-trimester abortion," by G. S. Berger, et al. AM J OBSTET GYNECOL 116:297-304, June 1, 1973.

"Termination of pregnancy with intrauterine devices. A comparative study of coils, coils and balsa, and catheters," by B. Mullick, et al. AM J OBSTET GYNECOL 116:305-308, June 1, 1973.

"Use of laminaria tents with hypertonic saline amnioinfusion," by J. H. Lischke, et al. AM J OBSTET GYNECOL 116:586-587, June 15, 1973.

"Uterine contractility and placental histology in abortion by laminaria and metreurynter," by Y. Manabe, et al. OBSTET GYNECOL 41:753-759, May, 1973.

"Uterine evacuation by aspiration," by J. Delgado Urdapilleta, et al. GINECOL OBSTET MEX 32:607-609, December, 1972.

"Vacuum extraction of hydrocephalic fetus," by T. G. Price. J OBSTET GYNAECOL BR COMMONW 79:1053, November, 1972.

"Water vacuum suction curettage (WVSC): one year's experience," by J. R. Woods, Jr., et al. OBSTET GYNECOL 41:720-725, May, 1973.

THERAPEUTIC ABORTION

"Abortion. The first five years at North Carolina Memorial Hospital," by W. E. Easterling, Jr., et al. TEX MED 69:61-67, April, 1973.

"Abortion applicants in Arkansas," by F. O. Henker, III. J ARKANSAS MED SOC 69:293-295, March, 1973.

"Abortion clinics and operating sessions," by A. E. R. Buckle. NURS MIRROR 136:36-38, March 9, 1973.

"Adolescent sexuality," by M. G. Wolfish. PRACTITIONER 210:226-231, February, 1973.

"The Anker dilator in therapeutic abortion," by B. von Friesen. ACTA OBSTET GYNECOL SCAND 52:191-192, 1973.

"Attitudes of obstetric and gynecologic residents toward abortion," by P. R. Mascovich, et al. CALIF MED 119:29-34, August, 1973.

"Cervical migration of laminaria tents," by F. W. Hanson, et al. AM J OBSTET GYNECOL 114:835-837, November 15, 1972.

"Changes in uterine volume following the intra-amniotic injection of hypertonic saline. Reply to comments of Dr. Goodlin," by M. O. Pulkkinen, et al. ACTA OBSTET GYNECOL SCAND 52:93-95, 1973.

"Combination of prostaglandin F 2 and paracervical block in the missed abortion and intrauterine fetal death," by E. J. Hickl, et al. KLIN

WOCHENSCHR 51:140-141, February 1, 1973.

"Complication rates associated with abortion," by G. Joslin. MED J AUST 1:1165, June 9, 1973.

"Considerable increase of renal HCS-clearance after the removal of fetus and placenta," by W. Geiger, et al. ACTA ENDOCRINOL 173: 51, 1973.

"Consultation for therapeutic abortion," by L. Daligand, et al. MED LEG DOMM CORPOR 5:372-378, October-December, 1972.

"Continuous extra-amniotic prostaglandin E 2 for therapeutic termination and the effectiveness of various infusion rates and dosages," by A. Midwinter, et al. J OBSTET GYNAECOL BR COMMONW 80:371-373, April, 1973.

"Continuous intrauterine infusion of prostaglandin E 2 for termination of pregnancy," by A. Midwinter, et al. J OBSTET GYNAECOL BR COMMONW 79:807-809, September, 1972.

"Continuous prostaglandin-F 2 infusion for middle-trimester abortion," by N. H. Lauersen, et al. LANCET 813:1195, May 23, 1973.

"Contraindication for carrying pregnancy to full term from the hematologic viewpoint," by R. Stieglitz, et al. Z AERZTL FORTBILD 67:274-276, March 15, 1973.

"Counseling for elective abortion," by R. S. Sanders, et al. JOURNAL OF THE AMERICAN COLLEGE HEALTH ASSOCIATION 21,5:446-450, June, 1973.

"Critical examination of the indications of the so-called therapeutic abortion," by J. Garcia Orcoyen. AN R ACAD NACL MED 90:263-272, 1973.

"Critical judgment of the medical indications of therapeutic abortion," by F. Bonilla Marti. AN R ACAD NACL MED 90:273-284, 1973.

"A double-blind study of intra-amniotic urea and hypertonic saline for therapeutic abortion," by R. J. Smith, et al. J OBSTET GYNAECOL

BR COMMONW 80:135-137, February, 1973.

"The dynamics of therapeutic abortions in the town of Bucharest during the 1967-1969 period," by V. Coroi, et al. OBSTET GINECOL 20:267-272, 1972.

"Early termination of an encephalic pregnancy after detection by raised alpha-fetoprotein levels," by M. J. Seller, et al. LANCET 2:73, July 14, 1973.

"Emotional reactions in abortion services personnel," by F. J. Kane, Jr., et al. ARCH GEN PSYCHIATRY 28:409-411, March, 1973.

"An expediting procedure for late abortion," by J. F. Shipp, et al. OBSTET GYNECOL 41:477, March, 1973.

"Follow-up after therapeutic abortion in early adolescence," by M. G. Perez-Reyes, et al. ARCH GEN PSYCHIATRY 28:120-126, January, 1973.

"Hyperosmolal crisis following infusion of hypertonic sodium chloride for purposes of therapeutic abortion," by E. D. De Villota, et al. AM J MED 55:116-122, July, 1973.

"Hypertonic saline-induced abortion complicated by consumptive coagulopathy: a case report," by J. C. Morrison, et al. SOUTH MED J 66:561-562, May, 1973.

"Induction of therapeutic abortion with intra-amniotically administered prostaglandin F 2. A comparison of three repeated-injection dose schedules," by W. E. Brenner, et al. AM J OBSTET GYNECOL 116:923-930, August 1, 1973.

"Infection as a complication of therapeutic abortion," by A. H. DeCherney, et al. PA MED 75:49-52, December, 1972.

"Injuries of the cervix after induced midtrimester abortion," by P. J. Bradley-Watson, et al. J OBSTET GYNAECOL BR COMMONW 80:284-285, March, 1973.

"Intra-amniotic administration of prostaglandin F 2 for induction of

therapeutic abortion. A comparison of four dosage schedules," by
W. E. Brenner, et al. J REPROD MED 9:456-463, December, 1972.

"Intra-amniotic administration of prostaglandin F2a to induce therapeutic abortion: Efficacy and tolerance of two dosage schedules," by W.
E. Brenner, et al. AM J OBSTET GYNECOL 114:781-787, 1972.

"Intrauterine extra-amniotic administration of prostaglandin F2a for
therapeutic abortion: early myometrial effects," by J. T. Braaksma, et
al. AM J OBSTET GYNECOL 114:511-515, 1972.

"Laminaria: an underutilized clinical adjunct," by R. W. Hale, et al.
CLIN OBSTET GYNECOL 15:829-850, September, 1972.

"Laparoscopic tubal sterilization coincident with therapeutic abortion
by suction curettage," by L. G. Whitson, et al. OBSTET GYNECOL
41:677-680, May, 1973.

"Latent morbidity after abortion." BR MED J 2:611, June 9, 1973.

"Maternal death due to DIC after saline abortion," by S. R. Lemkin, et
al. OBSTET GYNECOL 42:233-235, August, 1973.

"Maternal plasma oestrogen and progesterone levels during therapeutic
abortion induced by intra-amniotic injection of prostaglandin F 2," by
E. M. Symonds, et al. J OBSTET GYNAECOL BR COMMONW 79:976-
980, November, 1972.

"The mental health of the prospective father: a new indication for
therapeutic abortion?" by R. Lacoursiere. BULL MENNINGER CLIN
36:645-650, November, 1972.

"A methodology for the planning of therapeutic abortion services," by
S. J. Williams. HEALTH SERV REP 87:983-991, December, 1972.

"Midtrimester abortion using intra-amniotic prostaglandin F2 alpha with
intravenous Syntocinon," by G. G. Anderson, et al. J REPROD MED
9:434-436, December, 1972.

"Midtrimester abortion using prostaglandin F2alpha, oxytocin, and
laminaria," by T. Engel, et al. FERTIL STERIL 24:565-568, August,

1973.

"Motivational factors in abortion patients," by F. J. Kane, Jr., et al. AM J PSYCHIATRY 130:290-293, 1973.

"A note on the effects of maternal or fetal injection of flumethasone and of thyroidectomy on the termination of pregnancy," by J. M. Van Der Westhuysen. S AFR J ANIM SCI 1:67, 1971.

"Nurse and the abortion patient," by B. Clancy. NURSING CLIN N AMER 8:469-478, September, 1973.

"Organizing on abortion service," by A. H. Danon. NURS OUTLOOK 21:460-464, July, 1973.

"Postabortal posterior colpotomy and sterilization," by S. S. Sheth, et al. J OBSTET GYNAECOL BR COMMONW 80:274-275, March, 1973.

"Postabortion attitudes," by D. A. Evans, et al. N C MED J 34:271-273, April, 1973.

"A primigravida in preparation for a therapeutic abortion," by D. M. Waselefsky. MATERNAL CHILD NURS J 2:67-77, Spring, 1973.

"Problem of pregnancy interruption as a question for the physician," by R. Reimann-Hunziker. PRAXIS 62:397-399, March 27, 1973.

"The prospects of PGs in postconceptional therapy," by A. I. Csapo. PROSTAGLANDINS 3:245-289, March, 1973.

"Prostaglandin administration for induction of mid-trimester abortion in complicated pregnancies," by M. Toppozada, et al. LANCET 2:1420-1421, December 30, 1972.

"Prostaglandins and therapeutic abortion: summary of present status," by C. H. Hendricks. J REPROD MED 9:466-468, December, 1972.

"Rubella vaccination and the termination of pregnancy." BR MED J 4:666, December 16, 1972.

"A safer cervical dilator," by C. Michael. MED J AUST 1:1254, June

23, 1973.

"The selective effect of therapeutic abortion when children thus eliminated are carriers of a recessive autosomic or x-chromosome-linked defect," by U. Pfandler, et al. J GENET HUM 20:135-150, June, 1972.

"Some psychiatric problems related to therapeutic abortion," by D. S. Werman, et al. N C MED J 34:274-275, April, 1973.

"Sterilization and therapeutic abortion counselling for the mentally retarded," by C. W. Smiley. INT J NURS STUD 10:137-141, May, 1973.

"Termination of pregnancy with 15 methyl analogues of prostaglandins E 2 and F 2," by S. M. Karim, et al. J REPROD MED 9:383-391, December, 1972.

"Termination of second trimester pregnancy with intra-amniotic administration of prostaglandins E 2 and F 2," by S. M. Karim, et al. J REPROD MED 9:427-433, December, 1972.

"Therapeutic abortion," by R. H. Christie. CENT AFR J MED 19:54-58, March, 1973.

"Therapeutic abortion," by A. Eistetter. CATH HOSP :3-4, January-February, 1973.

"Therapeutic abortion and its complications in Halifax, N. S.," by C. Resch, et al. NS MED BULL 52:67-70, April, 1973.

"Therapeutic abortion and a prior psychiatric history," by J. A. Ewing, et al. AMER J PSYCHIAT 130:37-40, January, 1973.

"Therapeutic abortion by extra-amniotic administration of prostaglandins," by M. P. Embrey, et al. J REPROD MED 9:420-424, December, 1972.

"Therapeutic abortion by intrauterine infusion of prostaglandin F2a," by T. H. Lippert, et al. ARCH GYNAEKOL 213:197-201, 1973.

"Therapeutic abortion employing the synergistic action of extra-amniotic prostaglandin E 2 and an intravenous infusion of oxytocin," by G. A. Morewood. J OBSTET GYNAECOL BR COMMONW 80:473-475, May, 1973.

"Therapeutic abortion in the second trimester by intra-amniotic pro-staglandin F2 alpha," by P. G. Gillett, et al. J REPROD MED 9:416-419, December, 1972.

"Therapeutic abortion: a multidisciplined approach to patient care from a social work perspective," by J. M. Rogers, et al. CANAD J PUBLIC HEALTH 64:254-259, May-June, 1973.

"Therapeutic abortion of early human gestation with vaginal supposi-tories of prostaglandin (F 2)," by D. R. Tredway, et al. AM J OBSTET GYNECOL 116:795-798, July 15, 1973.

"Therapeutic abortion on psychiatric grounds. A follow-up study," by J. A. Ewing, et al. NC MED J 34:265-270, April, 1973.

"Therapeutic abortion: a prospective study. II," by S. Meikle, et al. AM J OBSTET GYNECOL 115:339-346, February 1, 1973.

"Therapeutic abortion utilizing local application of prostaglandin F2alpha," by F. Naftolin, et al. J REPROD MED 9:437-441, Decem-ber, 1972.

"Therapeutic abortions in Siriraj Hospital," by S. Toongsuwan, et al. J MED ASSOC THAI 56:237-240, April, 1973.

"Therapeutic termination of pregnancy in private practice," by J. M. Miller. MED J AUST 1:831-834, April 28, 1973.

"Trends in therapeutic abortion in San Francisco," by P. Goldstein, et al. AM J PUBLIC HEALTH 62:695-699, 1972.

"An unusual surgical injury to the ureter," by M. P. Gangai. J UROL 109:32, January, 1973.

"Vacuum extraction of hydrocephalic fetus," by T. G. Price. J OBSTET GYNAECOL BR COMMONW 79:1053, November, 1972.

"Vaginal administration of prostaglandin F2a for inducing therapeutic abortion," by W. E. Brenner, et al. PROSTAGLANDINS 1:455-467, 1972.

THREATENED ABORTION

"Biochemical study of the amniotic fluid in threatened pregnancies," by R. H. Gevers, et al. NED TIJDSCHR GENEESKD 116:1969-1970, October 21, 1972.

"The bioelectrical activity of the brain in women with threatening interruption of pregnancy," by E. A. Panova. AKUSH GINEKOL 48: 32-34, September, 1972.

"Detection of fetal heart activity in first trimester," by O. Piiroinen. LANCET 2:508-509, September 1, 1973.

"Determination of urinary C.G.H. in spontaneous threatened abortion. Prognostic value " by R. Hechtermans, et al. J GYNECOL OBSTET BIOL REPROD 1:869-876, December, 1972.

"Diagnosis and therapy of threatened abortion--our experience," by B. Stambolovic, et al. ZENTRALBL GYNAEKOL 95:808-810, June 15, 1973.

"Endangered pregnancy--an important part of perinatal medicine," by Z. K. Stembera. CESK PEDIATR 28:1-2, January, 1973.

"Evaluation of the effects of chlormadinone in the treatment of threatened abortion," by J. Cardenas. GINECOL OBSTET MEX 33:121-124, January, 1973.

"Evaluation of the prognosis of threatened abortion from the peripneral plasma levels of progesterone, estradiol, and human chorionic gonadotropin," by K. G. Nygren, et al. AM J OBSTET GYNECOL 116: 916-922, August 1, 1973.

"Experience with Shirodkar's operation and postoperative alcohol treatment," by N. H. Lauersen, et al. ACTA OBSTET GYNECOL SCAND. 52:77-81, 1973.

"Extended indications for cervix cerclage uteri in pregnancy," by G. Widmaier, et al. ZENTRALBL GYNAEKOL 95:16-21, January 5, 1973.

"Hormone therapy of threatened abortion during the early stages of pregnancy," by S. Trepechov, et al. AKUSH GINEKOL 11:152-160, 1972.

"Human chorionic gonadotropin (HCG) in threatened abortion," by P. Baillie, et al. S AFR MED J 47:1293-1296, July 28, 1973.

"Imminent abortion," by H. J. Wallner. MED KLIN 68:497-500, April 20, 1973.

"Indices of the coagulant and anticoagulant systems of the blood in threatened and incipient abortion," by A. I. Zherzhov. VOPR OKHR MATERIN DET 17:85-86, August, 1972.

"New etiopathogenetic and therapeutic studies in threatened abortion," by M. Goisis, et al. MINERVA GINECOL 25:481-492, August, 1973.

"On the pathomorphism of threatened abortion (labor complications and fetal diseases)," by A. Weidenbach. MINERVA GINECOL 25:457-461, August, 1973.

"Placental lactogen levels in threatened abortion," by P. A. Niven, et al. PROC R SOC MED 66:188, February, 1973.

"Prevention of premature labor with beta receptor stimulants," by L. Kovacs, et al. ORV HETIL 114:2537-2538, October 21, 1973.

"Prognostic value of immunologic determinations of chorionic gonadotropins (C.G.H.) in threatened abortion," by D. Chouvacovic, et al. BULL FED SOC GYNECOL OBSTET LANG FR 23:629-630, November-December, 1971.

"Statistical analysis of 1021 abortions. Treatment of abortus imminens," by T. J. Horvath. MED WELT 23:1929-1930, December 16, 1972.

"Treatment with synthetic ACTA of threatened abortion in women with secondary hypophyseal insufficiency," by R. Klimek, et al. GINEKOL POL 44:25-29, January, 1973.

"Urinary excretion of various steroid hormones during the physiological course of pregnancy and in threatened spontaneous premature interruption," by L. V. Timoshenko, et al. PEDIATR AKUSH GINEKOL

5:38-40, October, 1972.

"Use of Alupent in obstetrics. Our personal experiences," by G. Di Terlizzi. MINERVA GINECOL 25:225-245, April, 1973.

"Use of isoxsuprine in the obstetrical pathology," by I. Signorelli, et al. ARCH OSTET GINECOL 77:115-128, April, 1972.

"Use of vaginal wall cytologic smears to predict abortion in high-risk pregnancies," by M. T. McLennan, et al. AM J OBSTET GYNECOL 114:857-860, December 1, 1972.

"Vaginal adenocarcinoma as a late result of treatment of threatened abortion with diethylstilbestrol," by J. Presl. CESK GYNEKOL 38: 473-474, July, 1973.

"Value of Salbutamol in obstetrics," by P. Dellenbach, et al. THERA-PEUTIQUE 48:671-675, December, 1972.

TOXOPLASMAS
see: Complications

TRIPLOIDY
"Histological analysis of spontaneous abortions with triploidy," by M. Geisler, et al. HUMANGENETIK 16:283-294, 1972.

"Spontaneous abortions and triploidy," by J. Levy, et al. REV FR GYNECOL OBSTET 67:327-342, May, 1972.

TRANSPLACENTAL HEMORRHAGE
see: Complications

VETERINARY ABORTIONS
see: Research

YOUTH
"Abortion and sexual behavior in college women," by K. J. Monsour, et al. AM J ORTHOPSYCHIATRY 43:804-814, October, 1973.

"Adolescent pregnancy: a study of aborters and non-aborters," by F. J. Kane, et al. AM J ORTHOPSYCHIATRY 43:796-803, October, 1973.

"Adolescent sexuality," by M. G. Wolfish. PRACTITIONER 210:226-231, February, 1973.

"Attitudes of unmarried college women toward abortion," by M. Vincent, et al. J SCH HEALTH 43:55-59, January, 1973.

"Constitutional law--minor's right to refuse court-ordered abortion," by SUFFOLK U L REV 7:1157-1173, Summer, 1973.

"Federal judge rules juveniles may not be denied abortions." NAT CATH REP 9:5, February 23, 1973.

"Follow-up after therapeutic abortion in early adolescence," by M. G. Perez-Reyea, et al. ARCH GEN PSYCHIAT 28:120-126, January, 1973.

"Minor cannot be compelled to have abortion: Maryland." NEWSLETTER 6:5, January, 1973.

"On abortion and the college woman," by K. J. Monsour. MADEMOISELLE 78:64 plus, November, 1973.

"Problems of reproduction in adolescence," by J. A. Grant, et al. WORLD MED J 20:57, May-June, 1973.

"Psychological problems of abortion for the unwed teenage girl," by C. D. Martin. GENET PSYCHOL MONOGR 88:23-110, August, 1973.

"Student opinion on legalized abortion at the University of Toronto," by F. M. Barrett, et al. CAN J PUBLIC HEALTH 64:294-299, May-June, 1973.

"The termination of adolescent out-of-wedlock pregnancies and the prospects for their primary prevention," by W. G. Cobliner, et al. AM J OBSTET GYNECOL 115:432-444, February 1, 1973.

AUTHOR INDEX

Abernethy, V. 9
Adamo, S. J. 42
Addelson, F. 44
Aiken, D. A. 73
Albe-Fessard, D. 62
Alberman, E. D. 52, 59
Aleskerov, G. S. 47
Alexander, S. 61
Allen, J. 15
al-Salihi, F. L. 55
Alsopp, M. 15
Altchek, A. 7
Altshuler, G. 70
Alvarez-Bravo, A. 60
Alvior, G. T., Jr. 63
Amin, H. K. 40
Anderson, D. 68
Anderson, G. G. 53
Arceo, J. R. 43
Ardrey, W. B. 31
Arroyo, R. O. 52
Atanasov, A. 33
Avirachan, S. 32

Badarau, L. 41
Badraoui, M. H. 24
Baillie, P. 42
Ballard, C. A. 54, 77
Barrett, F. M. 74
Barsotti, D. 55
Basu, H. K. 72

Baum, G. 11
Baumann, J. 1
Beaulieu, M. 19
Becker, W. 72
Beckmann, K. H. 36
Bedoya-Gonzalez, J. M. 25
Beguin, F. 18
Behrens, C. 40
Behrman, S. J. 54
Belden, E. L. 60
Bell, J. N. 48
Bell, W. R. 8
Beller, F. K. 48, 78
Bennett, O. 72
Berczy, J. 41
Berger, G. S. 58, 76
Berger, H. 33
Beric, B. 16
Beric, M. 50
Bermejillo, M. 54
Bernstein, A. H. 49
Berry, H. 30
Bhardwaj, K. S. 19
Bhasin, M. K. 29
Bianchi, E. 25
Billewicz, W. Z. 72
Blaes, S. M. 11, 51
Blair, R. G. 16
Blatchley, F. R. 34
Blice, P. 29
Bluett, D. G. 68, 76

228

Potts 3
Presl, J. 56, 81
Price, T. G. 81
Pulkkinen, M. O. 23, 45

Quelquejeu, B. 19

Rahmas, D. S. 4
Rall, H. J. S. 65
Ramsey, P. 14
Rao, I. B. 55
Rao, K. N. 8
Ratner, H. 7
Ratten, G. J. 68
Redford, M. H. 4
Redman, L. J. 9
Reed, G. E. 26
Reed, E. 4
Regan, W. A. 74
Rehnquist, W. 67
Reimann-Hunziker, R. 64
Renne, R. A. 52
Resch, C. 77
Revaz, C. 65
Ribes, B. 23, 32
Rice, C. E. 33
Rice, C. O. 58
Rieger, H. J. 50
Riga, P. 69
Rivet, M. 66
Robbins, J. C. 75
Roberts, N. 50
Robertson, F. J. 9
Roche, A. 57
Rodman, H. 4
Rogers, J. M. 77
Rosenberg, C. O. 14
Rott, H. D. 23
Roux, G. H. 49
Rovinsky, J. J. 43
Rozovskii, I. S. 31
Rozovsky, L. E. 69
Rudel, H. W. 4

Russell, R. G. 19
Ryle, E. 62
Ryzhova, R. K. 69

Safronenko, G. D. 63
Saldana, L. 58
Saltman, J. 4
Sanders, R. S. 28
Santesson, B. 54
Sanyal, M. C. 42
Sarvis, B. 4
Sato, T. 44, 61
Saunders, J. R. 35
Saunders, P. 48
Scheck, H. 58
Scheiber, R. 83
Schjerven, L. 16
Schlensker, K. H. 31
Schneider, J. 67
Schrader, E. S. 58
Schuhmann, R. 78
Schulman, H. 28
Schulte, E. J. 11
Schulz, S. 31
Schutte, A. P. 82
Schwenger, C. W. 12
Sedaghat, A. 32
Seewald, H. J. 24
Sehgal, N. 24
Sehovic, S. 38
Seiler, H. 1
Sele, V. 31
Sell, M. B. 55
Seller, M. J. 33
Seppala, M. 17, 37, 65
Sesboue, B. 23
Seward, P. N. 34
Shaffer, T. 14
Shaikh, A. A. 67
Shapiro, S. 67
Sharf, M. 49
Sharman, G. A. 74
Sharp, D. S. 76